# Sparta's Kings

# Sparta's Kings

## John C. Carr

Pen & Sword
**MILITARY**

First published in Great Britain in 2012 by
**PEN & SWORD MILITARY**
An imprint of
Pen & Sword Books Ltd
47 Church Street
Barnsley
South Yorkshire
S70 2AS

Copyright © John C. Carr 2012

ISBN 978-1-84884-849-8

A CIP catalogue record for this book is
available from the British Library.

Typeset by Concept, Huddersfield, West Yorkshire.

Printed and bound in England by
CPI Group (UK) Ltd, Croydon, CR0 4YY.


Pen & Sword Books Ltd incorporates the Imprints of Pen & Sword Aviation, Pen &
Sword Family History, Pen & Sword Maritime, Pen & Sword Military, Pen & Sword
Discovery, Wharncliffe Local History, Wharncliffe True Crime, Wharncliffe
Transport, Pen & Sword Select, Pen & Sword Military Classics, Leo Cooper, The
Praetorian Press, Remember When, Seaforth Publishing and Frontline Publishing.

For a complete list of Pen & Sword titles please contact
PEN & SWORD BOOKS LIMITED
47 Church Street, Barnsley, South Yorkshire, S70 2AS, England
E-mail: enquiries@pen-and-sword.co.uk
Website: www.pen-and-sword.co.uk

# Contents

*Call to arms* ........................................ vii

*List of illustrations* ................................. viii

*Maps* ............................................... ix

*Prologue* ........................................... xviii

**Chapter 1: Kings in the Mist** ..................... 1
  Lelex, Myles, Eurotas ........................... 2
  Lakedaimon, Amyklas, Kynortas, Oibalos ........... 2
  Tyndareos ...................................... 4
  Menelaos ....................................... 5
  Orestes and Tisamenos .......................... 11

**Chapter 2: Sons of Herakles** ..................... 12
  Eurysthenes and Prokles ......................... 12
  Agis I and Eurypon ............................. 15
  Echestratos and Prytanis ........................ 16
  Labotas to Charillos ............................ 17
  Teleklos and Nikandros .......................... 20

**Chapter 3: Forging the Spartan State** ............. 22
  Alkamenes ...................................... 22
  Polydoros and Theopompos ....................... 23
  Eurykrates to Agasikles ......................... 30
  Ariston ........................................ 34
  Anaxandridas II ................................ 35

**Chapter 4: The Politics of Defiance** .............. 39
  Kleomenes I .................................... 39
  Demaratos ...................................... 49

**Chapter 5: 'Come and Get Them!'** ................. 54
  Leonidas I ..................................... 54
  Leotychidas II ................................. 61

**Chapter 6: The Cold War Kings** . . . . . . . . . . . . . . . . . . . . .  69
    Pleistarchos . . . . . . . . . . . . . . . . . . . . . . . . . . . . . . . . . . .  69
    Pleistoanax . . . . . . . . . . . . . . . . . . . . . . . . . . . . . . . . . . . .  73
    Archidamos II . . . . . . . . . . . . . . . . . . . . . . . . . . . . . . . . . .  73

**Chapter 7: Projecting Power** . . . . . . . . . . . . . . . . . . . . . . . .  84
    Agis II . . . . . . . . . . . . . . . . . . . . . . . . . . . . . . . . . . . . . . .  84
    Pausanias . . . . . . . . . . . . . . . . . . . . . . . . . . . . . . . . . . . . .  98

**Chapter 8: Domination and Decline** . . . . . . . . . . . . . . . . . .  103
    Agesilaos II . . . . . . . . . . . . . . . . . . . . . . . . . . . . . . . . . . .  103
    Agesipolis I . . . . . . . . . . . . . . . . . . . . . . . . . . . . . . . . . . .  117
    Kleombrotos I . . . . . . . . . . . . . . . . . . . . . . . . . . . . . . . . . .  119

**Chapter 9: Retreat** . . . . . . . . . . . . . . . . . . . . . . . . . . . . . . .  123
    Agesipolis II and Kleomenes II . . . . . . . . . . . . . . . . . . . . . .  123
    Archidamos III . . . . . . . . . . . . . . . . . . . . . . . . . . . . . . . . .  124
    Agis III . . . . . . . . . . . . . . . . . . . . . . . . . . . . . . . . . . . . . .  124
    Eudamidas I . . . . . . . . . . . . . . . . . . . . . . . . . . . . . . . . . . .  131

**Chapter 10: The Hooded Flame** . . . . . . . . . . . . . . . . . . . . .  133
    Areus I to Leonidas II (including Kleombrotos II) . . . . . . . . . .  133
    Archidamos IV and Eudamidas II . . . . . . . . . . . . . . . . . . . . .  138

**Chapter 11: The Reformers** . . . . . . . . . . . . . . . . . . . . . . . . .  140
    Agis IV . . . . . . . . . . . . . . . . . . . . . . . . . . . . . . . . . . . . . .  140
    Eudamidas III and Archidamos V . . . . . . . . . . . . . . . . . . . . .  148
    Kleomenes III and Eukleidas . . . . . . . . . . . . . . . . . . . . . . . .  149

*Epilogue* . . . . . . . . . . . . . . . . . . . . . . . . . . . . . . . . . . . . . . . .  169
*Standing down* . . . . . . . . . . . . . . . . . . . . . . . . . . . . . . . . . . .  175
**Spartan kings: Timeline** . . . . . . . . . . . . . . . . . . . . . . . . . . .  176
**References and Chapter Notes** . . . . . . . . . . . . . . . . . . . . . .  178
**Index** . . . . . . . . . . . . . . . . . . . . . . . . . . . . . . . . . . . . . . . . .  183

# Call to arms

By midmorning most of the Spartan expeditionary force was already dead. Since dawn the invading Persians had been hurling masses of men against the Spartan defence at the pass of Thermopylai, whittling down the defenders to a mere handful of bloody and exhausted warriors.

King Leonidas I, right there in the front line, was still on his feet, but only just. Cascades of Persian arrows darkened the sky. Leonidas, his face contorted with the supreme effort, fought bravely on until a spear thudded into him and he crumpled slowly onto the corpses of his comrades.

And I was there to see it all happen.

The month was November of 1960 and I, a young schoolboy fresh from the grey skies of Yorkshire, stood transfixed as Twentieth Century Fox recreated the 480 BC Battle of Thermopylai on the shores of a lagoon near the Greek spa town of Loutraki. As my mother worked on the movie set I was given a rare chance to see history in the re-making.

'Cut!' yelled the director, and the last of the rubber-tipped arrows, fired from cannon-like cylinders out of camera range, flopped to the ground. Hollywood actor Richard Egan, playing Leonidas, eased himself up from the gravel. 'Is that a wrap?' he said in his California baritone, wiping the fake blood and real sweat from his bronzed arms and face.

'It sure is,' replied Spyros Skouras, the Greek-born boss of Twentieth Century Fox, who had flown in to see the climactic shooting of *The 300 Spartans*. Skouras had just been driven up in a massive black limousine that had drawn crowds of curious villagers on the dusty ten-kilometre route from Loutraki.

I had sat in the back of the limo with the Great Man, who took great pleasure in expounding to this young English lad the glories of Greek arms in the Persian Wars. I don't remember what I said in reply, but at one point Skouras turned to me and said: 'You're a smart boy, John. Why don't you come to Hollywood?'

For better or worse, I didn't become an actor. But now, half a century on, I feel I've done the next best thing by pursuing a career as a journalist and writer, helping bring to life in my own way some of those momentous events and people in Greek military history.

# List of Illustrations

1. The Menelaion [Author's photo]
2. Late Bronze Age remains near the Menelaion, possibly of Menelaos' palace complex [Author's photo]
3. Enthroned archaic male figure, possibly a king, on 6th century BC stele base [Sparta Archaeological Museum]
4. Menelaos stabbing Helen, on 6th century BC stele base [Sparta Archaeological Museum]
5. Kastor and Polydeukes (the Dioskouri), on late 6th century BC stele base [Sparta Archaeological Museum]
6. Mount Taygetos as seen from central Sparta [Author's photo]
7. The Eurotas River today [Author's photo]
8. Remains of the Acropolis of Sparta [Author's photo]
9. Remains of the theatre of Sparta [Author's photo]
10. A Spartan warrior often believed to be Leonidas I, 470s BC [Sparta Archaeological Museum]
11. Lysandros the general, Roman copy of original bust [Ekdotiki Athinon]
12. Archidamos III – the only extant likeness of a Spartan king [Ekdotiki Athinon]
13. The Leuktra battlefield and the restored Theban monument today [Ekdotiki Athinon]
14. Remains of the temple near Aulis where Agesilaos' sacrifices were abruptly halted in 396 BC [Ekdotiki Athinon]
15. Modern Sparta and its environs as seen from the Menelaion [Author's photo]
16. Spartan short sword and scabbard [Hellenic War Museum]
17. Troops in formation with the sarissa pike, adopted by Kleomenes III from the Macedonians [Hellenic War Museum]
18. The modern statue of Leonidas I in Sparta [Author's photo]
19. A high school student places a wreath at the Cenotaph of Leonidas in central Sparta, 27 October 2011 [Author's photo]
20. Author's news story from *The Times*, 13 March 1996

# Maps

1. The Greek World
2. The Peloponnese
3. Lakonia
4. Sparta City Plan
5. Battle of Thermopylai
6. Battle of Mantineia
7. Battle of Leuktra
8. Battle of Sellasia

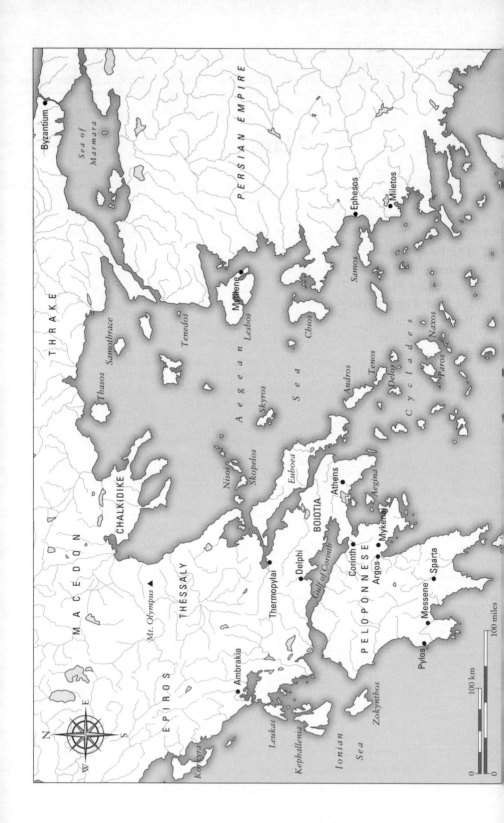

The Peloponnese

Patrai •

Aigion •

ACHAIA

ELIS

Olympia •

Sikyon •

Corinth •

Epidauros •

Argos •

Aigana

Hyora

Mantinea ✕

Tegea •

ARKADIA

Megalopolis •

Ithome ✕

MESSENIA

THYREATIS

LAKEDAIMON

Sparta •

Gytheion •

Kythera

Zakynthos

Ionian

Sea

50 km

50 miles

N
E
S
W

0

0

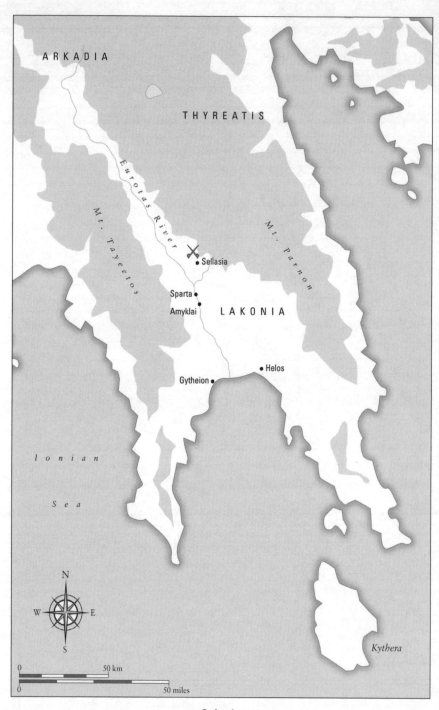

Lakonia

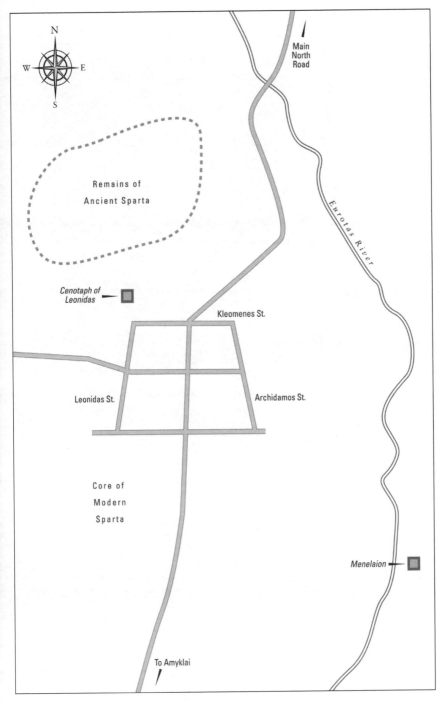

Sparta City Plan

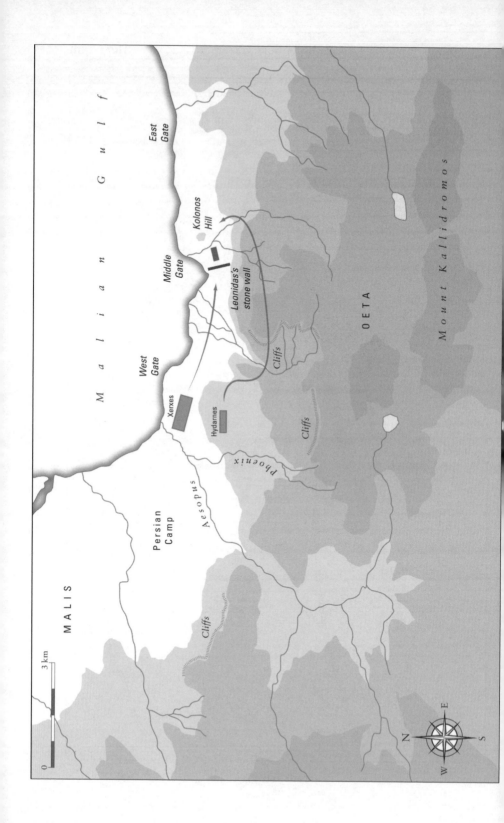

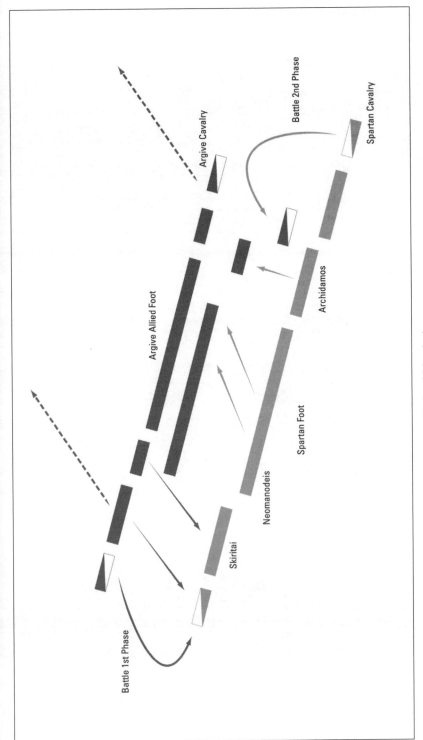

Battle of Mantineia

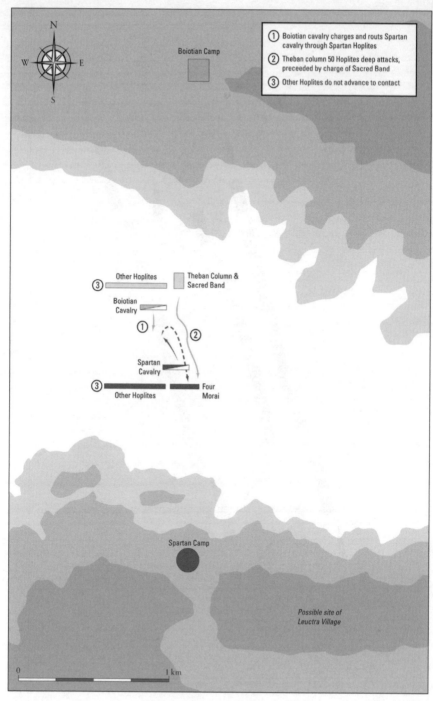

Battle of Leuktra

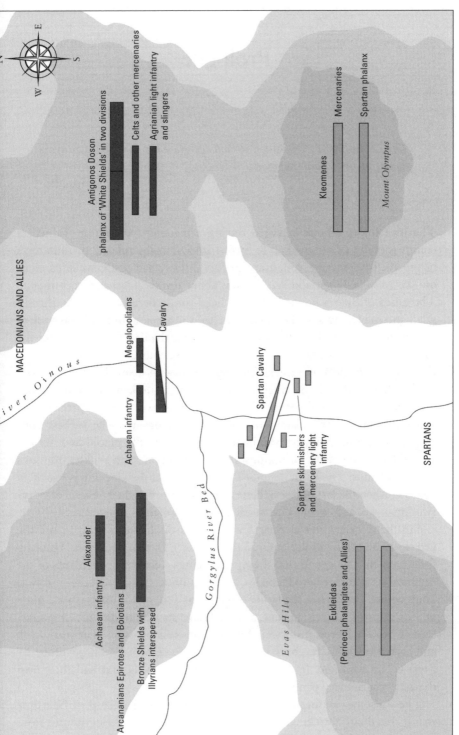

Battle of Sellasia

# Prologue

*There is no poetic composition to commemorate the doings of the royal
houses of the Lakedaimonians.*

Pausanias

The idea for this book emerged during a meeting with Philip Sidnell, a
commissioning editor for Pen & Sword Books, in the refined surroundings
of the British Museum restaurant in July 2011. I had just completed work
on *On Spartan Wings* and was casting about for some other Greek theme.
The kings of Sparta popped into my head somewhere between the shrimp
salad and the Dover sole. Days later we had the green light and I was back in
Greece dusting off my sources and pecking out the first few lines. Over the
following months the book was written amid a serious Greek economic crisis
that bid fair to turn all Greeks into Spartans, with a small s.

The kings of ancient Sparta ruled in an unbroken chain for about
900 years. I say 'about' because it's by no means easy to put a precise start
and finish line to the history of the Spartan kingship. The earliest conventional starting point for the historical era is usually placed at 1103 BC
with the creation of the twin kingship by Eurysthenes and Prokles, the sons
of Aristodemos. The latest date for the extinction of the kingship is probably
183 BC, when the last of Eurysthenes' descendants perished. A total of sixty-
two kings reigned, thirty-one in each of the two royal houses.

Yet there were kings at Sparta well before the historical era, before the
Greeks as an ethnic group entered the southern Balkan peninsula. Ignoring
for a moment the legend that the Spartan kings were the descendants of the
mythical semi-divine hero Herakles, ancient authors noted eight pre-historical
kings before Tyndareos, the father of Helen of Troy, who brings Sparta more
or less into the known ancient world. These ancient traditions, of course,
cannot be considered historical. Yet they are reliable signs that pre-Greek
and early Greek Sparta, back to 2,500 BC or even before, was governed by
royal rulers who may be little more than names to us, but had their own
dynastic continuity spanning the epochs.

The most fascinating aspect of the historical-era kingship of Sparta is
that it was dual. Two kings, one each from the Agiad and Eurypontid royal
houses, reigned concurrently. Rarely did the two houses intervene in each

other's affairs; each respected the other's autonomy and authority. Neither were Sparta's kings splendid monarchs as one might expect in the ancient world. With few ignoble exceptions they conspicuously shunned the grandeur and pomp of their equivalents in the Middle East or nearer regions such as Macedon.

Writing about the dual kingship presents an unusual difficulty in that the parallel reigns of the kings rarely, if ever, coincided chronologically. For example, the eventful thirty-nine-year reign of the Eurypontid king Agesilaos II in the first half of the fourth century BC overlapped no fewer than five reigns of the Agiad line. Such cases have necessitated a certain amount of back-and-forthing in the narrative, though I hope it has been kept to a minimum. As for the earliest kings, dating them with any degree of accuracy is an exercise fraught with hazard. I have had to allocate more or less arbitrary time-frames to the first thirty or so kings (fifteen from each house) between 1100 BC to about 520 BC when reliable records began to be kept, by the rule-of-thumb of thirty or so years per generation, and can only hope I'm not too far off the mark.

In the text I have preferred the term 'kingship' over 'monarchy' in that the latter term defines rule by a single sovereign. To replace it with something like 'dyarchy,' though semantically precise, would be pedantic and off-putting to many readers.

Source material becomes more plentiful for the classical and Hellenistic-era kings of Sparta, such as the justly-famous Leonidas I, Agesilaos II and Kleomenes III. Yet this presents its own set of problems. Only about half a dozen kings were written about extensively, mainly by Herodotus, Thucydides, Pausanias, Plutarch and Polybius. All later accounts are based on these. A conventional history of Sparta could sidestep this difficulty by emphasizing historical processes over the kings themselves. But in a book of this nature, which tries to deal with real people rather than processes, the problem of bringing them to life sometimes is acute. For example, the long reign of Kleomenes II in the fourth century BC is an impenetrable mystery, as prolific chroniclers such as Plutarch and Pausanias unaccountably ignore him completely. As with a few other kings in this narrative, I've had no choice but to write around them, an exercise like filling in a drawing around a blank face.

The ancient writers, of course, had their prejudices and like today's news reporters were prone to giving currency to improbable tales as long as they were sensational. It's every historian's task to put it all through a mental filter and hope that the reader's credulity won't be strained by what's left. One way of doing this, in cases of doubt, is to defer to standard histories of Greece to maintain a sense of perspective. Another is to mention conflicting accounts of a particular event and let the reader decide. I have done both, I hope not too inconsistently.

Since this is a book primarily about people as well as events, I have taken the calculated risk of including the ancient writers' reconstructed words of the kings and scraps of dialogue in the hope that they can enliven the narrative. All such reconstruction, as Thucydides readily admitted, involves some guesswork. My own yardstick of including such spoken material has been whether it seems 'in character.' (Plutarch's *Apophthegmata Laconica*, a collection of sayings by leading Spartans, is of great value here.) In this digital age I have inevitably made use of online sources, but the reader may rest assured that I have treated those sources with the utmost caution they require.

In the text I employ the Hellenic original rather than the old Latinized usage in Greek proper names (e.g. Perikles and Lysandros instead of Pericles and Lysander). The exceptions are where the Latinized or Anglicized form is too well-known (e.g. Homer, Herodotus, Thucydides, Philip, Alexander) to change without confusing the non-specialist reader. The same applies to the names of cities such as Sparta, Athens, Corinth and Thebes (which, if I were to be painfully consistent, I would have to render as Sparte, Athenai, Korinthos and Thebai, and that wouldn't help the majority of readers, either). Like many writers past and present, I use the terms 'Spartan' and 'Lakedaimonian' pretty much interchangeably. All dates are understood as being BC: therefore that suffix is omitted from the main text.

Besides Philip Sidnell, I owe a great deal of thanks to George Mermingas, a veritable repository of Greek historical material, be it ancient, Byzantine and modern. Yannis Korodimos of the Hellenic War Museum was very helpful, as were the directors of the Sparta Archaeological Museum and Maria Koursi of Ekdotike Athinon for kindly making available several of the illustrations. Nike Morgan helped weed out errors in the early drafts. Finally, as I am one of those writers who, when at work on a book, tends to blot out all else from his consciousness, I owe an apology to all those friends whose ears I repeatedly bent with the doings of the Spartan kings, yet who remained friends nonetheless.

JCC
Athens, November 2011

*Chapter 1*

# Kings In The Mist

Lelex, Myles, Eurotas
Lakedaimon, Amyklas, Kynortas, Oibalos
Tyndareos
Menelaos
Orestes and Tisamenos

*Today, among the scanty ruins of that ancient capital, hardly a torso or a
fallen pillar survives to declare that here there once lived Greeks.*[1]

Since the popular American historian Will Durant wrote those lines in the
1930s, not much has changed in Sparta, a town of some 20,000 people on
the west bank of the Eurotas River (now called the Evrotas). The river
valley winds lazily and empties itself between the easternmost two of the
three rocky promontories of the southern Peloponnese that protrude like
bony fingers into the Mediterranean Sea. Sparta rests on a low height between
the widest part of the river bed and the lower slopes of Mount Taygetos
to the west. The well-watered Eurotas plain is lush with olive and citrus
groves that make it one of the more idyllic of Greece's valleys.

Sparta's streets and squares today resound with the names of the ancient
kings and warriors – Leonidas, Agis, Archidamos, Lykourgos and Brasidas,
to name just the main ones. Yet the origin of the name Sparta itself is
disputed. It may have derived from Sparte, an early queen (see below), or
be a reference to the *spartos* bush that is still common in the area.[2] Mount
Taygetos, looming more than 7,000 feet over the city, and snow-capped for
most of the year, reflects the morning sun on its impressive crags. Bounding
the Eurotas valley to the east is Mount Parnon, not as formidable as Taygetos
but still enough of a presence to lend a sense of seclusion and exclusiveness to
the valley and the people who live in it that lingers even now. This exclusiveness was the foundation of the Spartan exceptionalism that helped the city
grow into the strongest power in the Greek world.

The wider region, including all the easternmost prong of the Peloponnese,
is called Lakonia. Even today, the Lakonians are among the more ruggedly

independent and conservative of Greeks, clinging to their valley home and blunt ways in defiance of globalization. Modern Sparta may have smart office and apartment buildings, modern hotels and good roads leading out of the town past the olive oil presses and fruit canneries, but the Lakonian valley has yet to see a railway or airport. Gytheion, the city's sea outlet forty-five kilometres to the south, still has the characteristics of a fishing village. There is no reason to suppose the scene was radically different in the third millennium before Christ, when the valley began to be populated on a permanent basis.

## Lelex, Myles, Eurotas (*c*. 2000–1500?)

The Spartans believed that the first king of the Lakonian valley was named Lelex, a native of the soil, after whom the local people named themselves Leleges. Lelex thus appears to have been the first to consolidate a viable and organized society in the valley on the foundation of Neolithic settlements. The Leleges were a pre-Greek people, one of a number of such tribes inhabiting the Balkan peninsula before about 1900, when the first Greeks began filtering in from the north.

The second century AD historian and traveller Pausanias, who is our sole source for this tradition, mentions Lelex as the first 'king' (*basileus*), without, however, explaining the term. Most likely Lelex was the first ruler who had the authority to bring together the settlers of the Lakonian valley into a unified entity. A political development such as the creation of a monarchy is usually a response to some external threat or internal instability.[3]

The earliest community of Sparta was probably not at the exact location of the classical or modern town. According to Pausanias, its earliest name was Therapne, after Lelex's daughter, and could have stood on a height on the east side of the Eurotas River. Lelex's rule must have been effective, as his son Myles became his heir, inaugurating Sparta's first dynasty. Myles was later credited with discovering the process of milling flour (the English word mill derives from his name). More likely is that the art of milling flour for bread reached mainland Europe from the Middle East while Myles was ruling and hence he got the credit. Myles was followed by his son Eurotas (meaning 'Good Flow'), who is said to have created Sparta's river by draining a stagnant lake in the middle of the valley to allow it to flow to the sea – and giving it his name.

## Lakedaimon, Amyklas, Kynortas, Oibalos (*c*. 1500–1250?)

In the tradition recorded by Pausanias, Eurotas had no male heir. His daughter Sparte was wed to one Lakedaimon, whose paternity was unknown but who became the next king. The name of Lakedaimon's mother Taygete was given to the adjacent mountain, suggesting that Lakedaimon's father, whoever he was, may have come from that area. The dynastic interruption personified by Lakedaimon seems to have accompanied a redefinition of the whole domain. This included changing its name to Lakedaimon, after himself. The tradition adds that he founded the chief town and named it Sparte (Sparta) after his wife, but as we have seen, there is some uncertainty on that point.

Lakedaimon's son and successor, Amyklas, seemingly inheriting his father's ambitious nature, built his own community a few kilometres down the valley, calling it Amyklai. Amyklas suffered a blow with the death of his youngest son Hyakinthos, remembered in local tradition as 'the most beautiful' of the king's sons, who was entombed in Amyklai; the tomb was still there more than 1,000 years later. When Amyklas died his eldest son Aigalos took the throne; after Aigalos came his son Kynortas, and then his son Oibalos.

Trying to put dates to this succession of names is impossible. We have no way of knowing, for example, in whose reign the Greeks entered the Peloponnese to either displace or merge with the pre-Greek inhabitants, or which of the listed kings from, say, Lakedaimon to Oibalos were pre-Greek and which were ethnic Greeks. A clue is afforded by the supposed dynastic break between Eurotas and Lakedaimon, whose name became that of the region, and whose unknown father could well have been one of the invaders who married into the local stock. Such a transition would have occurred very roughly between 1500 and 1400, some few centuries after the Greeks' appearance in the peninsula. By that time the Greeks of the Peloponnese had coalesced into a major Mediterranean power centring on the stronghold of Mykenai. Another stronghold, almost as mighty, rose at Pylos, dominating the western sea approaches to the Peloponnese and the rich Messenian plain on the other side of Mount Taygetos. The Messenian plain and its plentiful crops would soon provide a tempting target for the poorer Lakonians.

The Greeks of this period called themselves Achaians. From their chief base at Mykenai their seaborne armies raided the Aegean islands, Crete and the Anatolian coast. The Achaians were the Vikings of antiquity, landing on the shores of what is now Turkey and ravaging the countryside, carrying off livestock, slaves and women.

One reason for this aggressive tendency was that these Greek newcomers to the southern Balkan peninsula had discovered that their new and sunny land was not as rich in resources as they had thought. In an economy based on small-scale agriculture and stockbreeding, boom-and-bust cycles were especially pronounced. Times of prosperity would trigger spikes in population growth that quickly outstripped the slender agricultural resources of the land, straining the social fabric. The Achaians' overseas raids served as a safety valve to let off social steam and give restless and underemployed young men something to do to enrich themselves as well as the state. The theft of women from Asia Minor was – initially at least – probably a way of easing a dearth of child-bearing females at home. It would prove to have momentous consequences.

There is no evidence that the early kings of Sparta took part in these grand overseas raids by the Achaians. Yet by the middle of the thirteenth century overseas contacts had come to play an important part in Spartan political life. King Oibalos himself looked beyond the borders of Lakedaimon for a wife; probably he had an eye on securing an alliance with neighbouring Mykenai, the stronger power. His bride was Gorgophone, a high-born lady of Argos in the Mykenaian realm.

## Tyndareos (*c.* 1230–1200)

Oibalos and Gorgophone had at least two sons, who when they grew up quarrelled over the succession. Hippokoon, the elder, for some reason feared the power of Tyndareos, the younger. Pausanias tells us merely that Hippokoon enlisted the aid of some private armed force to eject Tyndareos from Sparta. Tyndareos fled, probably to Messenia on the other side of Taygetos, where he had a half-brother from his mother's side.

Pausanias' none-too-clear outline nonetheless gives us a few clues that enable us to fill in the picture a little. If we assume that the clash between Hippokoon and Tyndareos broke out on the death of Oibalos, it would tie in with the fact that Gorgophone also had a son by Perieres, a Messenian, who would have been her second husband. Tyndareos must have had some previous contact with Aphareus, Perieres's son, before fleeing to him. Whatever the truth, Tyndareos settled down to a country squire's life in leafy Messenia, marrying and having children.

Subsequently, reports Pausanias with admirable but frustrating brevity, Tyndareos was brought back by Herakles and recovered his throne.[4]

The reference to the mythical Herakles could be a reference to the Herakleidai clan who led the Dorians, a tougher and more aggressive breed of Greeks, southwards to take over the Achaian domains. But that didn't happen until several generations after Tyndareos. More likely a Spartan palace coup, possibly with the aid of Gorgophone, brought back her favourite son.

It was a time of prosperity for Lakedaimon, which shared in the general stability of the Mykenaian world. Out of about 130 stable settlements on the Greek mainland, about two dozen made up Lakedaimon between the ranges of Taygetos and Parnon. Tyndareos had two sons and two daughters. Pausanias says that the twin sons, Kastor and Polydeukes, also 'became kings,' though it's not clear of what. At least one may have briefly reigned in Sparta; in Greek tradition Kastor was the son of Tyndareos' wife Leda by Zeus the father of gods. If we discount the Zeus connection as obviously unhistorical, we may theorize that Kastor was illegitimate. As for Polydeukes, he may have been too young when the succession time came. More likely Tyndareos saw greater potential in his strong-minded elder daughter Helene who, when married off to a member of the neighbouring Mykenaian royal house, would guarantee Sparta's power and prosperity – not to mention an heir who might even unite the kingdoms. This Helene – Helen of Troy – would in fact do a great deal more than that.

Several versions of the alleged kidnapping of Helen were current in the historical era. Plutarch, for example, writing in Roman times, surmises that Enarsphoros, the son of Tyndareos' elder brother Hippokoon, wanted Helen and tried to carry her off by force while she was still a young girl. To keep her out of his nephew's clutches, Tyndareos put her in the care of the king of Athens, Theseus, whom some later accused of carrying out the abduction himself, though he was fifty years old at the time. Theseus supposedly employed a confederate to snatch Helen as she was dancing innocently in the temple of Artemis Orthia in Sparta. At Tegea, north of the boundaries of Lakedaimon, they drew lots for her and Theseus won.

Yet as Helen was still too young to be a bride, Theseus left her in the care of a friend at Aphidnai, a community about twenty-five kilometres northwest of Athens. In Theseus' absence a rival named Menestheus gained influence at Athens. Tyndareos in person led a Spartan army to Athens to demand Helen back. Menestheus replied that he had no idea where she was; Tyndareos didn't believe him, and the war was on. A man named Akademos – perhaps an Athenian, perhaps a Spartan – learned that Helen was at Aphidnai and told her father who sped there with his force and had little trouble taking the town.

Kastor and Polydeukes, who were with their father, entered Athens at the invitation of Menestheus, were feted as having stopped the war, and received recognition as *wanakes*, or supreme kings (see Menelaos below). According to one twist in the story, among those whom Tyndareos captured at Aphidnai was Theseus' mother Aithra, who was led off to Sparta to be a lady-in-waiting for Helen but not, apparently, treated dishonourably. Akademos, for his part, was honoured by Tyndareos; his home in Athens was called the Akademia – the origin of the word academy and the site of Plato's Academy in later years.[5]

## Menelaos (*c*. 1200–1150)

It may not be amiss at this point to speculate about Helen herself, as her effect on history was, for a woman, considerable. When she left Athens to be taken back to Sparta she was still very young, but already attractive enough to have started a brief Spartan-Athenian war. Add to this a strong character and will, and we have the ingredients for a turbulent career spanning seas and marriages. Having had early experience of being pursued for her beauty and intelligence, and having seen something of the wider world outside Lakedaimon, she must have chafed under the highly-regulated domesticity of a provincial royal house.

The husband chosen for Helen was Menelaos, a younger brother of the powerful Mykenaian king Agamemnon. He assumed the throne of Sparta sometime around 1200. We owe his image largely to Homer's *Iliad*, the 15,693-line epic poem that commemorates one of the final stages of the drawn-out conflict known as the Trojan War. This war, or something very like it, appears to have been a Greek expedition to clip the power of Wilusa, a power related to the Hittites, occupying what is now the north-western corner of Turkey. Wilusa is identifiable with Troy, against which Agamemnon moved about 1190 with a seaborne army drawn from all over the Greek world. Triggering the expedition, according to Homer, was the abduction of Helen by Paris, a smooth-tongued and notorious Trojan womanizer who had been on a diplomatic mission to Sparta, possibly to head off rising cross-Aegean tensions.

Menelaos sailed to Troy at the head of his contingent of sixty ships full of men from 'the swarming hollow of Lakedaimon, Pharis and Sparta ...'[6] The adjective 'swarming' in the line may be a propaganda piece inserted centuries later, when the final text of the *Iliad* was standardized during the period of Spartan and Athenian ascendancy. But there is little doubt that Lakedaimon at the time was enjoying a period of prosperity under the sovereignty of Mykenai.

As seen through Homer's lines, Menelaos is of medium height, well-built and with reddish hair. He is man of few but choice words and a courageous warrior, yet sensitive enough to still love Helen after her flight to Troy and declare himself ready to end the war if he can get her back. There is something of the honest, if unimaginative, country baron about him. He bursts onto the stage of the *Iliad* 'in the confidence of his valour, driving [his men] battleward, since above all his heart was eager to avenge' the gross injustice done to him.[7]

No late Bronze Age Greek king could have put up with such ignominy and survived politically. Revenge was not only a moral but also a political necessity. Menelaos, it must be remembered, was an outsider who had become the ruler of Sparta. He was driven by a need to prove himself in the eyes of the locals. Any sign of insecurity would have disappointed not only his people and army but also his beautiful and strong-minded wife. Helen was an exception to the rule that Greek women at that time, even high-born ones, were kept out of public affairs; on the contrary, this did not apply in more liberal and civilized societies such as Troy.[8] It would be far from surprising if Helen chafed under her benevolent but rather dull husband and succumbed to the Eastern charms of a good-looking stranger. As for Paris (or Pari-zitis in the Wilusa tongue), he would have had ample cause this way to avenge the Achaians' own theft of Asian women. Menelaos had no choice but to appeal to his elder brother Agamemnon, the supreme king, or *wanax*, of the Greek world. The Achaian kingdoms were well organized militarily, needing just a signal from Agamemnon to gather for what they imagined would be another profitable raid across the Aegean. Menelaos was just one of a number of *basileis*, or regional kings, to be called up with their contingents.

The Achaian Greek armies were organized in tens of units, with up to 200 soldiers per unit. A king's executive general was called the *lawagetas* (meaning 'leader of the people,' but in the field rather than in an administrative sense). The soldiers were almost all of the land-tilling yeoman class, the *moropa;* the term comes from an early Greek version of the verb *moirazo*, meaning to share out or allocate. Men of the *moropa* class had their family lands allocated to them. They had a physical share in the Spartan state, hence a definite stake in the fighting, either defending their own lands from invasion or hoping for booty in a foreign expedition, booty they could use to enrich their families and maintain their yeoman status. The soldiers were protected by full-body armour and boar's tusk helmets, and were expert in the use of the chariot, an invention that reached Greece from the east.

For a *basileus* such as Menelaos, who as such carried the entire prestige of Sparta on his person, heading an efficient army was not enough. He himself had to be in peak physical condition and possess considerable physical courage – and display those qualities at every possible opportunity. The *Iliad* is replete with examples of leading Greeks and Trojans challenging one another to sole physical combat. Such a feat of prowess and bravery was called an *aristeia* (meaning 'being the best') and counted enormously in the people's assessment of their kings and other leading personages.

According to Homer, Menelaos was called on to perform his own particular *aristeia* after nine years of constant warfare on the plain of Troy. We are in no position to know how long the Trojan War or its equivalent actually lasted. We don't even know whether the story that Homer hands down to us depicts a single, well-defined campaign or pulls together various soldiering memories hundreds of years after the actual events. On the assumption that Homer's conflict indeed was fought, Menelaos must have been away from Sparta, on the other side of the Aegean Sea, roughing it for several years at least. We don't know if any senior Greek king or officer ever availed himself of home leave; Homer mentions nothing. In the opening of Book III of the *Iliad* the Spartan king gets a crack at the man who stole his wife and shamed him before the entire Greek world. Paris himself pushes out from the front rank of the Trojan force and challenges to single combat any Greek who cares to take him up on it.

> Now as soon as Menelaos the warlike caught sight of him ... he was glad, like a lion who comes upon a mighty carcass ... thinking to punish the robber, straightaway in all his armour he sprang to the ground from his chariot.[9]

A great deal is riding on this encounter. Even allowing for the dramatization techniques of Homer and the bards who preceded him in shaping the story, the picture of Menelaos here rings true. As the wickedly handsome fellow who has humiliated him in two continents comes forward, Menelaos is confident. Rank upon rank of Greeks and Trojans watch the scene. Many war-weary Greeks hope that Paris' demise at the hands of the man he had wronged will end the long and bitter conflict and enable them to go home.

Paris, sensing all this, suffers an attack of nerves – a credible character trait in someone who has followed a make-love-not-war ethic in his life. As Menelaos jumps down from his chariot with blood in his eye, Paris shrinks back into the mass of Trojan soldiers, earning a rebuke from Hektor, the Trojan prince and leader, who has now been shamed in his turn. The rebuke brings Paris to his senses, and he renews his challenge.

Menelaos comes across as a reasonable man, unlike his brother Agamemnon, who is portrayed as autocratic and unfeeling, selfish and none too bright. Menelaos says he's willing to die in this encounter, if need be, if the Greeks and Trojans can be friends again. That's about the extent of his speech. Homer, probably for reasons of melodrama, has Helen taking her place on the walls of Troy to watch the fight for herself and see which way her fate will turn. Debating with herself, she bitterly regrets her fling with Paris, 'slut that I am.' The scene before her has the air of unreality. She asks herself: 'Did this ever happen?'[10] Below, in the space between the silent armies, Paris draws the lot to hurl his spear first. The spear strikes Menelaos' shield dead in the centre but fails to penetrate it. Menelaos has either the stronger arm or stronger spear, or both. His weapon slices through Paris' shield and the armour behind it, but Paris agilely twists away from the spear point before it can sink into his flesh. Menelaos now brings his sword down on Paris' helmet, but the sword breaks. Furious, he seizes the horse-hair plume of Paris' helmet and twists it until the strap cuts into Paris' throat, almost strangling him. There is no doubt here who is physically the stronger man.

Just when Menelaos is expected to win and get his long-delayed revenge, Homer brings in Aphrodite, the Greeks' goddess of love, who snaps her favourite Paris' helmet strip to free him, sweeps him up in a mist and transports him to Helen. But Helen calls him a coward; she secretly hoped her former husband would win and carry her back to Sparta. Menelaos comes out not only physically but also morally stronger as he is willing to take Helen back and let bygones be bygones. As he ranges over the field, wondering where his enemy has got to, he savours his moral victory.

The judgements of commentators ancient and modern have not been kind to Menelaos. Old Egyptian texts ridiculed him as 'feeble,' while one modern scholar dismisses him as 'second-rate' and 'faintly ridiculous.'[11] The basis for such judgements seems to be the Homeric picture of the goddess Aphrodite plucking Paris magically out of danger before Menelaos can destroy him in single combat – a sneaking suspicion that Homer could have invented the fantastic episode to explain away what actually may have been Menelaos' inability to overpower his more effete opponent.

Whatever his limitations as a soldier, Menelaos remained loyal to Agamemnon throughout, submerging his own wish for peace in the greater cause. He stayed awake with worry when things were going badly for the Greeks. His sense of wounded honour was slaked only when Paris was killed in action and he was given the opportunity to mistreat the corpse. Helen was married off to another Trojan, but Menelaos still wanted her back. And in the end, he got her, when around 1180 the Greeks finally sacked Troy and went home.

Homer's other epic poem, the *Odyssey*, affords us a few more glimpses of Menelaos in later years, enjoying the comforts of home with a contrite Helen who sounds too good to be true. In Book IV of the *Odyssey* we see Menelaos secure on his throne, recalling his years of combat before Troy yet not boasting about them. However, he doesn't fail to tell visitors that he was one of the Greeks waiting inside the wooden horse that was towed into Troy and proved that city's downfall. He sheds tears of remembrance for lost comrades and gives the impression of an ordinary king who has done his military duty and is well recompensed for it in later life.

Homer's version of events is, of course, unsupported by historical evidence. But that doesn't mean it must be rejected. There is no contrary evidence that those events did *not* happen or that Agamemnon, Menelaos and Paris were figments of the vivid Homeric imagination. If many generations of later Greeks were prepared to believe it, and they haven't so far been proved wrong, there is no reason why we should not.

Just east of Sparta, on a height overlooking the Eurotas, archaeologists have uncovered what is called the Menelaion, or shrine to Menelaos. By the grand standard of ancient Greek ruins it's unprepossessing, four sides of low masonry about 100 feet square, in the middle of which the remains of a higher wall rest on a mound. There is no incontrovertible sign that it was Menelaos' dwelling (in fact, it may have been built much later than the 12th century), but conversely there is no evidence that it was not, so there is no harm in imagining Menelaos living in middle-aged wedded bliss in that house.

Yet one very real relic jars with this scene. One of the exhibits of the Sparta Archaeological Museum is a marble stele about half a metre high, carved about the sixth century, featuring Menelaos in the act of stabbing Helen with a very large blade. Did he not manage to overcome his jealous wrath after all?

Another version of the Menelaos-and-Helen story was penned by Herodotus, the fifth century historian and traveller. When Herodotus was travelling in Egypt he was intrigued by a temple dedicated to 'Foreign Aphrodite' in the royal palace at Memphis. Egypt's ruler at the time was a king whom the Greeks called Proteus, the first of the New Kingdom's XX Dynasty. Employing what today might be called investigative journalism, Herodotus learned from Egyptian priests that Paris and Helen, after fleeing Greece, were blown off course, and ended up not at Troy but at one of the mouths of the Nile. Paris, a haughty and arrogant young noble, was in the habit of mistreating his servants, who took revenge by informing the Egyptian authorities of the kidnapping. The pharaoh ordered Paris out of Egypt, but kept back Helen and the Spartan treasure he had absconded with to give back to their rightful owner.

Menelaos, however, had no way of knowing this, and when he arrived at Troy he demanded back Helen and the stolen treasure, plus reparations. The Trojans strenuously denied having them. Herodotus casts doubt on Homer's narrative, figuring that if Helen indeed had been at Troy, the Trojan king Priam, being an honourable man, would have unhesitatingly handed her back to her husband. But Menelaos didn't believe the Trojans, and the Trojan War was on. When the war was finally over Menelaos decided to follow a clue which the Trojans had given him, namely, that Helen must be in Egypt. Menelaos sailed up the Nile to Memphis, found Helen and took her back with the Egyptian king's blessing. 'Foreign Aphrodite' was the Egyptians' term for Helen.

Menelaos' character appears consistent in both Homer's and Herodotus' stories, except for one jarring note in the latter. As contrary winds kept Menelaos from sailing back to Greece, he took a page out of his brother Agamemnon's book and sacrificed two Egyptian youths to get a favourable wind. Hearing of this crime, the Egyptian king's forces pursued Menelaos.

But he escaped first to Libya and then across the Mediterranean. Menelaos' apparent ruthlessness in performing a double human sacrifice would be in character with the possibility that he killed Helen, as the stele in the Sparta Archaeological Museum suggests.[12]

## Orestes and Tisamenos (*c.* 1150–1120?)

According to Pausanias, Menelaos had a daughter called Hermione. Presumably, given Helen's flight and the long years of his absence before Troy, he didn't have time to furnish himself with a son and heir. Therefore, probably to keep the political link with Mykenai intact, Hermione was married off to Orestes, the son of Agamemnon, who assumed the throne at Sparta. It was in the reign of Orestes' son Tisamenos, between about 1130 and 1120 at a very rough guess, that the whole Greek world, including the comfortable royal domesticity at Sparta, was abruptly overturned.

## Chapter 2

# Sons of Herakles

Eurysthenes and Prokles
Agis I and Eurypon
Echestratos and Prytanis
Labotas to Charillos
Teleklos and Nikandros

## Eurysthenes and Prokles (*c.* 1103–1060?)

After Tisamenos a thick fog of ignorance descends and legend very slowly begins to give place to history. It's as if we have been watching a film and the screen has suddenly gone dark, and now we're expecting real people to appear on the stage. But the theatre lights are still very dim, and we're not sure at which point those real people do begin appearing on the historical stage of Sparta, or even who they are.

The Trojan War or its equivalent had seriously upset Greece's domestic economy, eating up manpower and impoverishing the countryside. Diminishing resources had triggered mass migrations, mostly to the Middle East. The prestige and power of Mykenai, Sparta and other centres shrank amazingly quickly. Even within Menelaos' lifetime some of the once-prosperous communities of Lakonia were sputtering out. The remaining towns and villages were thus fair game for a hardier breed of Greeks called the Dorians, who were pushing down from the north.

The Spartans of later years, in order to explain and perhaps sanctify their extraordinary military proclivities, cultivated the myth that their rulers were direct descendants of Herakles, the legendary strongman. According to this narrative, when Herakles died and was taken up into the pantheon of gods, his sons – the Herakleidai – took refuge in Athens from persecution by their father's enemies. After seeing off those enemies by various means, the Herakleidai went on the counteroffensive and invaded the Peloponnese. Herakles' grandson Aristomachos was killed in the initial attempt to force the Isthmus near Corinth, the neck of land that connects the Peloponnese with the mainland, Greece's most strategic choke-point. Aristomachos' son Temenos took up the cause but invaded from another direction – across the narrowest point of the Gulf of Corinth at Rhion (now Rio). The Herakleidai clan was credited with leading the Dorians south to take over the weakened and defunct Achaian domains.

As the legitimation of every Spartan king, from the first to the last, hinged directly on his perceived pedigree from the line of Herakles, it's worth taking a closer look at this mythical man. Herakles in Greek legend was a son or son-in-law (the tradition is not clear here) of Zeus, which explains his extraordinary physical strength, a kind of Greek Samson-figure. Herakles is portrayed as essentially good-natured, more brawn than brain, but condemned to carrying out a series of near-impossible tasks for having angered the gods by being too good to people. He is one of several atonement-figures that appear in the traditions of the ancient world, a mythical embodiment of the harsh realities of human existence, where good and strong people often have to suffer precisely because of their goodness and strength.

Steeped in such a tradition, the kings of Sparta would see themselves as public servants rather than rulers. The attitude was most pronounced in the earlier centuries of the kingship, when the kings studiously avoided the more obvious pretensions of royal status such as palaces and vast wealth. At least until the fourth century almost all of them lived extremely simply, putting Sparta first and themselves second. In Greek tradition Herakles, as half-god and half-man, was credited with being able to overcome death.[1] Thus we have a quasi-religious underpinning for the Spartan kings' active engagement with death, especially on the battlefield. All male Spartans were taught that such a demise was far preferable to a slow death of old age at home – a message that got through to a good number of Spartan women as well.

But all this lay in the future as the Dorians began to descend in waves from the north. The Dorians were so named because they first appeared in a region of central Greece known as Doris. They seem to have been of Macedonian origin and eager to settle in the warmer Peloponnese, though Herodotus reports a rather dubious tradition that their real origin might have been Egypt. The Dorian invasion of southern Greece, which reached its apogee in the eleventh century, was no mere confluence of migrations by people seeking a warmer climate. It was a distinct and well-planned campaign of military conquest. The Peloponnese was the target of a precise three-pronged offensive aimed at the three main centres of Achaian power: Mykenai, Sparta and Pylos. After crossing the Gulf of Corinth the Dorians split into three waves. The westernmost wave occupied the lush Messenian plain, the easternmost smashed what was left of mighty Mykenai, and the centre column made a beeline for Lakedaimon and Sparta. The speed and surgical effectiveness of these incursions suggests that the Herakleidai had done a good job of briefing the Dorian leaders about the resources of the Achaian domains beforehand.

Some 2,000 Dorian Greeks under Aristodemos entered Sparta sometime between 1120 and 1105, deposing and driving out Tisamenos. Military morale in Sparta must already have been low. Tisamenos, whose subsequent fate is unknown, was replaced by the head man of the village of Amyklai to the south of Sparta, as Amyklai had allied itself with the Dorians from the outset, suggesting a certain pre-existing hostility to Sparta by some of the outlying Lakedaimonian communities. Who actually ruled Sparta in these turbulent years is not known. Aristodemos, since he co-opted a local man for that task, may have resisted the temptation to become a usurping king as a needless provocation. If that was his intention, it was a wise one, as it would have helped the newcomers settle peaceably into the older community.

Aristodemos seems to have been a devout man, a frequent visitor to the Oracle at Delphi from where he would get sound advice. Pausanias reports that he received divine approval for his twin sons, Eurysthenes and Prokles, to rule jointly after his death. According to Herodotus, who delved a little deeper into the family story, shortly after the twins were born Aristodemos was murdered while journeying to Delphi, possibly by relatives of the deposed Tisamenos, about 1103. The twins were raised by their mother Argeia who was the only one who could tell them apart. This threw the Spartan elders into a quandary, as only one firstborn could succeed Aristodemos. (This story would cast some doubt on the claim that Delphi urged a double kingship.) Argeia knew which child had exited the womb first, but was keeping it a secret. The Oracle at Delphi was again consulted, and the reply was that both twins indeed should reign together, though the 'elder,' again, should receive more honour.

Such an 'explanation' seems to be a clumsy attempt to reconcile the traditional idea of a single monarch with the alleged Delphic ruling – which of course solved nothing. A man from neighbouring Messene named Panites came up with the idea of keeping a watch on Argeia to see which twin she would habitually pick up and feed and wash first, on the logical grounds that it would be the 'elder.' The thus-favoured child turned out to be Eurysthenes. An uncle of the twins named Theras became the boys' guardian, but when the boys grew to manhood and claimed their rightful power Theras was unwilling to give it up, having 'become used to being the boss,' as Herodotus puts it. Theras was eventually forced out of Sparta to found a colony on the Aegean island of Thera (now Santorini), which took its name from him. As for Eurysthenes and Prokles, the controversy surrounding their infant status must have carried over into manhood, poisoning their relations. Later

Spartans credited them with being unbearably autocratic. Pausanias reports that they despised each other for the rest of their lives.[2]

## Agis I and Eurypon (*c.* 1050–1000?)

The dual kingship was retained by the sons of Eurysthenes and Prokles, Agis I and Eurypon respectively, who by common consent split the Herakleidai line and established the simultaneous Agiad and Eurypontid royal lines in an arrangement that worked, albeit with the inevitable strains, for the next 900 years. How exactly this was done is not known. These sons' names were believed to have been given to the respective royal houses in a reaction against the mutual loathing of their fathers which was seen as a bad omen for the continuation of both lines. In later years King Pleistarchos (480–459) would claim that as Eurysthenes and Prokles were absolute rulers and their successors rather more likeable figures, in keeping with Spartan tradition it wouldn't have been proper to name them as heads of dynasties. It's an 'explanation' that smacks of casuistry but it's the only one we have.

That, in short, is the Spartan founding myth. And like all such myths, it has come in for some robust criticism by later scholars. Some believe it was invented to paper over the very different origins of the Agiad and Eurypontid houses: the Agiads could have stemmed from the earlier Achaian dynasty of Tyndareos and Menelaos, while the Eurypontids were descendants of the Dorian invaders. It was thus in Sparta's interests, to prevent a potentially fatal split in Spartan society, that official propaganda give both houses a common ancestor in Herakles. The dual kingship turned out to be a durable and effective power-sharing deal. Buttressing this view is the historical fact that neither royal house ever intermarried with the other (though there would presumably have been many opportunities for it), and that each house retained its hereditary servants and burial place. This would argue for a strong underlying notion of tribal separateness. One latter-day Spartan scholar speculates that Eurysthenes and Prokles could have been fictitious figures, invented for propaganda purposes to connect Aristodemos with the eponymous originators of the Agiad and Eurypontid lines, Agis I and Eurypon.[3]

Towards the end of the eleventh century Agis I helped Sparta establish a port city on the north shore of the Peloponnese called Patrai (modern Patras). A grandson of Orestes named Gras sailed across the Aegean to found colonies in Asia Minor. These developments could be echoes of a budding overpopulation problem, complicated perhaps by persistent dynastic mutterings by relatives of the deposed Tisamenos. As for Prokles, his son Sous was relatively quickly succeeded by his grandson Eurypon, whose name was adopted for the royal house. We know nothing else about Eurypon except that, under his son Prytanis, Sparta began the task of consolidating its realm.

It's often assumed that the Dorian controlling class had little time for art and learning, except on a purely practical level. There is little hard evidence for this view, as Sparta in later years certainly had no lack of poetry, music and dance. Yet historians still commonly view the four centuries from the collapse of Mykenaian civilization to the birth of Homer and Greek literature as the equivalent of a Greek 'dark age.'

Whatever artistic or literary culture there was, however, was recruited into the maintenance of the Dorian city-state, a social and political structure designed to make the citizen feel a part of something larger than himself, to safeguard the local economy and to instil a sense of civic pride and discipline.

## Echestratos and Prytanis (*c.* 1000–950?)

What is remarkable in these years is that the dual kingship held together, seemingly unaffected by the inevitable interpersonal conflicts and power drives which must have made up a good part of Spartan royal politics. One factor in this stability was the ceremonial respect which the royal houses now claimed. Sparta had yet to form itself into a territorial unity; the town was just one of several communities in Lakedaimon jealously guarding their independence. The two kings therefore had the vital function of representing and personifying the wider state in the absence of a centralized administration. Their precise duties at this stage, except for ceremonial and military functions, are but vaguely known. If we extrapolate from the historical tendency for the Spartan kings to gradually give up some of their powers until about the fourth century, we can assume that their power in the tenth century was considerable. We know of no countervailing authority that could provide a check on them. But neither do we know of any serious abuse of power on their part. We can, however, be fairly sure that they upheld the distinct and unchanging sense of military destiny that was a key part of Sparta's Dorian ideology, and which by the eighth century had earned Sparta considerable dividends in territory and influence.

King Echestratos, the son of Agis I, and Prytanis of the Eurypontid house, organized expeditions to take over Kynouria, the coastal stretch of the eastern Peloponnese between Lakonia and Mykenai, which as a military and commercial power was under the control of Argos. For some time lawless bands had been raiding lands in Argive territory, and as Sparta was an ally of Argos, Echestratos rounded up all the Kynourian men of military age and transferred them to Lakedaimon to work the land as serfs and keep them out of mischief.[4] Kynouria had a strategic importance for Lakedaimon since the main northbound road ran perilously close to that lawless region. Sparta could not rest until Echestratos and Prytanis had secured it as a buffer zone. Yet the reduction of Kynouria awoke anxieties in neighbouring Argos about Sparta's military capabilities.

The Spartan military reputation actually masked the uncomfortable fact that the Spartan kingdom in its early years was small and vulnerable. The four townships making up Sparta proper stretched for just eight or so kilometres along the Eurotas River. To the south lay the community of Amyklai, flaunting an aggressive independence going back to the days of Amyklas. To the north the communities of Pellana and Sellasia sat astride the narrow part of the Lakonian plain between the northernmost spurs of Mounts Taygetos and Parnon. These were still inhabited by pre-Dorian subject populations with whom the Spartans could never feel quite comfortable, rightly suspecting that they could at any time rebel. The strategy of Sparta in the ninth century was to secure these potentially unsafe neighbouring areas. After the reduction of Kynouria, it was the turn of Pellana and Sellasia, and their fertile fields, to come under Sparta's heel.

## Labotas to Charillos (*c.* 950–760?)

Echestratos' reign seems not to have been a long one; his son Labotas assumed the Agiad throne. Argos in the meantime had repudiated its earlier friendship with Sparta and had begun to counter-occupy Kynouria, fomenting anti-Spartan revolts among the peasantry. Labotas moved to correct this state of affairs. Tradition credits him with securing Pellana and Sellasia, the two communities at the northern approaches to Sparta. Pausanias reports that Labotas' son Doryssos, and Doryssos' son Agesilaos I, were both killed early in their reigns. Mystery surrounds their deaths. They may be presumed to have been killed in battle, yet our sources assure us that the corresponding Eurypontid kings of the time, Eunomos and Polydektes, presided over 'a period of peace.'[5] The alternatives are that Doryssos and Agesilaos I may have been assassinated, or deposed as unsuitable.

These early campaigns to bring Sparta's neighbours to heel were not simply annexations of fertile land but a systematic extension of political influence designed to last a long time. The owners of the conquered lands were allowed to keep and cultivate them as long as they remained available for conscription in Sparta's army. These populations were called the *perioikoi*, or 'dwellers-around,' and given a distinctly second-class status. The early kings of Sparta preferred to be militarily strong rather than well-fed. By the eighth century Sparta's northern approaches were secure enough for the next step: control of the southern part of Lakedaimon, including the seaport at Gytheion.

If several kings appear in previous paragraphs as mere transient names, it is because next to nothing is known about them. That being the case, it's the delicate task of the chronicler to fill in as much of the largely blank canvas as possible on evidence that is sometimes highly circumstantial. For example, it's a reasonable conclusion that the Spartan kings of this period must have varied in character and military competence. In the main they were solid enough men to maintain the royal office when Sparta was most vulnerable. Character was highly important. The ascendancy of Tyndareos over his elder brother Hippokoon may well have turned on the fact that Tyndareos was the stronger character. The era of the powerful Achaian *wanax* suzerain was long gone. A regional king, a *basileus*, was expected to be in full and total command of his own domain. The myth of the Spartan kings' descent from Herakles must have helped. By this reasoning it is also worth speculating whether the 'one-line' kings such as Doryssos, Agesilaos I and Polydektes had weaker characters which in the old chroniclers' view diminished their historical importance, and perhaps even had them ejected from office.

Sparta's kings, it must be pointed out, had nothing of the divine or awe-inspiring attached to them, in contrast to Middle Eastern absolute rulers such as Egypt's pharaohs. Their personal qualities alone ensured their political survival. They lived off the proceeds of their properties, which cannot have been very lavish at the best of times. The royal revenues took the form of a fixed tribute from the *perioikoi* and other levies in kind, plus war booty. Archaeologists have yet to come up with any Spartan palatial ruins to match even the modest dimensions of the Menelaion. Nowhere do we hear of any sumptuous royal living, of any of the elaborate accoutrements of other ancient kingdoms such as lavish entourages and legions of praetorian guards. If we are to believe Herodotus, some of the early Spartan kings lived in such noble simplicity that 'their own wives baked the bread of the house.'[6] With the passage of centuries they continued to live as aristocrats of modest means, shunning display of any kind and setting a strong moral example for upholding the rigid class-based system. When new territory came under Sparta's control the kings made sure to give each Spartan citizen a share of new land so as to maintain the citizens' stake in the permanence of the regime.

It would be wrong, however, to think of Sparta's kings as likeable but pretty much powerless figureheads on today's British or Scandinavian model. Some may indeed have been such figures by inclination, confining themselves to their ceremonial duties as priests of Zeus Lakedaimonios and Zeus Ouranios, two forms of the father of gods. Others were more activist. The kings were the only officials entitled to declare war. Plutarch cites one un-named 'ancient king' as enshrining the principle that the Spartans should never ask how many their enemies were, but *where* they were, a dictum that gained wide currency for a long time. The kings kept in close touch with the Oracle at Delphi, which they later sought to control, yet nevertheless never ceased to hold in awe. Wherever they went they each were entitled to three upper-class aides-de-camp and a cavalry bodyguard of 100 picked men. When a king died representatives of the whole Lakedaimonian population had to attend his funeral, the women beating pots in a ritual dirge. Anyone refusing to mourn in this way could be severely punished. If a king fell on the battlefield he was buried there; back at home his effigy was placed in a flower-bedecked coffin and put in a cenotaph, or empty tomb. (This ritual was later changed.) For ten days afterwards, no Spartan was allowed to buy or sell or conduct any state business. The symbolic reverence attached to the kings indicates their vital function as the administrative connection between Sparta proper and its outlying domains, much as the British monarch used to be the official link between Britain and its Empire.[7] All had to play the unceasing see-saw game of power with the controlling classes, sometimes losing and sometimes winning, according to the character and abilities of each particular king.

The short reign of the Agiad Agesilaos I was followed by that of Arkesilaos, of whom we know nothing save that he himself was succeeded by Agesilaos' son Archelaos, suggesting that Archelaos was a minor at the time of his father's death and Arkesilaos served as a regent. Pausanias, however, clearly refers to Arkesilaos' term as a 'reign,' implying that he may have usurped the throne, only to be displaced later by its rightful occupant. The reign of Arkesilaos, however long or short it might have been, saw a solidifying of Sparta's political structure as a city-state, perhaps as a consequence of the dynastic irregularity. In the Eurypontid house, Prytanis was succeeded by Eunomos, who according to Plutarch was slain in an outburst of civil unrest after what Pausanias claims was a peaceful reign. Eunomos was followed by his son Polydektes, also described as a man of peace.

Polydektes died before his son and successor Charillos (sometimes referred to as Charilaos) was born. Looking after the Eurypontid house at the time, according to an uncertain tradition, was one Lykourgos – possibly a younger brother of the late Polydektes – who became the infant king's guardian. 'A Spartan king is born!' Lykourgos announced to the elders when Charillos came into the world. The Spartan people were happy it was a male child, hence his name, meaning 'Joy of the People'. Plutarch here puts a fly in the ointment, claiming that though a male baby was greeted with glee by the people, it was the last thing his mother wanted, and she plotted to have him done away with. Her aim was to make Lykourgos king and marry him. Some-how the plot failed and Charillos grew up determined to make his mark. He led seriously destructive expeditions against Argos, now seen as Sparta's prime foe. Tegea, a central Peloponnesian state to the north of Sparta (near modern Tripoli) was next on Charillos' list but he failed to take it because he probably misinterpreted a Delphic oracle which he had taken care to obtain beforehand. It was a mistake that more than one Spartan king would make.

Charillos in later times was credited with being one of the Spartan sage-kings. Plutarch quotes him as saying Sparta needed few laws because they were enough for a people of few words. He continued the Spartan men's tradition of wearing the hair long 'as a natural and inexpensive form of decoration.' He touched on an aspect of Spartan sexual politics when someone asked him why the Spartans took their unmarried girls into public places unveiled but kept their wives covered up. 'The girls have to find husbands,' he said, 'while the married women have to keep theirs!' Charillos' ideal form of government, he said, was one where 'the greatest number of citizens are willing, without civil strife, to vie with one another in virtue.'[8]

The reign of Charillos has become associated with the rise of Lykourgos, Sparta's greatest social and political reformer. This would place him in the early eighth century. Authorities differ over when Lykourgos carried out his reforms, but the reigns of Charillos and the next two Eurypontid kings are the most likely time-frame. This theory, however, requires that Lykourgos had to have a fifty-year career at least and live to be a very old man.

Be that as it may, tradition agrees that as soon as Charillos came of age Lykourgos left Sparta, determined to expand his mind. He studied the administration of the Dorian city-states of Crete and sailed to Asia Minor and even Egypt in search of more ideas on efficient statecraft. Returning to Sparta determined to overhaul the state from top to bottom, he made such a dramatic entry into the city armed to the teeth, according to Plutarch, that he sent Charillos running to a sanctuary in terror. The incident, if true, might explain the opposition of Charillos' mother to Lykourgos who, moreover, didn't want to become her second husband. Yet once the king, 'a good man and lover of his country',[9] got over his initial shock he was a willing accomplice in Lykourgos' design to overhaul Sparta along the lines of state militarism, strict social discipline and a ban on a money economy. (See Polydoros and Theopompos below.)

## Teleklos and Nikandros (*c.* 790–750?)

Charillos' son and successor Nikandros kept the army in shape by continuing to ravage the lands around Argos. While he was thus occupied, the Agiad house was producing some able men. One of them was Archelaos' son

Teleklos, the first Spartan king whose reign can be dated with some degree of precision (*c.* 790–*c.* 760).

Teleklos was a vigorous champion of the drive for more land. After a long struggle he seized Amyklai to the south, plus Pharis and Geronthrai (now Geraki) in the folds of Mount Parnon which had been inhabited by descendants of the old Achaeans for at least three centuries and lay outside the Dorian state structure. Amyklai became the fifth borough of Sparta proper. The people of Pharis and Geronthrai agreed to leave the Peloponnese and seek new homes, possibly in Athens, which was becoming the chief city of the Ionian branch of Greeks.

Teleklos' next project was to secure the approaches to the rich and tempting Messenian plain to the west, on the other side of Mount Taygetos. As a first step he occupied Dentheliatis overlooking the plain. From there one could look northwest to the Spartans' ultimate objective. This was the very fertile plain of Stenyklaros, a breadbasket if ever there was one.

Teleklos may have been a good military man, but he had a cunning and ruthless streak. As Stenyklaros was a longish distance from Sparta and bounded on the south by Messenian territory, some kind of hardball was needed to discourage the Messenians from trying to seize it. Teleklos' plot was to lure a group of high-ranking Messenians to the shrine at Dentheliatis. There he set among them some beardless Spartan boys disguised as 'hospitality girls.' Under their skirts they carried daggers. They had orders to pounce on the Messenians on a predetermined signal and kill them. Something went horribly wrong, however, and it was the Spartan boys who ended up being butchered, along with Teleklos himself.[10]

Against this evidence for a proclivity for plotting, Plutarch has preserved some instances that show Teleklos to have been a stern judge of character. When, for example, Teleklos was told that his own father was speaking against him, his modest response was that his father must have some good reason for it – a sign that he was quite aware of his failings. He never, to anyone's knowledge, sought to acquire land or goods beyond what he needed, and insisted that young men rise in the presence of their elders in order to learn how to 'pay greater honour to their parents.'[11]

# Chapter 3

# Forging the Spartan State

Alkamenes
Poydoros and Theopompos
Eurykrates to Agasikles
Ariston
Anaxandridas II

## Alkamenes (*c.* 750–730)

Teleklos' son and successor Alkamenes understandably decided to give Stenyklaros a miss for the time being; there was general agreement that Sparta had brought its predicament on itself through Teleklos' misplaced craftiness. Alkamenes therefore concentrated his energies on completing the control of Sparta's southern approaches. In the late eight century he captured Helos, a village on the Lakonian coast (near present Molai), putting its inhabitants to work on Spartan lands as Helots – a term henceforth used for a subservient class whose condition was little different from slavery.

Under Alkamenes the Spartan-controlled domains took up not only Lakedaimon and the Eurotas valley 'home counties,' as it were, but also the entire rugged middle peninsula of the southern Peloponnese – later to become known as Mani – and the borders of mountainous Arkadia to the north. Some 4,500 Spartan property-owning households totalling 32,000 citizens formed the upper layer of society, ruling about 120,000 subject *perioikoi* in the middle and some 200,000 Helots at the bottom to do the menial jobs. At the end of his reign Alkamenes took an active part in the First Messenian War (see below) but didn't live beyond the war's opening campaigns.

Alkamenes was a modest man who lived up to the frugal ideal of the Spartan kingship by insisting on living simply, despite owning a good deal of property. He was also incorruptible. When the Messenians tried to bribe him to stay away from their territory he refused the gifts, saying it would be illegal to accept them, and if he broke the law in that way 'it would be impossible to maintain peace' at home. Alkamenes was later credited with the saying that it was a noble thing 'to live according to reason and not according to desires.'[1]

## Polydoros and Theopompos (*c.* 730–700)

It was under Alkamenes' son and successor in the Agiad line, Polydoros ('He Of Many Gifts'), that the Spartan polity took its first steps towards forging itself into the *par excellence* militaristic state of the ancient Greek world. Much of the credit for this must go to Lykourgos (see Labotas to Charillos above). There were several motives for thoroughgoing reform in the eighth century. One was the continuing hostility of the Messenians in the west and the realization that they would be dangerous foes for a long time to come. Another motive lay probably in the Lakedaimonian heartland itself, not as lushly fertile as Messenia and hence innately economically weak. There was also a need for a backup to the kings themselves, who were vulnerable to being killed on campaign and might thus deprive Sparta of leadership at crucial moments. The Spartiate upper class, which fought the wars and owned most of the land, demanded a greater say in the running of the state. The way to overcome these liabilities was to clothe the Dorian-type city-state in iron. Just when this happened is a vexed question. Against Plutarch's claim that Lykourgos began his reforms in the reign of Charillos, there is a more modern consensus that they didn't begin until Polydoros.

If the royal houses at first looked favourably on Lykourgos, they soon had reason to feel some alarm, as his overhauling of the state greatly diluted the royal power in favour of the elites who were demanding greater representation. One of Lykourgos' first moves to cement social cohesion was to create a new arm of government in the form of a thirty-man Gerousia or senate, charged with drawing up bills to be voted on by the assembly of citizens, the Apella. The two kings were co-opted as senior members of the Gerousia, which means literally an 'assembly of old men.' None of the lay Gerousia were under sixty years of age, and younger kings might well feel intimidated in their august presence. It must have been a distinct come-down for the kings to be made into mere senators, though they could have derived some consolation from the fact that the Apella had voting rights only, and no authority to debate or initiate issues.

Keeping the Apella weak could well have been the price of royal support for the new constitution, as we know that around the middle of the eighth century Alkamenes and his co-king, the Eurypontid Theopompos ('Sent by God'), pulled rank to thwart an attempt by the Apella to assume debating and amendment powers.[2] The Apella remained little more than a rubber stamp, but the kings needn't have worried. They would soon have plenty to do.

Under Lykourgos' new regimen there was nothing resembling the 'private sphere' of today's culture, not even for the kings. All spheres were public. Every person, from the highest Spartiates to the lowliest Helot, occupied a precisely-defined post in the state hierarchy and was supposed to devote his and her life to that structure. The top Spartiates citizen class was reserved for the supreme task of providing the state's soldiers and administrators. Selection for a Spartiates boy's military career began precisely at birth, ruled by relentless eugenics. The problem of sickly infants was effectively dealt with by exposing them in the Kaiadas ravine on Mount Taygetos for the vultures to eat. Healthy children were allowed to live with their parents until the age of seven, when boys and girls were segregated and assigned to their respective *agelai*, or 'herds,' to undergo the *agoge*, or training schedule.

Much has been written about the *agoge* over the ages, much of it false. It's generally assumed that Lykourgos invented it, and that for Spartan youth it was a living hell of flogging and constant mistreatment, calculated to drive all humanity out of the average Spartiates boy and turn him into a brutal fighting machine. That is a hopelessly distorted picture. First, there is no extant contemporary source for the *agoge* in the eighth to the fifth centuries. Second, the earliest sources are the historians Herodotus, Xenophon and Plutarch, who describe nothing more than a rigorous system of public education for both sexes. Sparta was the only Greek state to have this facility. Parents paid fees in kind to the schools.

The youngsters were put in uniform and taught how to live on slender means by being fed at just over the minimum subsistence level. They do not seem to have been starved, as later writers claim, in order to encourage them to steal. They wore a single garment for all weathers and were taught sports and military drill. They had to bathe daily in the Eurotas River in all seasons. At some point, perhaps in their mid-teens, they were given a sort of bivouac training, in which their prowess as hunters was tested. Some of the wilder or more resourceful spirits might steal from farms, but there is no evidence that the practice was encouraged or had become a social problem.

It is often claimed that the Spartiates boy between seven and twenty-one could be flogged on the slightest pretext, merely to toughen him up. Such a practice, in fact, seems not to have appeared until the third century under Kleomenes III, who attempted a revival of what he believed were the old Lykourgan virtues (see Kleomenes III below). 'Spartan education,' says one modern authority, 'was designed to turn the graduates of the *agoge* into good soldiers.'[3] The staple Spartan diet was very basic, consisting of barley bread and an eye-watering concoction called 'black broth' (*melas zomos*), made of pork fragments, pig's blood, salt and vinegar. As a source of protein and an aid in digestion, black broth may have been effective, but it definitely was an acquired taste, as whenever other Greeks tried it they would spit it out in disgust. However, on the reasonable assumption that any nourishment would have been welcome after a hard morning of exercising and drill, black broth remained a main item on the Spartan menu for centuries.

The most controversial aspect of the final stage of the *agoge* regimen, applicable at age eighteen, was the infamous *krypteia*, or secret service. For two years a young Spartiate was authorized to harass any member of the inferior peasant or slave classes and even murder any suspected of plotting revolt. The *krypteia* accomplished two aims: to hone the Spartiates' field skills and keep the serfs and Helots cowed. Yet the picture of a continually terrorized countryside cannot be an accurate one. We might better imagine the *krypteia* as a police training course that only in extreme cases would have resorted to a licence to kill – like modern police forces anywhere. At twenty-one the young Spartiates settled down to nine years of barracks life and war service. Assuming he survived that, at thirty he was allowed to marry and become a lifelong member of the Spartan assembly. But his married life was far from ideal. By day he associated with his fellow Spartiates, going home to his wife only in the evenings. From then until he turned sixty he was liable at any time for combat or rear-echelon duty. To keep his mind on his duties, and himself personally incorruptible, at no time was a full Spartan citizen permitted to engage in trade or industry or handle gold and silver coinage. In fact, the Spartiates exercised no profession besides that of arms. He didn't produce anything, but lived off the labours of those he was called on to protect.

There was also a considerable mystic element in Spartan society. In the psychological sphere a state obsessed with the military way of life must come to terms with those awesome forces that come to the fore in such a way of life – fear and death. As both needed to be propitiated, both had temples erected to them. The Temple of Fear, for example, was a recognition that fear can be a healthy emotion if it is channelled into the common good. The Spartans, Plutarch observed much later, 'worship Fear.' This is not as bizarre as it might sound today. Throughout the ages, thoughtful men and the greatest soldiers have said that courage is not an absence of fear; on the contrary, it lies in doing one's duty even when fear is overwhelming. A degree of fear is necessary to be able to think wisely in dangerous situations. The Temple of Death was built for a similar purpose – to familiarize people with the idea of death and thus provide an antidote to worldly materialism and overweening ambition.[4]

The lingering Messenian wars, more than anything else, created the need for a backup to the royal authority. As both kings more often than not were away campaigning, someone had to stay at home to run the state. At first the kings picked their own close associates for the job, but it wasn't long before these men began to arrogate more power to themselves than was originally intended. They morphed into a permanent magistracy, taking the name of Ephors (*ephoroi*), literally Overseers. They appear as a distinct government department in 754 in the reign of Theopompos, consisting of one man from each of Sparta's five boroughs. We know the name of the first chief Ephor, one Elatos. They were initially charged with duties of divination and star-gazing to seek the gods' will for projected campaigns, and the gods' explanations for failures. Harmless enough, one might think. Yet the Ephorate represented one more slice off the royal prerogatives; within a few hundred years it would assume hugely greater powers, threatening to eclipse the royal authority. (In modern Greek, incidentally, the term *ephoros* has come to mean the taxman – again not a favourite state functionary.)

Sifting through the scanty historical evidence, we may conclude with some degree of confidence that some kings didn't take kindly to Lykourgos' Spartan constitution. Correspondingly, the Gerousia and later the Ephors tried to erode the royal authority whenever they could. But there wasn't much a discontented king could do. As a descendant of the Herakleidai he would have to be careful not to display either greed or a lust for power. He had to tread carefully. None of the kings were wealthy in the ordinary sense of the word and they didn't live in grand palaces. In return for not rocking the state boat, the young heirs-apparent of the royal houses were exempt from the rigours of the *agoge*. Nevertheless, they were inevitably the objects of envy from the more ambitious members of the Spartan elite.

Timomachos was one such upper-crust Spartiates who had commanded the successful campaign to reduce Amyklai. Connected to the royals by marriage, Timomachos was widely admired as having reorganized the Spartan army along more efficient lines. But his rapid rise earned him the enmity of other Spartiates with the result that he fled to exile on the island of Thera. Amid these signs of social tension, the kings trod carefully. As for Lykourgos, the greatest praise due to him may be that he didn't try to usurp the kingship for himself, as he might easily have done with considerable prospects of success. On the contrary, it was said that after reinventing the Spartan state he retired to the haunting crags of Delphi, shut himself away and starved himself to death. He regarded his mission at an end, and thus himself as of no further use.

As Sparta's population grew in size and prosperity, so did its requirements for food. Despite a vigorous trade with other Greek states, with the islands and Asia Minor, and even with Egypt, Sparta preferred to have the fertile assets of its neighbour Messenia. Political memories among the Greeks have always been long, and so we can confidently expect that the assassination of King Teleklos by the Messenians, however justified, still rankled. The fields and orchards of Stenyklaros remained out of reach. The Messenians were keenly aware of the Spartans' designs and made moves to counter them. King Phintias of Messenia hired a famous bard to travel Greece to sing about the Spartan threat – one of the first uses of mass media to stoke inter-state tensions. Phintias' two successors, his sons Antiochos and Androkles, disagreed over how to handle the threat, with Antiochos urging a tough anti-Spartan line. The dispute turned violent, and in the resulting strife Androkles was killed. But his brother did not long outlive him, so around 735, about the time of the eleventh Olympiad, when Antiochos' heir was still a minor, Alkamenes judged that Messenia was in a weakened state and that the time was ripe for its conquest once and for all.

The Messenians, though Dorian in origin, had become used to the good life that their rich plains had provided. They had blended easily with the more numerous indigenous people and their prosperity seemed assured. Sparta, on the other hand, was being squeezed by a Malthusian problem of a grow-ing population on fixed landholdings. Just as importantly young Spartans, brought up by the *agoge* to consider themselves warriors first and foremost, 'could not abide the monotonous life of peace.'[5] The ingredients were in place for the First Messenian War.

Alkamenes and the younger Theopompos, plus Alkamenes' son Polydoros, marched their well-drilled Spartan columns northwards up the Eurotas valley, wheeling the army west at Aigytis hugging the northern end of Mount Taygetos. It may have been on this occasion that someone asked Polydoros how he felt going out to fight his Dorian brethren in Messenia. 'All I'm doing is claiming unassigned portions of the land,' he said in a smooth rationalization that has been used by aggressors from that day to this.[6] The Spartans surprised a Messenian garrison at Ampheia and massacred it along with its non-combatants. Ampheia became a Spartan base from which raid-ing parties set out to seize crops for the next three years.

In 732 Antiochos' heir Euphaes came of age and showed it by attack-ing the Spartans, but inconclusively. The following year Theopompos and Polydoros, who had now succeeded Alkamenes, marched with a bigger force into the Messenian plain. When the two armies came within sight of each other south of Mount Ithome, Theopompos (as presumably the senior king) halted the Spartans to give them a brief pep talk on what a noble feat of arms the conquest of Messenia would be. Then he took up his position on the right of the line, with Polydoros commanding the left.

Euphaes led an impetuous charge, slamming at full speed into Theopompos' solid wing of spears and shields and caving it inwards. In the struggle to maintain his battle order Theopompos manoeuvred for position to strike at Euphaes directly, but the Messenian leader evaded, keeping up the intense pressure on Theopompos' units with desperate energy. The Messenians fought, in Pausanias' words, 'in a frenzy of despair near to madness,' so resolved were they to repel the Spartan invader. On the Spartan left Polydoros was faring rather better, but as soon as he saw his co-king's difficulty he wheeled round to stiffen the right. Battle raged for hours until nightfall, when the Messenians had to retire from the field with Euphaes mortally wounded. In the morning, appalled by the carnage of the previous day, the Spartans too pulled back.

The casualties of the battle of Ithome were in part a consequence of large armies operating without what might be called military science. Tactics were rudimentary. The art of war had yet to become distinguished from the natural act of aggression. A Spartan regular soldier, known as a hoplite ('weapon-carrier'), carried a two-metre-long spear and a round shield. He wore a helmet, body armour and greaves, and marched and fought in a spread-out line formation. A typical battle might begin with a line of Spartan hoplites advancing unhurriedly towards the enemy line to the music of flutes. The hoplites would be accompanied by lighter-armed members of the *perioikoi* class who also had orderly and rear-echelon duties. (Much later, able-bodied Helots would also be recruited into the Spartan fighting ranks.) After the lines engaged it would be essentially a trial of brute strength to see which line would break first. The Spartans, thanks to their superior discipline and endurance, more often than not would win. On the other hand, line-battle with hoplites carried with it a serious risk. It was natural for each advancing hoplite, as he neared the enemy, to subconsciously seek the security of his neighbour's shield for his own unprotected right side. This would cause the whole line to shift to the right. Here a smart Spartan officer could make a difference, as a drifting front line could this way wrap around an enemy's exposed left flank, but such initiatives seemed to be still in the future.

After Euphaes' death the Messenians elected Aristodemos, a popular general, king in his place. For five years both sides sniped at each other in the hills of Ithome. Attempts by the Spartans to chase the partisans into the hills were costly. In 722 the war flared up again as the Arkadians of the mid-Peloponnese had decided to aid their Messenian neighbours. Argos, seeing Sparta discomfited, joined the list. Sparta in return secured the help of the strong trading city of Corinth in the north Peloponnese. In this war of attrition, the Messenians broke first. In the twentieth year of the war Aristodemos committed suicide and the Messenian leadership gave up the fight.

In Sparta the two kings were showered with gratitude. 'To our king beloved of the gods, Theopompos,' ran a ditty composed at the time, 'through whom we took Messene with its wide plains.'[7] Theopompos' abilities in peace seem to have been equal to his prowess in war. He believed, according to Plutarch, that the way to keeping a kingdom was to ensure that 'the subjects are not allowed to be wronged.' He realized that in the last analysis it wasn't a king who ruled, but his subjects in whom he could inculcate a willing obedience. He correctly assessed the merits of patriotism when he advised a Greek from another city who claimed to love Sparta that he should love his own country first. A strong city-state, he said, had no need of walls 'where only women live.'[8] Theopompos lived to an old age that towards the end was saddened when his son and heir-apparent Archidamos died before him. When Sparta renewed the fight with Argos over Thyreatis, Theopompos played no part in it.

Polydoros, as we have seen, gave early signs of his talent for politics. With many square kilometres of Messenian land now available for Sparta to cultivate, he lost little time in handing out at least 3,000 Messenian farms to Spartan citizens. Messenia itself was reduced to dependent status, though it retained some of the trappings of statehood, including the right to send athletes to the Olympic Games which had been instituted some sixty years before. But the long First Messenian War had cost Sparta, and not only in manpower. While Polydoros and Theopompos had been spending time in the field, the Spartan Apella gathered to itself more power. By about 715 the Apella had acquired the right to amend laws prepared by the Gerousia. When the upper chambers resisted, the two kings threw their weight behind them by threatening to block any legislation altered arbitrarily by the Apella.

Polydoros here was treading on thinning ice. His valiant record in the First Messenian War and his genial character had secured him great popularity with the masses. 'He never did a violent act or said an insulting word to anyone,' reports Pausanias, 'while as a judge he was both upright and humane.' Plutarch adds that Polydoros attributed Spartan success in arms to the fact that 'the Spartans have learned to respect their commanders and not to fear them.'[9]

This was the first sign of what would become a lasting division between the Spartan royal houses. Polydoros, being an Agiad, was presumably descended from the indigenous Achaians who ruled Sparta before the Dorian invasion. Founding myths aside, could the Agiad royals have been aware of their antecedents to the extent that they felt they owed the lower orders more support against the Dorian-origin upper crust? A more recent analogy would be England after the Norman conquest, where the Norman newcomers (like the Dorians) established their aristocracy on the backs of the earlier Anglo-Saxons (equivalent to the poorer Spartans and the *perioikoi*). It would explain the historical fact that for several hundred years to come the Agiad kings would display rather more 'democratic' tendencies than the conservative Eurypontids. Polydoros could have found himself sandwiched between a bumptious Apella, boosted by victorious soldiers, and the reactionary Ephors and Gerousia. Some of the Spartan aristocracy felt cheated out of its rightful gains in the Messenian war, believing that the lower orders had been given more land than their political status warranted. They smarted as Polydoros' fame spread throughout Greece. Shortly after the end of the war a hot-tempered aristocrat named Polemarchos assassinated him. The Apella promptly honoured the fallen king by erecting a bust of him in the centre of Sparta. His visage graced the new great seal of the state.

At this point there occurred the strange case of the 'Virgin Boys.' These were an undetermined number of sons born to Spartan women whose husbands had been away too long fighting in Messenia, and sired either by other Spartan citizens or Helots. The Spartan woman, then and later, was not one to live a passive husband-circumscribed existence, especially when her husband was away fighting much of the time, and for all she knew, she would never seen him again. The education and training she enjoyed as a teenager bred an independence of spirit that often found an outlet in a sexual liberty that the rest of Greece considered shocking. These young men were termed Virgin Boys apparently as a politically correct way of avoiding mention of their dubious fathering. When they grew to manhood they demanded land and civil rights. The demand was refused, and so about 708 they agreed to quit Sparta and found the city's only overseas colony, Taras in southern Italy (now Taranto).

## Eurykrates to Agasikles (*c.* 700–550?)

Polydoros was succeeded by his son Eurykrates, in whose longish reign the subjugated Messenians gave little trouble and the frontier with Argos was quiet. Matters seem not to have been so stable in the Eurypontid house, where Theopompos' grandson Zeuxidamos made way in short order for his own son Anaxandridas I. Pausanias, our sole source for this chink in the Spartan royal history, is vague on whether Zeuxidamos actually got to reign. His name, meaning 'placer of the yoke upon the people,' well indicates the anti-populist inclinations of the Eurypontid house. What we don't know is whether Zeuxidamos was given time to live up to his name. Given this uncertainty, conventional lists of the kings of Sparta do not include him.

The growing rift between the royal houses was part of a more general unsettlement of politics in Sparta. Before the unrest could get out of hand, about the time of the twenty-sixth Olympiad in 676, cooler minds invited a famous bard from the island of Lesbos named Terpandros to reconcile the Spartan factions with his musical talents – perhaps the world's sole case of settlement of political disputes through a music festival. Terpandros sang of his new employers as the city of 'youth in peak condition' and 'home of justice.' His efforts just may have had their effect. Contrary to what is popularly believed, Sparta was no mere dull military state. Music and poetry flourished, and artists from around Greece were welcomed. After the death of Polydoros, wiser heads recognized that the Apella, the main source of hoplites, could not be kept down if Sparta wished to maintain its security in the face of a ring of hostile Peloponnesian neighbours. Donations of land to the landless also reduced social tensions.

In the reign of Anaxandridas I, about 640, the Messenians revolted again, triggering the Second Messenian War. They were encouraged by a heavy Spartan defeat at the hands of the Argives in a terrible battle at Hysiai in 669. For nineteen years Sparta again struggled to keep the Messenians down; the conflict may have cut short the careers of Anaxilas, Leotychidas I and Hippokratidas of the Eurypontids, who as kings would have had to march to battle, with all its attendant risks. We know nothing of these three except that they intervened between Anaxandridas' son Archidamos I and his son Agasikles. All we have of Leotychidas I, for example, are a few philosophical insights attributed to him by Plutarch. He was prone to changing his mind often, which he regarded as a virtue; only base people, he said, never did so. He was an adherent of strict instruction for boys to help them become men sooner, and claimed that the Spartans drank little 'so that others may not deliberate over us, but we over others.'[10]

A royal Spartan army in the field was an awe-inspiring sight. The uniform of the Spartiate soldier in the Second Messenian War and later conflicts was a scarlet cloak over a bronze breastplate, and a bronze helmet. In his left hand he carried a bronze shield large enough to protect his shoulders, abdomen and thighs; in his right hand he wielded a six-foot spear. A short slashing sword hung at his waist. The main combat unit was the *mora*, each divided into five battalions. Each battalion consisted of five companies of fifty men each, with each company divided into four squads (*enomotiai*). Five or six *morai* made up a typical Spartan army in the field, acting as divisions, though an individual *mora* could number anything between 600 and 1,000 men. The cavalry was made up of two squadrons (*oulamoi*) of fifty horsemen each, assigned to cover the wings. Crack units included the Skiritai, a 600-strong band of redoubtable fighters from the mountains of Arkadia who were always placed on the left of the battle line. The commanders of all units, from the *morai* to the lowliest squad, had the privilege of camping with the kings.

Three years into the Second Messenian War the Spartan effort began to flag. A new Messenian leader, Aristomenes, began winning battles. It was an unlikely character who ended up reviving Spartan military morale – a lame schoolmaster from Athens named Tyrtaios. We don't know how Tyrtaios came to be in Sparta. But his inspired martial poetry has survived as the supreme glorification of men in combat. He appeared on the scene as the Spartans were falling back under the attacks of Aristomenes and his Messenians. His public performances as a poet, flute-player and singer roused young Spartans to battle fever:

> It is a fine thing for a brave man to die in the front rank of those who fight for their country ... Let each one, standing squarely on his feet, rooted to the ground and biting his lips, keep firm ... Let the warriors press breast to breast, each sword and spear-point meeting in the shock of battle ...

The effect of such lyrics on the Spartan soldiery was electric. Singing them, they drove the Messenians back. By 657 almost all the territory Sparta had lost in the Second Messenian War had been regained. Poetry as well as spears put the city of Lykourgos back in control of the Peloponnese. For the rest of the seventh century life in Sparta gradually improved. Trade flourished. There was little, if any, of the squabbling over conquered lands that had characterized Spartan society after the First Messenian War, though the Messenians were not well and truly subdued until about 600. Aristocrats and the Apella got on reasonably well – at the expense of the dual king-ship, which saw its powers dwindling in proportion. The kings' status had declined to the point at which the Ephors could fine Archidamos I, the son of Anaxandridas I, for marrying a short woman. The physical stature of future kings must not be in jeopardy! As a Eurypontid, Archidamos was compliant with the Ephors' demands. 'Superiority,' he is reported to have said, 'lies with him who is reared in the severest school.' According to Pausanias, the reigns of Archidamos I and Agasikles were peaceful ones, 'undisturbed by any wars.'[11]

Eurykrates was succeeded by his son Anaxandros, whose reign witnessed a flowering of Spartan prosperity, culture and art. All we know of Anaxandros is that he was personally honest in economic matters. When asked why the Spartans did not amass funds in the royal treasury, he replied that if they did, 'the guardians of it might become corrupt' – a telling commentary on the risks of state banking.[12] Around 570 Sparta, as the dominant power in the Peloponnese, gained control of the Olympic Games which were in their fifty-second Olympiad and as popular and prestigious as ever. Following Anaxandros in the Agiad line were his son Eurykratidas, followed by Leon and Anaxandridas II. In the case of the last-named, it was the first time that the scion of one royal house was named after an ancestor of the other, as the first Anaxandridas had been a Eurypontid. Perhaps the royal houses were conscious of a common threat from the powerful aristocracy and sought a symbolic way of coming together.

Leon and Agasikles, who reigned in roughly the same time-frame, faced a serious problem in Tegea, the only Peloponnesian state that seemed undefeatable by Spartan arms. Tegea (corresponding roughly to modern Tripoli) sat astride part of the main northward road from Sparta, threatening it from the west as Argos did from the east. To get the gods' all-important opinion the Spartans sent a mission to Delphi and returned with the following pronouncement from the all-knowing priestess:

> I will give you Tegea where you can prance about, and its pleasant plain which you can measure with the rod.[13]

On the face of it, the pronouncement appeared favourable. But the Tegeates beat off a Spartan attack and put the captured Spartans to work in the fields with the very measuring rods the Oracle had mentioned; the chains which the Spartans had brought to shackle their prisoners with were now fastened on themselves. As on many occasions in the future, no-one could say the Delphic Oracle was wrong – it was just misinterpreted by wishful thinking.

Leon is another shadowy figure, given some visibility only by Plutarch, who preserves a few scraps of what he was about. Like most Spartan kings of his time he valued justice and moderation. He defined the ideal city-state as one 'where the people shall have neither too much nor too little, and where right shall be strong and wrong shall be weak.' Once at the Olympic Games he noticed that the runners jostled for advantage at the starting line, and lamented that the principle of fair play was being abused (even then). He is described as easy-going and not given to fruitless debate about nonessential issues.[14]

Agasikles was considered something of a sage in his time, a fan of learning and educated discourse. Yet only the tiniest fragments of his personality have come down to us. For example, Plutarch reports that such was Agasikles' inner calm that he habitually walked around without a bodyguard. When asked how he could do this without fear, he replied that he ruled his subjects 'like fathers rule their sons.'[15] Comments such as this show that Sparta, even in very early times, was far from the intellectual backwater it is often assumed to have been. As the example of Agasikles shows, there was no lack of wise rule at the top when needed.

These scraps of statements from rulers such as Leon and Agasikles, to take just two examples, show that the underlying philosophy of what makes a stable and successful state was already well-developed in the Sparta of the late eighth century. Justice, moderation and a respect for the law were the cornerstones. These were Dorian Greek qualities that took longer to mature in the Ionian Greek cities such as Athens, where spirits were rather freer and less amenable to regimentation. Almost all the royal Spartan sayings preserved by Plutarch and others have one underlying theme – moderation and self-discipline. In the ancient civilizations of the time, only the discipline and exclusiveness of the Jews came close. These would much later be enshrined as virtues by philosophers such as Plato and Aristotle – both of whom, in fact, admired Spartan institutions and detested the excesses of Athenian democracy. The Spartan principles were to be deepened yet later by Christianity as part of the bedrock of the Western polity.

## Ariston (*c*. 550?–515)

'Ariston was the best king who ever ruled in Sparta.' These are the words of Herodotus, who never lavished praise where none was needed. Yet as we have little concrete evidence for such a sweeping claim, we may assume that Ariston was a more than usually just and capable king, as well as a competent soldier. Taking the Eurypontid throne around 550, Ariston early in his reign could not produce an heir. Two successive wives failed to solve the problem. Then he was smitten by the young wife of his best friend Agetos.

Herodotus relates that this woman, whose name we don't know, was reported to have started life as the ugliest little duckling in Spartan society, an embarrassment to her parents. So that she could have a reasonable chance of finding a husband, the girl's governess handed her over to the beauticians attached to the Temple of Helen for a complete makeover. The beautification worked well enough to enchant Ariston. According to Herodotus' story, which rather stretches credulity, Ariston made a deal with the unsuspecting Agetos to exchange whatever each friend had that was most valuable. In this way Agetos was honour-bound to hand over his wife.

Seven months after the nuptials, Ariston's new wife bore him a son. The news was brought to him as he was sitting in council with the Ephors. Ariston was embarrassed, as everyone knew how many months had elapsed since his latest marriage. He at once protested, in the Ephors' hearing, that the child could not possibly be his. Yet in view of the barrenness of his past wives, the political pressure on Ariston to produce an heir was overwhelming. All Lakedaimon, in fact, had been praying for it. The boy was thus named Demaratos, or 'Prayed For By The People,' and took his lawful place in line for the Eurypontid throne. Classical authors conclude that Demaratos was not illegitimate but merely premature. The Ephors, though, wouldn't forget

Ariston's unguarded cry when the child was born. And neither would the rival Agiad house.

## Anaxandridas II (*c.* 550?-520)

It fell to Leon's successor in the Agiad line, Anaxandridas II, to realize that the power rivalry between the kings and Ephors could turn into political hardball. His reign coincided with the rise to prominence of Chilon, a strong-willed Ephor who around the fifty-sixth Olympiad (556) decided that the Ephorate should become fully the equal of the kings in prestige and power. Chilon acquired influence over Anaxandridas, obtaining his help in toppling Aischines, the tyrant of Sikyon in the northern Peloponnese. That done, however, the king found he had to pay a price for Chilon's continuing friendship. Anaxandridas so far had been childless and Chilon, fearing that the Agiad line might become either extinct or embroiled in succession tussles, pressured the king to divorce his wife who was blamed for being barren. Anaxandridas at first refused; he may well have loved his wife, and moreover, Spartan women were no wilting wallflowers and she could have made an unqueenly but quite understandable fuss. Chilon and the Ephors nonetheless kept up the pressure until Anaxandridas came up with a compromise, taking a second wife to procreate while remaining technically married to the first. It was all strictly illegal, but Chilon had made his subtle point – that the kings needed to be reminded that they weren't the centre of the universe and that their elders sometimes knew better about dynastic issues. Anaxandridas emerged with some credit from the episode, as he had diplomatically neutralized a governmental intrusion into his personal life.

Anaxandridas' wife number two promptly gave birth to a boy named Kleomenes. Then, to everyone's consternation, wife number one turned out not to have been barren at all. From the same Anaxandridas she turned out three boys in close succession: Dorieus, Leonidas and Kleombrotos. Kleomenes, the eldest of the four sons, was nonetheless groomed for the Agiad succession. Yet something about this improbable sequence of events arouses suspicion. Was Chilon playing a long-term political game? The Agiad line, to which Anaxandridas belonged, by now had developed a strong pro-Apella bias. Yet here was Chilon displaying a strong concern for the *continuation* of that Agiad line. Was this a way of trying to bring both the royal houses together in a show of unity for the Peloponnesian conquests that the Spartan government was planning? The kings above all were *ex officio* commanding generals, both of whom were required on campaign, and a hiccup in one of the houses could translate into military weakness at the wrong moment. With the somewhat contradictory facts at hand, we may conclude that Anaxandridas' first wife just happened to take a worryingly long time to get pregnant, a situation that caused the panicky Ephors to take steps that in the end weren't needed, but which were to sow dragon's teeth in both the royal houses for the next fifty or so years.

Not much is known about Anaxandridas' character except that he was a stern sort who valued effort and drive. Plutarch reports that when someone asked him why the Spartan soldiers marched so fearlessly into battle, he replied, 'It's because we train ourselves to have regard for life, and not, like others, to be timid about it.' In short, only those who are afraid of life are afraid of death. He was a stickler for justice, insisting that capital cases be tried over several days to give the defendant fewer chances of being executed hastily or in error. It was common for an accused Spartan to flee to a neighbouring state rather than face a trial at home. When one of them loudly complained about having to do it, Anaxandridas corrected him: 'Don't be sad at being an outcast from your country but at being an exile from justice.'[16]

Tegea, the scene of the great Spartan humiliation under Leon and Agasikles, was the great unfinished business. Around 560 the Spartan state circulated a propaganda story according to which Sparta was the legitimate heir to the old Achaian domain of Agamemnon, through Menelaos and his heir. This historically shaky claim pointedly ignored the uncomfortable fact that the Dorian invasion had all but wiped out Menelaos' actual line. But it was enough to alarm the Argives who, living in the old Mykenaian heartland, had perhaps a more valid claim to it. Tegea had to be dealt with first. The town and its environs had become a refuge for escaped Helots and other foes of the Spartan establishment. Past attempts to reduce Tegea by force had failed. It was now time for words to temporarily replace the sword.

The sacred Oracle at Delphi was recruited into the cause again, this time with a pronouncement that Spartan arms would never succeed against Tegea unless Sparta recovered the bones of Orestes, the son of Agamemnon, believed to be buried near the town. Most modern commentators believe that Sparta controlled the Oracle and its pronunciamentos. The whole institution of Spartan kingship, in fact, was tightly bound up with it; each king had on his staff two *pythii* whose task was to represent them at Delphi whenever the priestess's lights were sought.[17] The sheer weight of wealth deposited at Delphi by all the Greek states must inevitably have corrupted many of the oracular responses. We don't know if this happened in the case of Sparta's plans for Tegea, but the Oracle's influence, however obtained, was simply too important to ignore.

An enterprising Spartan named Lichas duly discovered a well at Tegea at the bottom of which lay a large coffin with the sought-after bones inside. Lichas dug the casket out and took it to Sparta in triumph. The exploits of the Greeks' Homeric ancestors were very much in people's minds at that time. In Athens Homer's *Iliad* and *Odyssey* were being edited and set down in their definitive forms. Poets and bards were often invited to perform in Sparta, and doubtless some of their inspiration seeped into official policymaking. With Orestes' bones now securely in Sparta's possession, Anaxandridas fulfilled the Oracle by defeating Tegea in a land battle. Sparta now controlled two-fifths of the Peloponnese, but still it wasn't enough.

With its military pride intact, Sparta wisely decided not to antagonize Tegea too much, as the main foe was always considered to be Argos. After Anaxandridas' campaign Sparta forced Tegea into a defensive alliance that freed Spartan arms for a fresh incursion into Thyreatis in 546. The campaign seems to have been a stalemate, as eventually the opposing armies agreed to settle the issue by ranging 300 of their best warriors on each side, in the best Homeric tradition, to fight it out to the death. The carnage lasted all day and into the night. Two Argives remained to run home to announce victory. Unknown to them, a single Spartan had also survived, claiming victory on the grounds that he was only one to remain on the field. The dispute gave rise to another, more general, battle which the Spartans this time won. The Argives, stung by the loss of the province of Thyreatis, decreed that no man could grow his hair long and no woman could wear jewellery until the province was regained – an early and colourful example of the populist irredentism that continues to poison international relations up to our own time.

Meanwhile, news of events in other Greek city-states had filtered down to the Lakedaimonian lower orders to give them a spark of hope that their lot might be lightened. In Athens an able and energetic soldier called Peisistratos had taken power, backed by a vigorous and enterprising commercial and artisan population. Peisistratos ruthlessly clipped the wings of the old landed aristocracy and built up an Athenian business class that laid the economic foundations for that city's future greatness. Leaders such as Peisistratos, in Athens and other cities such as Corinth, were known as *tyrannoi*, translated today as tyrants. The word then didn't carry any connotation of despotism; it meant simply 'one-man rule.' Tyrants, of course, could be benevolent like Peisistratos, or truly cruel as the modern term indicates. But the Spartan Ephors invariably feared all tyrants of whatever stripe as potential examples for revolt by the *perioikoi* and Helots, not to mention liberators of a city's moneyed and business power. In the sixth century it became a cardinal rule of Spartan policy to topple them wherever possible.

It was in this way that Sparta, the austere kingdom nestling in the Lakonian valley, became known across the Aegean Sea, where a number of Greek city-states were coming under threat from a power much more formidable than any Greek tyrant. This was the Persian Empire, newly consolidated under the extremely capable Cyrus the Great. From its cradle in present-day Iran, Cyrus' domain pushed outwards to include most of what is now Turkey. By the latter half of the sixth century the Persians were at the doors of the Ionian Greek cities on the Asia Minor seaboard and the eastern Aegean islands. Between Cyrus and the Ionian Greeks stood a non-Greek state, Lydia, whose king, the fabulously wealthy Croesus, topped Cyrus' conquest agenda.

Croesus appealed to Sparta for aid. This was the first time that Sparta's claim to be the champion of Greek independence anywhere came under serious test. Would Sparta send its armies across the sea or, overcome by an innate isolationism, turn its back on the chance to fight a tyrant and lose its reputation? Honour, of course, demanded the former. Sparta was already a member of a loose alliance that included powers as diverse as Babylon and Egypt. Croesus' money could have provided another powerful incentive. We don't know where Anaxandridas or Ariston stood on this. The decision was made to intervene, but it shows signs of having been half-hearted; there was still a great deal of ethnic prejudice in Dorian Sparta against the Ionian Greeks who had been displaced centuries before. Before the Spartans could set out to aid their wealthy ally, the news arrived that Croesus had been overthrown and the preparations were halted.

*Chapter 4*

# The Politics of Defiance

Kleomenes I
Demaratos

### Kleomenes I (*c.* 520–490)

The middle of the sixth century marks the beginning of a new era of Spartan assertiveness. It's difficult to determine whether the Gerousia, the Ephors or the kings were the prime movers of this muscular policy, or whether it was a joint effort. The kings probably had little say in decision-making at this stage, especially as any Spartan success, military or diplomatic, would reflect favourably on them anyway. The kings, as commanders of the army in time of war, basked in the credit of securing control over potentially harmful neighbours such as Messenia and Tegea. The population of Lakedaimon was increasing along with its power. At this time it stood at about 10,000 full citizens, or Spartiates, with perhaps 30,000 women and minors, and 150,000 *perioikoi* and Helots.

Ariston's self-conscious cry of concern over his child's premature birth and Anaxandridas II's caving in to the Ephors over his family life show how eroded their authority had become over the previous 200 or so years. Depending on circumstances, they were either order-taking generals or mere senators and ceremonial high priests of Lakedaimonian Zeus and Zeus Ouranios. Their military and religious duties were not as different as we might imagine them in our time. Not only in Sparta, but throughout the Greek world, the decision to go to war was made only after diviners secured favourable omens from their arcane rites, such as splitting open animals and scanning the steaming entrails for some sign of divine favour. Both kings had to take the field at the same time, even at the risk of both being slain (though this rule was later to change). But even on campaign, the commanding king was not the real boss; he had to submit to the oversight of the Ephors, who placed 'commissars' in the army to keep an eye on what the king was doing or not doing, as the case may be.

To make up for their lack of real power, the kings enjoyed several peace-time perks. They were given the best seats at athletic contests, and at state feasts they were served first and with double portions to boot. Every seventh of the month and new moon they each received a meat animal, a bushel of grain and a quart of wine courtesy of the state. By the time of Kleomenes I they had few judicial powers left; among them, however, were the right to administer the public roads and issue rulings in some inheritance cases.

Despite Anaxandridas II's run-in with Chilon and the Ephors, there is little evidence that the Eurypontid house seriously concerned itself with matters of power at that stage. What we do know is that by the close of the sixth century the kings of both houses were compelled every month to renew an oath to the Ephors 'to reign according to the laws of the city.' When the oath was duly given, the Ephors in turn would promise each king that essentially he would not be sacked as long as he toed the Ephors' line. The power balance in Sparta was tilting heavily in the Gerousia's favour, while the Apella was growing in numbers and influence. There may also have been a sneaking suspicion among the aristocracy that the kings might be magnets for movements by the disaffected and underprivileged. As ceremonial and military figureheads they could be tolerated. But the government didn't count on the son of Anaxandridas II's second wife.

When Kleomenes I, the son and successor of Anaxandridas II, assumed the Agiad throne about 520, he had already given rise to a problem. While growing to maturity he had displayed worrying signs of mental instability to the point at which, on the death of his father, the Ephors were most reluctant to confirm him on the throne. They far preferred Dorieus, the first of Anaxandridas' three sons by his first wife, whom they also considered a better soldier. But as the law of succession of the eldest was iron-clad, the Ephors could find no way around it. Kleomenes duly became the Agiad king.

According to the sober Pausanias, Kleomenes was 'subject to fits of mad excitement.' The condition emerged in various ways, including what today we might call a passion for human rights. As soon as he assumed the throne he took it upon himself to personify Sparta's anti-tyrant policy. His first target was Athens. Peisistratos, the tyrant of Athens, had been dead for seven years and power there was in the hands of his two sons, Hippias and Hipparchos. In 514 Hipparchos was assassinated, which made his elder brother Hippias harden his rule into a true tyranny in the classic sense.

Sparta already had some experience in tackling a Greek tyrant. Around 524 it had sent an expedition against Polykrates, the ruler of the island of Samos off the Asia Minor coast. Samos had benefited from trade between the Ionian Greek cities of Asia Minor and the mainland by building up a powerful navy. The backbone of the Samian navy was the trireme. Designed with the help of Phoenician shipwrights, the trireme was a sleek fighting machine propelled by up to 170 oars in three tiers, hence its name, with a pointed ram in the bow. Polykrates was competent, diabolically clever and ruthless. He and his regime were propped up by the trireme navy and a personal guard of well-paid mercenaries and 1,000 archers. He may have remained secure in his power had he not allowed his ships to commit the occasional act of piracy, threatening Peloponnesian commercial interests.

Polykrates' cruelties at home forced a band of rebels to seek aid from Sparta to overthrow him. Their reception was disappointing. Kleomenes, having listened to their appeal, confessed that it didn't make sense to him. 'What you said at the beginning I don't remember, so I couldn't understand the middle part, and I don't approve the conclusion,' was Plutarch's summation of what was really a right royal put-down.[1] The Samians might be forgiven for thinking they were in the presence of a lunatic. But there was very likely a method in Kleomenes' seeming madness. Since the episode of Croesus a note of realism had crept into Spartan foreign policy: the Spartans might hate tyrants, but also didn't like the idea of sailing over the Aegean to tangle in other people's quarrels. The Samian rebels then tried a piece of political theatre. They displayed an empty sack before the Apella, telling them it was in need of flour. The crass symbolism may have made its point, as in 524 a Spartan force sailed against Samos on ships provided and manned by Corinth. The siege of Samos lasted for a month. Two Spartan soldiers, Archias and Lykopes, breached the walls and charged into the town with no hope of relief until they were slain. Despite these individual feats of valour, the Spartan expeditionary force eventually had to admit defeat. Polykrates himself fought valiantly in the front line defending the wall towers.

When the Persians did away with Polykrates, his successor Maiandrios escaped to Sparta with a considerable quantity of gold and silver which he had managed to salvage. Maiandrios invited Kleomenes to his lodgings, making sure to have his servants polish the gleaming bowls and cups while he was there. Herodotus reports that when Kleomenes marvelled at the wealth he saw before him, Maiandrios (with what could well have been a knowing wink) casually told the king he could help himself to whatever took his fancy. Not only did Kleomenes refuse to be bought in this way, but he also thwarted the possibility of Maiandrios' corrupting the Spartans by warning the Ephors that the Samian could get them embroiled in an overseas war if they weren't careful. Maiandrios was booted out of Sparta.[2]

In this way Kleomenes showed that despite his mental instability he possessed a diplomatic cunning which the Ephors found they could turn to their advantage in the case of Athens. Hippias was rapidly becoming unpopular with the Athenian landed aristocracy who were the natural conservative allies of a regime such as Sparta's. The influential Delphic Oracle was fulminating against Hippias. To be fair, it's almost certain that the Oracle – the ancient equivalent of a 'bad press' – had been recruited by Kleomenes as his own mouthpiece.[3] More damningly, Hippias was believed to be cultivating the friendship of Argos. Soon after becoming king, Kleomenes marched at the head of an army northwards across the Isthmus in the direction of Athens. The immediate cause for this expedition is unclear, unless we assume that it was a show of strength for diplomatic purposes. While on the expedition he was approached by a delegation from Plataia, a town in Boiotia to the north, which felt threatened by its stronger neighbour Thebes and sought a link with Sparta to protect itself. Kleomenes refused to take the bait, advising the Plataians to seek their help from Athens. This way, Herodotus says, the Spartan king hoped to sow discord between Athens and Thebes to Sparta's advantage.

Meanwhile, Kleomenes had to deal with the enmity of his half-brother Dorieus, the eldest son of his father Anaxandridas' first wife. Though preferred by the Spartan establishment, Dorieus could see no legitimate way to replace Kleomenes. So rather than serve under what he considered a half-mad half-brother, Dorieus organized a colonizing expedition to Libya. The colony disintegrated under attacks by the native Libyans and Carthaginians. Dorieus returned to Sparta to fit out another expedition, this time to western Sicily, where he was killed fighting the natives.

In 512, feeling stronger after about eight years of reign, Kleomenes took his first real crack at Hippias of Athens. A Spartan seaborne expeditionary force under Anchimolos was first sent to land at Phaleron Bay on the Athenian coast. Hippias, however, got wind of the plan, recruited 1,000 cavalrymen from Thessaly in the central mainland and cut down the trees on the plain of Phaleron to give the horsemen a free field of operations. The landing was beaten back and Anchimolos was killed.

Kleomenes himself followed up with a punitive expedition by land, defeated the Thessalians in a pitched battle at Eleusis, and marched up to the very ramparts of the Athenian Acropolis, where Hippias, his family and a force of mercenaries were holed up with plenty of provisions. Kleomenes probably hadn't planned for a long siege; there was grumbling in the ranks, and he was mulling over whether or not he should withdraw, when Hippias tried to sneak his children out. The escape was bungled; the children fell into the hands of Kleomenes, who now had an ace which he promptly employed to force Hippias off the Acropolis on a safe-conduct and deliver Athens into the hands of the pro-Spartan aristocracy. Kleomenes struck up a personal friendship with Isagoras, the head of Athens' aristocratic faction. Hippias exiled himself to Asia Minor, but it wouldn't be the last that Athens heard of him.

Kleomenes had certainly pulled off a coup for Sparta, one which resounded throughout the Greek world. He brought with him to Sparta the records of divine oracles – almost certainly spurious – that supposedly predicted 'great evils' in store for Sparta at the hands of the Athenians. Yet neither the Ephors nor anyone else could have realized at the time that Kleomenes and his army had been the catalyst for a momentous development in the Greek world. For as a direct result of the Spartan intervention, politics in Athens took an unexpected turn. A noble named Kleisthenes considered it shameful that the Athenian upper class had to rely on the Spartans' spears to maintain power. He decided that the common citizens of Athens deserved more of a say in affairs than they had so far been entitled to. A series of smart political manoeuvres enabled him to bring to birth the world's first democratic government. At this the Spartans took sudden alarm: a democracy, even the restricted ancient sense, would negate everything the Spartan state stood for. In the interests of Sparta, Kleomenes' friend Isagoras had to be reinstalled at Athens.

So in 508 Kleomenes led his Spartan hoplites to Athens a second time. Acting in concert with Isagoras and the Athenian aristocratic party, he took control of the city, exiling Kleisthenes along with 700 democratic families. (Herodotus cheekily gives us an additional motive for Kleomenes' eagerness to visit Athens again, namely, that he was having an affair with Isagoras' wife.) Kleomenes' next step was to suppress the fledgling democratic government consisting of the 500-member *boule* (parliament) and replace it with 300 of his own unelected supporters.

But the *boule*, to its credit, put up a stout resistance. As Kleomenes and his pliant Athenian supporters occupied the Acropolis they found themselves under siege by a mass of Athenian citizenry. Herodotus tells us that as Kleomenes stepped into the inner sanctum of the temple on the Acropolis the priestess met him at the threshold with the stern words: 'Foreign Lakedaimonian, step back. No Dorians are allowed in here.' The king lied that he was not a Dorian but a descendant of the old Achaians of Menelaos, echoing the standard Spartan propaganda line. But neither people nor priestess would budge. Kleomenes this time had badly misjudged the mood of the Athenians. After a two-day stand-off on the Acropolis he secured a safe-conduct for himself out of Athenian territory, abandoning his own local supporters to the untender mercies of the democrats. Kleisthenes returned and proceeded to consolidate the democracy which would prove to be one of the brightest jewels in the crown of classical Athens.

The abortive campaign against Athens in 508 showed up a facet of Kleomenes' complex personality. He could be resolute, but his resolution was unstable. When matters were going well for him he was unstoppable.

But the first serious difficulty would plunge him into uncertainty. His wavering during the first siege of the Acropolis, and his precipitate flight from Athens in the face of the democrats in 508, contrast oddly with the famed Spartan cult of immovable courage in the field. Spartan wives and mothers expected their men folk, when marching to war, to return 'with your shield or on it' – that is, either victors or dead. But was Kleomenes, a king, thus expendable? He apparently thought not. Vain or flamboyant men, however impressive on the outside, often shrink from the possibilities of personal extinction. Whatever the story he told to the Ephors on his return, there is no evidence that he was penalized or shamed in any way.

Kleomenes' interventionist tendency, in fact, dovetailed nicely with the foreign policy of the Gerousia and Ephors, who were willing to overlook the Agiad house's affinity for populism as long as Sparta gained victories. The setback at Athens, however, showed the limitations of a purely values-driven foreign policy. There were many in Sparta, including King Demaratos of the Eurypontid house, who thought Kleomenes was going too far. They saw nothing wrong in Persian control of the east Aegean seaboard as long as it brought with it economic and political stability and didn't rock the trade boat.

Whatever Kleomenes' domestic opponents thought, they couldn't prevent a further burst of libertarian meddling. He spent two years putting together a powerful Peloponnesian alliance, backed up by forces from Thebes and Chalkis, and led them to Athens with the aim of suppressing the newly-minted democracy in that city. The Athenians were faced with attacks on two fronts – the main one by the Spartans and their allies on the plain of Eleusis, and a secondary one to the north, from the Boiotians and Chalkidians. They decided to take on Kleomenes first. Kleomenes' own conduct in the campaign, if we are to believe the hostile Herodotus, left a lot to be desired. The king reportedly had failed to inform his Corinthian allies of the real object of the campaign, which was to re-occupy Athens. When the Corinthians learned what was afoot they refused to harm a city with which they had no quarrel, and packed up and left.

Watching them go was Demaratos, who had dutifully, if unwillingly, led his own contingent alongside his co-king. Herodotus claims that Demaratos, too, was kept in the dark about the campaign's real objective, and that when he found out, he picked up his own detachment and followed the Corinthians out. But Demaratos almost certainly would not have dared to withdraw from the field if he didn't believe the Ephors supported him. This in turn suggests there had been a change of heart in Sparta; the elders could have feared the consequences of a vigorously democratic Athens inflicting a stinging defeat on Spartan arms. With the army disintegrating before his eyes, Kleomenes had no choice but to retreat. Before he withdrew he devastated a part of the Eleusinian plain. Was he perhaps showing signs of sympathy with the Athenian democrats? It would fit in with the populist tendencies of his Agiad house, and perhaps also explain why Demaratos was assigned to keep a close eye on him.

Again, there is no evidence that Kleomenes' stature was diminished by this latest reverse. One concrete consequence was that the Ephors changed the law on kings campaigning to keep one king always at home while the other was in the field. But bigger problems were now looming. The Ionian Greek cities of Asia Minor, centres of prosperity and learning, were being extinguished one by one by the Persian advance. Around 499 Aristagoras, the tyrant of Miletos (on the Asia Minor coast opposite the island of Samos) placed himself at the head of a general revolt of Ionian Greeks against Persian overlordship. He travelled to Sparta, the perceived foe of despotism everywhere, to seek help. Aristagoras' meeting with Kleomenes, went (according to Herodotus who cannot have been far wrong) something like this:

'Don't be surprised at my haste in coming here,' Aristagoras told Kleomenes at their first encounter. The Milesian leader had in his hand a bronze plaque with a map of the known world etched on it. 'The sons of the Ionians are enslaved, and that should shame you, too, who are the leading power in Greece.' Aristagoras knew how to flatter someone such as Kleomenes by playing on Spartan military pride. He made a point of stressing that Ionian and Dorian Greeks were still 'one blood,' and proceeded to disparage Asian soldiers as outlandish laggards in baggy pants but sitting on reserves of untold wealth if only the Greeks would rouse themselves to go after it. After all, Aristagoras wheedled craftily, what would Sparta do with its few acres of rocky soil when the riches of Asia were there for the taking? It was a clever pitch.

'Milesian foreigner,' Kleomenes replied in the formal mode of address usual for the time, 'I will answer you in two days.'

Two days later the king still hadn't decided. We don't know whether, during these two days, Kleomenes consulted the Ephors or anyone but himself. It would certainly have been unusual for him not to seek official advice, considering the sheer importance of the Gerousia and Ephorate in policymaking and what was at stake – a major military expedition into unknown lands. Herodotus, our sole source for this episode, is silent on that score. We are left to presume either that Kleomenes was a strong enough character to be able to negotiate on his own or, equally if not more likely, that the government was giving him rope to figuratively hang himself somewhere in the wilds of Asia. He must have had his poker face on when he turned up for his next meeting with Aristagoras to ask him the distance from the Asia Minor coast to the palace of the Great King of Persia. Aristagoras, thinking he had the Spartans in the bag, slipped up and truthfully replied that it was three months' march. He was still talking when Kleomenes interrupted him: 'Milesian foreigner, get yourself beyond the frontier of Sparta before sunset.'

Aristagoras panicked. He would surely meet a grisly end at Persian hands if he went back home with nothing accomplished, so he rushed back to Kleomenes' royal residence – this time as a supplicant, who under Greek hospitality laws could not be turned away. The king agreed to hear him out a third time.

At Kleomenes' side was his daughter of eight or nine years, Gorgo. Aristagoras asked if the two men could be alone. 'Speak freely and don't mind the child,' Kleomenes said. As a royal only child and intelligent at that, Gorgo was apparently being groomed to become familiar with affairs of state at an early age. Aristagoras went straight into heavy-duty bribery. First he offered the king ten talents, a not-so-small fortune, to authorize a Spartan expedition. Kleomenes refused; we can imagine him turning up his chin and closing his eyes in the way of wordless refusal that still prevails in modern Greece. Aristagoras upped the offer, to twenty, thirty, forty and fifty talents.[4] Aristagoras surely knew that Spartan citizens, particularly of the higher class, were forbidden to own gold or silver coinage. Yet he may have been canny enough to also know that the ban was often honoured in the breach. But before Aristagoras could say any more, little Gorgo piped up: 'Father, if you don't go away this foreigner will corrupt you.' Kleomenes left the room and Aristagoras knew the game was up.[5]

Scholars, inevitably, have taken a long and critical look at Herodotus' edifying account. There are doubts based on the premise that it would have been inconceivable for Kleomenes to have made such a unilateral decision without the consent of Demaratos on the one hand, and the Ephors, the Gerousia and the Apella on the other. Could the Ephors have circulated the story to discredit Kleomenes as supposedly ready to have been bribed if Gorgo hadn't spoken up?[6] The jury on that point must remain out.

Sparta wisely held back from expending its power in the limitless wastes of Asia Minor, and Darius I, the Persian Great King, had no trouble reconquering the rebellious Greek cities. As for Kleomenes, he disappears from the stage for a few years, reappearing in 494 at the head of an army marching to attack arch-foe Argos. Ever since the infamous Battle of the Six Hundred and its sequel, the Argives had nursed revenge. As Kleomenes reached the bank of the Erasinos River which marked the frontier with Argos, his diviners stared into the entrails of their slaughtered beasts to see if the gods favoured an advance. The gods, or the innards, said no. Intelligence reports from Argos also could have indicated that the Argives were in a furious fighting mood. A land campaign was out; but what about a seaborne attack? To find out the prospects a bull was slaughtered on the coast and examined. This time the signs were favourable.

It was at this point that Kleomenes displayed a ruthlessness not tempered by law or ordinary human considerations. He had been a keen student of the *Iliad* and perhaps took too much to heart its combative messages. The might-makes-right doctrine reached in him its fullest expression. During his first campaign against Argos he made plain that he had no time for oaths or other such promises. 'Whatever ill one can do to one's enemies is regarded, among both gods and men, as something vastly higher than justice,' Plutarch reports him as saying. When the Argives protested against such callousness, he replied, 'You have the power to speak ill of me, but I have the power to do ill to you.'[7]

As soon as Kleomenes and his Spartans landed on the Argive coast at Tiryns (near modern Nafplion) the Argive army formed up to meet them. The Argives, by no means confident that they could beat the Spartans in a fair fight, thought up a trick: in order to confuse the enemy, whatever commands the Spartan officers were heard to call were to be obeyed by the Argives. It's not clear what was to be tactically accomplished by this, except perhaps a degree of battlefield confusion. Kleomenes' intelligence got wind of the ruse. He ordered that when the call went out for mealtime, the troops should not sit down to eat but charge the enemy. The result was a bloody lunchtime defeat for Argives. Their survivors found themselves bottled up in a wooded grove, where Kleomenes displayed the needless cruelty which earned him the contempt of Herodotus. He called on the Argives in the grove to surrender in return for a safe-conduct home. Those who believed him emerged, to be promptly put to the sword. The rest refused to come out, so Kleomenes set the wood on fire and burned them to death.

If the erratic king thought he would be praised on his return to Sparta, he was mistaken. The Ephors were furious, not only at his unnecessary barbarism but also at his failure to occupy Argos, which had been the ostensible purpose of the campaign. They had been willing to put up with his eccentricities as long as they served Spartan strategic purposes, but now he was causing the state definite harm. Those with long memories recalled that as Kleomenes was leaving the outskirts of Athens after the abortive campaign of 506 he had burned down a sacred grove, thereby incurring ritual pollution. Had his usefulness come to an end?

The Ephors' chance came in 491, three years after the atrocity at Argos, when Athens asked Sparta's help to neutralize Aigina, an island state within sight of Athens. Aigina was alarmingly pro-Persian. Kleomenes took with him

Demaratos' cousin and heir-apparent to the Eurypontid throne, Leotychidas. Once there, they delivered Aigina's pro-Persian leaders in chains to Athens. But events at home tripped Kleomenes up. He of course cannot have led a force to Aigina without the government's green light. Yet as soon as he sailed, Demaratos began bad-mouthing him at home. He messaged the Aiginetans that Kleomenes was acting entirely on his own, with no official sanction whatsoever. This stiffened the Aiginetans who sent Kleomenes and the young Leotychidas packing.

Back in Sparta Kleomenes engaged in increasingly erratic behaviour. While attending a public lecture on bravery, at one point he laughed out loud. 'Why do you laugh, Kleomenes, especially as you are a king?' the offended speaker asked.

'If a swallow spoke of bravery I would laugh,' the king shot back. 'But if it had been an eagle speaking I would have kept quiet.' When someone accused him of being lazy and addicted to luxury, he replied that it was better than being unjust. When someone praised a musician, he responded by praising his soup-chef, implying that neither one was better than the other.[8]

He was now the sworn enemy of Demaratos. In a series of obscure political manoeuvres, that included the *de rigueur* consultation of the Oracle of Delphi, Kleomenes hit back at Demaratos, stigmatizing him as illegitimate. It had never been forgotten that Demaratos' father Ariston, unpleasantly surprised by the birth of his son just seven months into his marriage, had publicly at the time protested that Demaratos was not his. Kleomenes got the Oracle to repeat and legitimize the charge. With the heavy weight of Delphi in the balance against him, Demaratos was forced to flee, leaving the Eurypontid throne to his heir, a great-grandson of King Hippokratidas, who became Leotychidas II. Neither was Leotychidas free from complicity, as he, too, had faithfully parroted the line of Demaratos' supposed illegitimacy.

The Ephors' blood was now up. They openly accused Kleomenes of having bribed the priestess at Delphi (an accusation repeated by Pausanias, who adds that no other Spartan king ever dared do anything of the kind). His life now in danger, Kleomenes fled to Thessaly and later to Arkadia, the mountainous centre of the Peloponnese north of Lakedaimon. In Arkadia he set about raising a force to invade Sparta and overthrow its government; he may have included Helots in his force, planning a social as well as a political revolution. According to Herodotus, Kleomenes was now quite insane. A contributing factor could have been a chronic alcoholism which began when he developed a taste for strong unwatered wine during a visit by a delegation of barbarian Scythians. Fearing that he might make uncontrolled mischief in Arkadia, the Ephors recalled him to Sparta in about 490 to keep an eye on him. In the streets he would strike people in the face with his stick, a habit which got him fastened in the stocks with his family's consent. Thus immobilized, he cajoled his jailer, a humble Helot, into giving him a knife. With it he began systematically hacking himself to death, starting first from his legs, then proceeding up to slash his abdomen and ribs.[9] Another tradition claims he was quietly disposed of by the Ephors.

## Demaratos (*c.* 515–491)

'So Demaratos was deposed,' writes Pausanias, 'not rightfully, but because Kleomenes hated him.' Who was this marginal Eurypontid king who nevertheless looms curiously large in Spartan history?

Demaratos ascended the Eurypontid throne about 515, some five years after Kleomenes' accession, and was known as a competent king. At some point early in his reign he won a four-horse chariot race at the Olympic Games, the only Spartan king ever to win such a distinction. Yet the stars in their courses marched against him. He could never come out from under the never-proven suspicion of illegitimacy that hung over him like a persistent black cloud. No-one in Sparta forgot – and Kleomenes made sure they wouldn't forget – the careless cry of his father Ariston at his birth. Ariston had later regretted his outburst, but it was too late. A particularly malicious twist in the rumour mill had it that Ariston himself had been unable to procreate and that Demaratos was in fact the son of a humble donkey-herder.

Demaratos, it must be admitted, didn't make things easier for himself. He was emotional and prone to errors of judgement. But he didn't suffer fools gladly and like a true Spartan was spare in speech. In one conference he remained silent and was asked, none too politely, whether it was because he was stupid. (A Spartan king could be talked to like that with impunity.) 'A fool,' he replied, 'would not have been able to hold his tongue.' He seems to have had little time for the arts, remarking of a musician he was listening to that 'he seems to do his silly task fairly well.'[10] The lingering doubts about his legitimacy cannot have been easy on him. For some twenty years he bore the burden until Kleomenes delivered his *coup de grâce* by influencing the high priestess at Delphi, one Perialla, to place the official stamp of illegitimacy on Demaratos. It made no difference that Perialla was later suspended from her post for incompetence; the Oracle had spoken through her and had to be respected.

Deposed from the Eurypontid throne, Demaratos was given another unspecified state office in compensation. One day he was sitting in the theatre watching a young people's athletics display when Leotychidas II, who had replaced him, looked down from his royal seat and sent an aide to ask him the barbed question of what it felt like to have to look up at the officials instead of down. Demaratos retorted that, unlike Leotychidas, he had experience of both views. His humiliation, though, can be imagined, as after delivering his reply, 'he covered his face with his cloak, left the theatre and went home.'

After sacrificing an ox to Zeus, Demaratos sent for his mother. There is no reason to suppose what was said, as Herodotus imagines it, to be very far from the truth. 'In the name of the gods, mother,' Demaratos implored, 'I beg you to tell me the truth about who my real father is. Leotychidas says you were already pregnant from your previous husband before you went to Ariston.' (The onetime ugly duckling, as we have seen, had been married to Agetos before Ariston took her over by none-too-delicate means.) 'Others are even saying that you went with a donkey-herder, and that I'm his child.'

His mother told him that he was simply a premature seven-month baby. 'Don't listen to anyone else,' she said. 'As for the donkey-herders, let the wives of Leotychidas and his ilk try them out!'

Despite his mother's spirited reply, Demaratos had had enough of the poisoned atmosphere. Perhaps he suspected his mother of not wanting to rock the boat at that point. Telling everyone he intended to journey to Delphi for a second opinion, he fled instead to Elis in the northwest Peloponnese. But Spartan agents followed him there. He evaded them by crossing over to the island of Zakynthos, though his pursuers captured his entourage. From Zakynthos he found his way eastwards to the court of Darius, who heaped him with honours and wealth.

Generations of readers of Greek history have felt a *frisson* of disappointment and even disbelief at the spectacle of a Spartan king, the embodiment of Greek discipline and love of liberty, transferring his allegiance to the court of an Oriental despot. To use an analogy from modern history, it would have been like Winston Churchill defecting to Nazi Germany just before the Second World War. But the analogy can be taken too far. Demaratos shared Sparta's pride in its achievements and independence, yet he was no fan of democracy or popular rule in any form. Moreover, as seen from mainland Greece in the early fifth century, the Persian Empire was not all bad, as its many Greek supporters would attest. Its administration of conquered lands had attained a peak of efficiency not seen again until the Roman Empire five centuries later. The Persian elites were a genteel class not unlike the Spartiate class but with a good deal more refinement and the ability to enjoy life.

The secure structure of Persian court life appealed to Demaratos, who in poor Sparta could look forward only to a lifetime of political intrigues and perhaps assassination. For the next ten years he occupied an honoured place as adviser to Darius I on Greek affairs. Darius's plans to conquer the Greek mainland and turn it into a major trading foothold in Europe were well advanced. Shortly after Demaratos arrived at his court, Darius set in motion his expedition against Athens, to punish that city for supporting the Ionian Greeks' revolt and to restore Hippias to power in Athens as a Persian puppet. In September 490 a large Persian invading force landed at Marathon north of Athens, to be routed by an Athenian defending force outnumbered six to one, in one of the most pivotal battles in history.

Ten years passed before Xerxes, Darius' son, made his own vengeful attempt on Greece. By this time Demaratos was probably feeling the pangs of homesickness. Hippias may have been thwarted in his scheme to rule again at Athens, but Demaratos still nursed hopes of regaining his throne at Sparta, even if on the tips of Persian spears. The impetuous Xerxes had put the finishing touches to what he fancied would be the campaign to end all campaigns, and was inspecting his fleet on the Asia Minor coast, when he turned to Demaratos who was with him. 'You're a Greek, Demaratos,' Herodotus reports the Great King as saying. 'Do you think your fellow-Greeks or anyone in the West can stand up to all this?'

'Shall I tell you the truth or that which will please you?' Demaratos replied, revealing his Spartan character. 'There's no way anyone in Lakedaimon will agree to your subjugating them, and will resist you even if alone. Even if a mere thousand remain, they'll fight you.'

Xerxes couldn't get his head around that one. To him, free men simply weren't as capable of fighting as his own subjects who were driven forward by the lash. Any one of his crack soldiers, he boasted, could take on three Greeks. Demaratos didn't have to remind Xerxes of his own beef against the Spartans, but he did anyway. 'Sire,' he said, 'they deprived me of my power and drove me from my land, turning me into a fugitive without a country ... The Lakedaimonians are free, it is true, but not absolutely, for they have a tyrant, Law, which they fear far more than your subjects fear you. This Law keeps them from retreating in battle, and makes them either win or die at their posts.' Xerxes laughed, but the laugh must have been hollow.[11]

When Xerxes' massive juggernaut invaded Greece in the summer of 480, Demaratos rode with the entourage. His motives for doing so are not clear. Almost certainly Xerxes had ordered him to go along; he needed his Greek adviser. But if Demaratos expected to be reinstated as king in Sparta as a Persian puppet, he ought to have known that he would be a despised figure. Was his motive pure revenge? Perhaps, but he must surely have had the wit to realize that it would eventually lead nowhere. Herodotus himself, usually perceptive where motives are concerned, professes himself baffled by Demaratos. If the Spartan indeed despised his countrymen so much, and with good reason, why then did he warn them of Xerxes' impending invasion by sending home a secret message to that effect? In Herodotus' account,

Demaratos scratched the message on a folding wooden board and covered the letters with melted wax. Somehow the board got to Sparta, where the authorities puzzled over it until Gorgo, the wife of Leonidas, had the idea of scraping the wax off – the second time she is known to have displayed unusual intelligence in an affair of state.

Not surprisingly, some of Xerxes' top men could not quite bring themselves to trust Demaratos. Could he have reconciled his conflicting emotions by deciding to become a double agent? Xerxes' brother Achaimenes, the commander of the Persian navy, nursed a strong suspicion of Demaratos as a potential traitor to the Great King's cause, and told his brother. But Xerxes would not hear anything against his favourite Greek. He ordered that 'no-one henceforth shall speak ill of Demaratos, who is my guest.'[12]

Herodotus notes other signs of Demaratos' complex character. After the battle at Thermopylai and as Xerxes' hordes were putting Athens to the torch, Demaratos was in the plain of Eleusis watching the smoke rising on the other side of Mount Aigaleos. He noticed a large whirlwind of dust sweeping across the plain, as if raised by 'thirty thousand soldiers.' He and an Athenian renegade with him strained to see what was causing the huge cloud of dust, but they could see nothing, though they thought they could hear human cries and sacred chants. 'Demaratos,' the Athenian said, 'if Athens is deserted, then this must be the voice of God going to help the Athenians. The Great King's army is going to meet with disaster.'

'Don't tell this to anyone,' Herodotus reports Demaratos as replying. 'If the Great King hears this, it will cost you your head and neither I nor anyone else will be able to save you. Let the gods see to the army.' The dire forecast proved correct at Salamis (see Leotychidas II below), and Demaratos retired with Xerxes to Persia to live out his days and leave a good number of descendants. He was occasionally jeered at as an exile by high-born Persians at court, to which he would sadly concur, admitting that 'I have squandered my position in life.'

Plutarch tells us that when Themistokles the Athenian fled to the Persian court after blotting his political copybook at home after the Persian Wars, he got to know Demaratos well. While Themistokles was adjusting to Oriental life in a big way, enjoying conspicuous royal favours, Demaratos may have felt his unofficial position as chief-Greek-at-court was under threat. When the Great King was feeling generous and inclined to give some additional honour to Demaratos and asked him what he wanted, Demaratos replied that he would like the privilege of wearing his tiara upright on his head when he rode into town, as the Persian kings did. Whereupon one of the Great King's cousins patted Demaratos' noble headgear, saying, 'This tiara of yours has no brains to cover. You won't become Zeus simply by taking hold of his thunderbolt!'[13]

But all this was in the future as Xerxes' colossal army in the summer of 480 came to a halt in front of the narrow strategic pass of Thermopylai which was being held by the Spartans and other Greeks. Xerxes called for Demaratos to ask his opinion on whether the pass would be difficult to force. Demaratos must have smiled ruefully. 'Sire,' Herodotus reports him as replying, 'you're facing the finest soldiers in Greece.' Throughout, Demaratos of the Eurypontid house remained a Spartan in spirit. No less a Spartan, in fact, than Kleomenes I's successor in the Agiad line, who was now a few miles away manning the rampart at Thermopylai for what would soon be the Spartan kings' finest hour.

# Chapter 5

# 'Come and Get Them!'

**Leonidas I**

**Leotychidas II**

## Leonidas I (490–480)

With Kleomenes I dead and Demaratos banished, the Ephors and the Spartan Gerousia were more powerful than ever before. As the war clouds darkened on the eastern horizon, they had their work cut out for them. For many years the Persians had been making no secret of their contempt for the Greeks. Cyrus the Great, the founder of the Persian Empire, had dismissed a Spartan mission warning him against trampling on Greek liberties by retorting that he had no time for 'a people who gather in a space in the centre of their towns where they cheat one another on oath.' This sneering reference to the Greeks' trading and democratic proclivities is reminiscent of Napoleon's put-down of the English as a nation of shopkeepers. Cyrus' successor-but-one, Darius, had a similar view, as did Xerxes, who hoped that the Greeks' trading talents could be put to good use to expand the Persian Empire in Europe.

Succeeding Kleomenes was his half-brother Leonidas I, who married Kleomenes' precocious daughter Gorgo, an only child. The union was probably just within the bounds of legitimacy, as Leonidas was the second son of Anaxandridas II and his first wife, after Dorieus. In his youth, with two older heirs-apparent in line before him, Leonidas scarcely expected to become a king, and Herodotus says that he didn't think much about it anyway. He was thus not entitled to the exemption from the *agoge* enjoyed by royal heirs, but went through its full rigours. It was said that he enjoyed the martial songs of Tyrtaios. When Dorieus ended up in self-exile, Leonidas unexpectedly found himself occupying the Agiad throne.

Despite his towering reputation, frustratingly little is known of Leonidas as a person. His training forced his character into the classic Spartan mould, tough, steadfast and courageous, just in time for the momentous role he was called on to play. Leonidas' character showed in his bearing, as shortly after his accession a jealous Spartan who had gone through the *agoge* with him accosted him. 'Except for being king,' the Spartan said, 'you are not superior to us.'

'If I were not better than you,' Leonidas shot back, 'I wouldn't be king.' Whatever the Ephors thought of Leonidas, he certainly deserved the job. He would have witnessed a dramatic episode in the late summer of 490 when an Athenian courier arrived in Sparta after having run more than 200 kilometres from Athens to appeal for help against Darius' invasion force encamped on the plain of Marathon, placing Athens in deadly danger.

The courier was Philippides (or Pheidippides), and if he had been expecting the Spartans to mobilize forthwith, he was disappointed. The Spartan government appeared to be in paralysis. Kleomenes may still have been alive, and some of the army was busy putting down one of the incessant Messenian peasant revolts. Moreover, an important festival called the Karneia was in progress. The Karneia, instituted during the twenty-sixth Olympiad in 676, was essentially a military celebration commemorating the Dorian invasion. During the nine days it lasted, the Spartan army was forbidden to march. When Philippides arrived the feast had six days yet to run. The Ephors and Gerousia promised the Athenian that they would mobilize immediately afterwards. Was the reason genuine, or did the conservative faction in Sparta hope that the Persians would eliminate Athens as a rival? To this day, the doubt persists.

The valour of the Athenians at Marathon saved their city, and perhaps all Greece. The day after the victory 2,000 Spartans turned up at the scene after a forced march. According to Herodotus, the Spartans surveyed the battlefield, congratulated the Athenians on their superb tactics and went home, no doubt wondering whether the Athenians' new military prowess might someday eclipse their own.

Marathon, it seems, had taught the Persians nothing. Xerxes' invasion force ten years later tried to make up in numbers for what its king lacked in strategic sense. Herodotus calculated it, including the multitudes of camp-followers, at well over five million men. That number is now agreed to be hugely exaggerated, with the probable figure something under half a million – still immense for the time. Sparta, as Greece's strongest land power, issued a call to all Greek states to cement a grand defensive alliance against the new Persian threat. It was in Sparta's interest to get as many Greek states 'on side' as possible. Besides, a newly-confident Athens under Themistokles, one of the commanders at Marathon, was busy building up a strong navy, a service in which Sparta was quite backward.

The defensive alliance held, but only just. Leonidas and Leotychidas seem to have been 'good boys' as far as the Ephors and Gerousia were concerned, not causing undue problems. Restiveness among the Helots and the subject Messenians was always bubbling under the surface, and had every chance of erupting whenever the Spartan army was away on campaign. This could have been an unstated reason why Sparta was reluctant to send a relief force to Marathon. Argos might have been subdued for the time being, but there was no telling when it might rise to strike again. A fear of Demaratos' possible return with the Persians also collected the royal minds.

In this time of uncertainty Sparta sent mixed signals to the Persians. When Darius had sent heralds to Sparta requesting 'earth and water,' meaning authorization to march over its land, the heralds had been thrown down a well to find their 'earth and water' the hard way. It was an unnecessarily dishonourable, not to say foolhardy, action, and there was plenty of hand-wringing afterwards. To make amends two Spartan volunteers, Sperthias and Boulis, were sent to the Great King's court to be killed in return for the Persian heralds' murder. Instead, the pair were treated courteously. When Xerxes tried to recruit them as Persian agents, promising them high office in occupied Greece, they rejected the offer in true Spartan fashion: 'If you had tasted freedom,' Herodotus quotes them as telling the court official who made them the offer, 'you would advise us to make war not only with spears but also with axes.' Sperthias and Boulis steadfastly refused to kowtow before Xerxes, even under threats. They insisted on being executed for Sparta's treatment of the Persian heralds; it was, after all, what they were there for, and death was preferable to humiliating servitude. Impressed by their courage, Xerxes allowed them to go home to Sparta. It was another valuable lesson in the Spartan character, yet Xerxes showed no sign of learning it.

As Greek spies returned with harrowing accounts of uncounted soldiers and horsemen pouring in from all parts of the far-flung Persian domains, the Greek League of thirty-one states, at a grand conference at Corinth, agreed on a division of labour: Athens would handle naval strategy while Sparta would run the land campaign and be in general command of both services. King Leonidas would command the army; Eurybiades, a Spartan officer, would be in nominal command of the Greek naval forces, though his second-in-command, the Athenian Themistokles, would be the real boss at sea.

Thessaly, the big plain in the middle of mainland Greece, was also a big question mark. Besides possessing Greece's best cavalry corps, Thessaly was one of Greece's extended breadbaskets. If Xerxes got control of it, its food would sustain the Persian forces for a long time. The League agreed to send a force through Thessaly to the strategic Tempe Pass, a gorge running between Mount Olympus and Mount Ossa. But from the locals the commanders learned that there were other routes the Persians could use as detours, so there seemed to be little sense in setting up a defensive line at Tempe. As the

Greek League force withdrew back south, the disappointed Thessalians felt they had little choice but to offer 'earth and water' to Xerxes. A surprising number of Greek states followed suit, most alarmingly Thebes, whose traditional animosity to Athens went back a long time. Argos, too, would not have hesitated to join a Persian attack on Sparta if the Isthmus defences were breached.

With Thessaly given up, the Spartans and Athenians disagreed on where the line of defence should be. The Spartans preferred to defend the Isthmus. But that, of course, would leave Athens exposed. The Athenians, who would be the first to feel Xerxes' fire and sword, urged a line much farther north. Themistokles might boast that if the chips were finally down Athens would be able to depend on its 'wooden walls,' meaning its big new fleet. But sound strategy dictated that any effective defence should also take advantage of Greece's mountainous and defile-ridden terrain. A defence against superior numbers was best handled on a narrow front where the enemy could not bring his maximum strength to bear. Greece is full of such geographical bottlenecks. Eventually the narrow passage at Thermopylai ('Hot Springs') on the east coast was agreed on. Leonidas was assigned to march to Thermopylai, while the fleet sailed in support to Artemision just off the coast. As Leonidas was setting out knowing that he probably wouldn't come back, he turned to his wife Gorgo. If he was killed, he said, she should 'marry a good man who will treat you well, bear his children and live a good life.'

The sea has receded at Thermopylai now, and acres of farmland lie where once the waters of the Aegean lapped. But in August 480, when Leonidas and his men arrived, Thermopylai was a seven-kilometre ribbon of land squeezed between the sea to the north and the towering spurs of Mount Kallidromos to the south. The value of this stretch of scrub – a mere two metres wide at its narrowest point – was that it contained the only uninterrupted road connecting central and southern Greece. Any invading army had no choice but to traverse it. The Persian fleet, correspondingly, had to snake through the adjacent narrows at Artemision.

Leonidas set up camp at the Thermopylai pass with some 6,000 Greek troops. They included 300 picked Spartiates, the cream of the force, chosen specifically from among those who had sons so that in case of a soldier's death his family line would continue; about 1,000 conscripted Peloponnesian *perioikoi*, 500 men from Tegea, 500 from Mantineia, 1,200 from the mountains of Arkadia, 400 Corinthians, 200 from Phlious, 80 from old Mykenai, 700 Thespians, 400 Thebans and 1,000 Phokians and Opuntian Lokrians from the nearby region. Was the Spartan elite force of 300 far too small for the task at hand? Again, as at Marathon exactly ten years before, the Karneia festival in Sparta was in full swing, not to mention the seventy-fifth Olympic

Games at Olympia, and Spartan armies were forbidden to mobilize fully. Were more Spartans to be rushed up to Thermopylai as soon as the festivities were over? We simply do not know.

It has often been remarked that Leonidas took too small a force to Thermopylai, especially as it was common knowledge that Xerxes was descending with a colossal army. Any suspicion that the Ephors might have deliberately engineered it that way is put to rest by Plutarch, who reports that they actually protested at the smallness of the Spartan contingent. 'There are too many for the job *we're* to do,' Leonidas is said to have replied, reinforcing the theory that he must have known he was on a suicide mission or something close to it. His parting words to Gorgo (if Herodotus transmits them correctly) are in the same vein. Though in terms of numbers alone 'all Greece' wouldn't be enough to stop Xerxes, Leonidas was depending on 'men's valour, for which this number will do.' When he was warned that his men might be all killed, he said that in that case it would be a good thing, as the casualty count would be low.[1]

Leonidas' relations with the Ephors and Gerousia can only be a matter of conjecture. As an Agiad, he could have been expected to follow that house's liberal tendencies. Yet we have no evidence of any political tensions along those lines. All sources unanimously portray him as a brave and pure soldier knowing or caring little for politics, committed to defending Greece and prepared to unhesitatingly face death in Sparta's service.

At Thermopylai he built a wall across the western entrance about fifty feet wide, stationing a small Spartan detachment in front, and the rest of the force behind. He sent out his Phokian contingent to block a mountain path around Mount Kallidromos on his left that could conceivably be used to turn his position. At the same time about 300 Athenian and allied triremes assembled off Artemision.

It was Xerxes' original intention to assault Thermopylai without delay. But he and his great army had to wait four days for his navy which had been badly mauled by a storm and a skirmish with the Greeks, reducing its strength by one-third. These four days were vital for Themistokles and the Greek fleet. His nominal boss, Eurybiades, according to Herodotus, nearly panicked at the sight of the Persian navy and was kept in line only by a bribe from Themistokles. Even Leonidas' men were sobered at the sight. Yet there was never any question of flight. One of Herodotus' more edifying vignettes says that when on the fifth day of his arrival on the field, Xerxes decided to attack, he sent a scout to check out the Greek lines. The scout reported back that far from being spooked, the Greeks were sitting around at leisure, combing their hair. Ex-king Demaratos heard the report and smiled to himself. He knew his Spartans. He knew that their calmness meant that they had already decided to die at their posts. And he surely wasn't surprised when Xerxes sent heralds to demand the Greeks' arms in surrender, to receive Leonidas' superbly laconic reply: 'Come and get them!' ('*Molon labe!*')

It's overwhelmingly tempting to accept this phrase as authentic. But is it? It has gone down in book after book, in innumerable documentaries and at least two Hollywood films. Yet Herodotus, our prime source for the battle and so much else, mentions no such utterance. It derives from Plutarch, who wrote several centuries later when legends had plenty of time to take hold.[2] We may nevertheless be confident that, employing some phraseology or other, even if not quite as pithy as what has been reported, Leonidas rejected Xerxes' ultimatum.

Xerxes launched wave after wave of attacks against the Spartans' stone wall, only to be hurled back with heavy loss each time. Persian bodies carpeted the ground for acres. The Greeks were able to hold the position partly because their long spears could stab the Persians before they got to the wall. Xerxes' most elite unit, including a crack regiment called the Immortals, failed to dent the Spartan line. Leonidas performed prodigies of courage while revealing himself to be a smart tactician. He would lead his Three Hundred against the Persian line, pull back in feigned retreat, and as the jubilant Asiatics surged forward, about turn and massacre them. Herodotus reports that Xerxes, observing these actions, jumped three times from his throne in anguish. His Immortals had proved themselves considerably mortal.

On the second day more human waves broke against the Greek position, which remained intact as Leonidas rotated his units, sending fatigued ones to the rear and bringing up rested troops. Asiatic corpses again piled up in front of the stone wall. According to one source Demaratos suggested that the Persians ought to give up the head-butting at Thermopylai and move against Lakedaimon by sea from the south, forcing the Spartans to split their own forces. It was a tactic that might very well have worked, but Xerxes, it seems, was set upon a frontal assault.[3] Then on the afternoon of the second day, a desperate Xerxes received help from an unexpected quarter. A local peasant named Ephialtes presented himself saying there was a footpath around the back of Mount Kallidromos that offered a way for Thermopylai to be turned.

Before the battle began Leonidas had sent a Phokian contingent to block that very route, known as the Anopaia path. What he could not have known was that the Phokians would be of little use. After dark, the Immortals under their commander Hydarnes filed up the Anopaia path, with Ephialtes (one imagines considerably wealthier now) leading the way. The Phokians, hearing the rustle of leaves and twigs underfoot, sprang up in alarm. Hydarnes halted his men and ordered his archers to shower the Phokian position with arrows. The Phokians withdrew up the slope, leaving the Anopian path unguarded. This blunder sealed the Greeks' fate.

The Greek defenders learned at dawn that the pass had been turned. The Corinthian, Arkadian and other Peloponnesian contingents plus the Phokians and Lokrians – three-quarters of the force – decided the game was up and pulled out through the southern entrance to the pass. Leonidas and his Three Hundred felt duty-bound to stay; electing to stay with him were the Thespians, Thebans and Mykenaians. Few had any illusions about what was in store for them. Megistias, the army's chief diviner, had read the portents of doom in his morning sacrifices. 'Eat your breakfast as if it's dinner in the next world,' Leonidas advised his men with supreme aplomb. According to Herodotus one Dienekes gave the perfect reply to an alarmist who described the Persian arrows as so thick they hid the sun. 'Good,' Dienekes deadpanned, 'then we'll fight in the shade.' Leonidas had the idea of detailing three of his younger men to return to Sparta with secret despatches and give them a chance of survival, but they wouldn't hear of it. 'I didn't come to carry messages but to fight,' one of them said, and that was that.[4]

Leonidas' mission, far from holding up the Persians, was now to inflict as much damage on them as possible before dying. There may have been no such distinction in his mind from the outset. There was absolutely no thought of retreat; the Spartans at home would never forgive them for it. In the morning Leonidas moved his force out from the western end of the pass, stretching them out in classic line formation and leaving a handful of men to guard the stone wall. He had no reserves.

The Persians were not long in coming. Not surprisingly, given the carnage of the previous days, many of them had to be whipped along by their officers. Fighting with the calm and deadly efficiency of men who have come to terms with death, Leonidas' men once more mowed down the attackers. When their spears shattered under the strain, they fought with their bare hands. Leonidas fought in front of the rest, and when he fell there followed a savage struggle for his body in which two of Xerxes' own brothers were slain. The Spartans finally secured the body and took it to a temporarily safe place in the narrowest point of the pass where a small hillock, the Kolonos, commands the path. There they drew up in a defensive circle, spear points outwards, prepared to fight to the last with their fists and teeth. Hydarnes' heavily-armed Immortals had come up in their rear. The exhausted Thebans had already thrown down their weapons and surrendered. From a safe distance the Persians rained spears and arrows on the remnants of the Three Hundred until none was left. Xerxes ordered Leonidas' body decapitated and hung on a cross. What became of it later is not known. It would be pleasing, in the absence of any evidence, to think that Leonidas might at last have been buried with his men under Kolonos hill, topped by a commemorative plaque, that still guards the main road northwards. Today's plaque is a copy of the ancient one that bore a couplet by the poet Simonides:

> *Stranger, go and tell the Lakedaimonians that here*
> *We lie, in obedience to their laws.*

One of Leonidas' men survived Thermopylai. This was Aristodemos, who at the time of the final battle was lying in a field hospital with an eye ailment. When news of the Spartans' extremity reached the hospital his friend Eurytos, also ill, nonetheless grabbed his weapons and ran to his death at the front line. Aristodemos saw fit to stay where he was. When he returned to Sparta he got a rude shock; as the only one of the Three Hundred not to die with their king, he was treated as the lowliest of outcasts. No-one would talk to him except to hurl jeers such as 'Aristodemos the Unmanly.' His life became utterly miserable. Ephialtes, for his part, wisely made himself scarce for a few years, but when he returned to the area he was murdered. The Spartans honoured the slayer.

Plutarch had the last word on Leonidas by quoting his reply when he was asked why the best men prefer a glorious death to an inglorious life. 'It's because the first is nature's gift,' he said.[5] Yet Leonidas I, credited with being the bravest of Sparta's kings, was denied even the honour of a funeral at home. In the centre of modern Sparta, in a small square bounded by shops and cafes, stand the ruins of a classical-era stone edifice, revered today as the Cenotaph of Leonidas, and honoured each October in a patriotic ceremony.

## Leotychidas II (491–469)

When young Leotychidas II, soon after his accession, was given the task of trying to persuade Athens to send back the Aiginetan hostages taken in 491, it was probably as a diplomatic exercise to cut his teeth on. He failed, and Athens and Aigina became embroiled in a bitter naval war for the next few years. Leotychidas had a son named Zeuxidamos, who died before his father but left him a grandson, Archidamos. To provide security for the boy, Leotychidas took a second wife; the resulting daughter, named Lampito, was betrothed to Archidamos and so the cement of the Eurypontid house was kept together.

At the time of Thermopylai, Leotychidas had been kept back to hold the fort at Sparta, as on the Agiad side Leonidas' son Pleistarchos was still a young boy. Pleistarchos was placed under the regency of his uncle Kleombrotos, Leonidas' younger brother. Kleombrotos commanded the force guarding the Isthmus which the Spartans believed was the only place where Xerxes could finally be halted, and Leotychidas was sent to join him there. By now Xerxes was burning Athens. The Greek fleet was still unscathed, awaiting the invaders at Salamis, an island separated from Athens by a narrow channel.

Eurybiades the Spartan, the admiral in command at Salamis, was in a grim mood. He may have been formally termed admiral (*nauarchos*), but he was simply a land general assigned to command ships. Naval warfare had never been the Spartans' strong suit. The treacherous sea was still alien to them, and they saw no point in staying at Salamis, bobbing at anchor among unfamiliar inlets and channels, when the columns of smoke from burning Athens could be clearly seen. Eurybiades himself was not one to see the other person's point of view. In the pages of Herodotus and Thucydides he comes across as blinkered, stubborn, rude and hidebound – a Colonel Blimp of the ancient world.

Eurybiades' relations with Themistokles were less than cordial. The Athenian, for his part, couldn't bear the thought of leaving his home waters to the enemy, and believed the Greeks had a sporting chance of hammering the Persian fleet inside the twisty channel of Salamis, which he knew well. Eurybiades, the sullen pessimist, wanted to withdraw to the waters by the Isthmus as soon as possible. He was also under pressure from other Peloponnesian crews such as the Corinthians. During an argument the two men almost came to blows as the Spartan raised his mace. 'Hit me if you want,' Plutarch reports Themistokles as saying, 'but listen to me anyway.' The channel at Salamis, he argued, would neutralize the size of the Persian fleet that had assembled at Phaleron where Anchimolos the Spartan had met his end a few decades before. Eurybiades reluctantly conceded the point. Herodotus reports that Themistokles duped the Persians through an ingenious bit of disinformation into attacking quickly, before Eurybiades changed his mind.

Themistokles' daring and foresight paid off brilliantly. In the early dawn, as the five-kilometre-long Persian fleet, numbering about 1,000 vessels, nosed into the channel and Xerxes himself had taken up an observer's position on Mount Aigaleos on the north side, a sharp bugle note sounded. It was the *paian*, the Greek battle cry:

> *Sons of the Greeks, liberate your lands,*
> *Free your wives and your children,*
> *The gods of your lands and fathers ...*
> *Now the fight is for all.*

At Eurybiades' command the Greeks ships sailed out to meet the enemy. The encounter was long and bitter. Sixteen Spartan ships formed the right of the Greek line, fighting as eagerly as the Athenians on the left. The Persian hulls proved unwieldy in the channel as a stiff breeze upset their formation and left them sitting ducks for the Greeks' rams. For the better part of a day the Salamis channel echoed with the battle yells of the Greek crews, the cries of the wounded and drowning and the splintering of ship timbers. Xerxes, as he had done at Thermopylai, leapt from his throne in anguish. While Themistokles dealt with the Persian right, the Spartan ships smashed the left. By sundown at least 200 Persian warships had gone down, to about forty Greek.

King Leotychidas waited at the Isthmus for the Persians to appear over the coast road from Athens, but they never did. The brilliant victory at Salamis had finally stopped the Persian Great King in his tracks. With his support fleet wiped out, Xerxes had no choice but to go home. He left 150,000 men in Thessaly under Mardonius as the advance guard for another planned incursion the following summer.

Salamis was a wake-up call for Sparta. For the second time in ten years a Greek power, Athens, had proved itself able to supply the equal of the Spartan fighting man. Athens was on an unstoppable rise. Its use of innovative land tactics at Marathon was now matched by its naval prowess at Salamis. More-over, the battle was a signal that naval warfare had become a necessary skill for any self-respecting city-state, even one with little naval tradition, such as Sparta. Eurybiades realized this when he vetoed Themistokles' idea of pursuing the remnants of the Persian fleet all the way to the Dardanelles. Themistokles made a triumphal visit to Sparta and was given the best chariot the city could provide. He and Eurybiades were awarded the supreme prize of olive wreaths. At the seventy-sixth Olympic Games in 476, four years later, the spectators paid more attention to him than to the sporting events.

When campaigning weather re-opened in the spring of 479, and Mardonius' Persian cohorts began to move south, Leotychidas – more confident in command now – got together 100 triremes and assembled them off Aigina to await orders. The Spartans had improved their naval skills over the winter. The Persians this time tried diplomacy to win over the resisting Greeks before employing force. To this end they sent one of their puppet rulers, King Alexander I of Macedon, to the Athenians with the advice that the Great King was magnanimously prepared to forgive their past 'mistakes' and reimburse them for their losses if they would submit. A Spartan delegation happened to be in Athens at the time and listened with satisfaction to the Athenians' defiant reply: 'Nowhere on earth is there enough gold to induce us to ... enslave Greece.' And then came the clincher: 'The Greeks are all of one blood and one tongue, with common temples and sacrifices, common customs.'

If something like it was indeed uttered, as Herodotus says it was, it marked a basic change in the Greeks' war attitudes. So far the attitude of the various Greek states to the Persian threat had differed: some had submitted, some had fought and some had sat on the fence, all in accordance with their perceived interests. Yet a more general Greek patriotism was bubbling under the surface. Salamis had instilled great pride in all the Greeks who had fought in it, together with a dawning realization that liberty was indeed sweet when fought for.

None of this, of course, registered with Xerxes. In the spring of 479 Mardonius burst into Athens and sacked the city for the second time in ten months. The Spartans felt justified in keeping their defensive position at the Isthmus in view of the fate of Leonidas and his Three Hundred. Any other loss on such a scale could sink the city. There had been a change of command at the Isthmus. Kleombrotos, the guardian of the young King Pleistarchos, had died, to be replaced by his son Pausanias – Leonidas' nephew – who was already old enough to command an army. The fortifications at the Isthmus were almost completed, and the Athenians fretted that the Spartans might well abandon all the Greek states north of the Isthmus to their fate.

It was not an unreasonable fear. King Leotychidas, the original fortifier of the Isthmus, was shunted aside in favour of Pausanias the regent. Sparta appeared to be on the verge of abandoning all of Greece outside the Peloponnese when a diplomat from Tegea named Chileos somehow convinced the Ephors that Athens was worth preserving after all. When an exasperated Athenian mission complained about Spartan inaction, they were pleasantly surprised to learn that Pausanias had decided to cross the Isthmus with 35,000 Spartan and other Peloponnesian infantry.

Hearing of the move, Mardonius retired from Athens northwards to the rolling plain south of Thebes. He intended to draw the Greeks into a trap where his cavalry would have free play in the battle he knew would come. Pausanias, meanwhile, gathered other allied troops on his march through the territory of Megara and the defiles of Mount Kithairon. When he caught up with the Persians on the plain of the Asopos River, some 8,000 Athenians had joined him, bringing his force up to 110,000, probably the biggest single Greek military force ever assembled up to that time.

On the northern bank of the Asopos River the Persians were encamped with the city of Thebes at their rear. Their Asiatic divisions were beefed up by Greeks allied to their cause, such as Macedonians, Thessalians and Thebans. Mardonius had a palisade built, behind which he could station his archers to fire at the Greeks from comparative safety. During an initial attack by the Persians, however, Masistius, the Persian cavalry commander, was killed; his body was paraded along the cheering Greek lines. For the next twelve days both sides glowered at each other across the river, probing for weaknesses. Mardonius hoped for a Greek attack so that he could decimate it with his archers and horsemen. On the other side, Pausanias rearranged his forces for better access to the Gargaphia spring, a key source of water for the army.

There was some temporary confusion when Pausanias courteously offered the Athenians the position directly opposite the main ethnic Persian force, on the grounds that the victors of Marathon would be better acquainted with Persian tactics. The Athenians under Aristides, who had been a division commander at Marathon, agreed. When the Tegeates protested, Aristides tried to calm matters. 'Whatever position you give us, we will hold with honour,' Plutarch reports him telling Pausanias. 'We didn't come here to quarrel with our allies, but to fight our enemies [and] to show courage in defence of Greece.'[6] But Pausanias agreed to the exchange of positions – a potentially hazardous manoeuvre given the closeness of the enemy. As it was underway it was observed by the enemy, who realized what was afoot and began altering their own positions accordingly. Seeing this, the Greeks resumed their original deployments, and the Persians again did likewise, so all that was accomplished was a lot of unnecessary toing and froing.

On the twelfth day the Persians captured and fouled the Gargaphia spring. Their flying columns massacred a supply train behind the Greek lines, making the Greek position even more precarious. Their frontal attack of that day stove in the Corinthians in the Greek centre, throwing Pausanias' whole defensive formation into disorder. The Spartans fell back more slowly than the others. Darkness saved the Greeks, whose various contingents managed to find themselves new positions to the left of the old ones. At daybreak the following day the Spartans still had not taken up their new position in the foothills of Mount Kithairon, where the Persian horse would be less effective. The reason was strenuous opposition by Amompharetos, an impetuous young front-line company commander who couldn't bring himself to withdraw in the face of the enemy, and told Pausanias so to his face. The general snapped at Amompharetos that he was a fool, and began the repositioning anyway.

As the acrimonious exchange was in progress, a Persian arrow whistled behind the lines and hit Kallikrates, a Spartan hoplite, between the ribs. Mortally wounded, Kallikrates gasped that he didn't mind dying for his country, but it was a shame that it couldn't be in the front line. Pausanias ordered his diviners to sacrifice animal after animal, but the signs came out negative each time. Reduced to tears of frustration, he prayed that if the gods were against him, the Greeks at least should go down fighting. At that moment, says Plutarch, the latest batch of innards was favourable and the diviner forecast victory. At about this time Amompharetos' company reluctantly joined the main line. Mardonius observed that straggling movement, and believing it to be part of a general Greek pullback, he ordered a frontal assault. The Persian cavalry splashed across the Asopos and bore down on Amompharetos' company just as it was rejoining the Spartan line. At the same time a Theban unit in Persian service engaged the Athenian front, preventing it from going to the aid of the Spartans. As the Greeks were now on uneven ground unsuitable for cavalry operations, the Persians switched to infantry charges.

Mardonius flung his elite units, including the Immortals, against the Spartan flank. Moments before the lines engaged, Persian archers sent volleys of arrows against the Spartan and Tegeate positions. The Greeks held their shields over their heads, and the arrows bounced harmlessly away. After the first volleys were spent Pausanias ordered a counterattack. First the Tegeates and then the Spartans cut a bloody swath through the formations of enemy archers; some of the Asiatics displayed desperate courage by seizing the Spartan spearheads with their bare hands and snapping them off. Arimnestos, a Spartan, penetrated Mardonius' bodyguard of 1,000 men to despatch the Persian general himself. With Mardonius gone, the fight went out of the Persians who fled back over the river. In the Spartan ranks was Aristodemos the Unmanly, the soldier who had not got up the nerve to join his comrades at Thermopylai. At about this hour, or a little later, he ended his lonely life – as he no doubt intended to do – performing deeds of reckless courage. Herodotus later erased Aristodemos' shame by according him recognition as 'the best soldier of them all.'

The Athenians on the left were hard pressed for a while, but the Spartan victory on the right ensured a Greek triumph at Plataia. The fleeing Persians attempted to regroup in a stockade but the Athenian contingent burst in, slaughtering all inside. The number of Persians who fell at Plataia is not reliably known, but it must have been many thousands. Ancient writers claim it took ten days to bury the dead of both sides. The Persian casualty figure was surely far in excess of the Greek, which came to about 1,300, including ninety-one Spartans. One of the fallen was the valiant Amompharetos (whose name means 'He of the Unstained Virtue'). Fifty-two Athenians also fell. The Spartans buried their battle dead in three common graves: one for the Spartiates, one for the *perioikoi* and one for the Helots. As the Persians retreated northwards, never again to set foot in Greece, Pausanias punished Thebes for siding with the invader, executing its leaders.[7]

The momentous consequences of the smashing victory at Plataia were not immediately apparent to the Spartans, or to the Greeks in general, who fully expected Xerxes to make another effort as soon as he could regroup his forces. King Leotychidas was thus with the Greek fleet of 110 triremes which sailed from its station at Aigina to Delos in the middle of the Aegean, to keep an eye on the main Persian fleet at Samos. A delegation of Samians led by one Hegesistratos called at Delos to inform Leotychidas and the Athenian commander Xanthippos that the Greeks of Asia Minor, heartened by Xerxes' reverses in mainland Greece, were on verge of revolt again. Leotychidas was in favour of an immediate expedition – he is said to have perceived the name of the Samian delegation leader Hegesistratos, which means 'Leader of the Army', as a good omen for action.

The Persian troops occupying the Aegean seaboard, Hegesistratos said, numbered not more than 60,000. These included many Ionian Greek conscripts who would desert at the first opportunity. The Persian fleet at Samos numbered about 300 ships, but the Greeks meanwhile had gathered some 250, and were better sailors anyway. Leotychidas and Xanthippos needed no more convincing. As they bore down on Samos, the Persian ships withdrew, lining up on the beach at Cape Mykale on the nearby mainland. The Greeks chased them there, securing the beachhead with 5,000 marines. The Athenians and Corinthians on the left attacked first, but found it hard going until King Leotychidas and his Spartans stormed ashore on the right. News had just reached them of the victory at Plataia, and their *elan* was decisive, hurling the enemy back into the hills while rebelling Ionian Greeks attacked the Persians from the rear.

So decisive were the twin victories at Plataia and Mykale that the Persian Empire would cease to be a strategic threat to Greece for the next fifty years. The way was open for Athens in particular to embark upon that half-century of glory and achievement which history knows as the Golden Age of Greece. As for Sparta, Kings Leonidas and Leotychidas, not to mention Pausanias the general (and even the gloomy Eurybiades) had kept Spartan battlefield honour at a high shine. If ever there was a time for Sparta to rest on its laurels for a time, this was it. Leotychidas may have had this in mind when immediately after Mykale he suggested that the Ionian Greeks emigrate *en masse* from Asia and resettle in the Greek mainland where they would cease to be vulnerable to Persian conquest. Behind this thinking lay the old Spartan distaste for overseas adventurism. Besides, autumn was approaching, rough seas would soon roil the Aegean, and the Spartan soldiery was eager to go home and get in the harvest – a key consideration in any strategic planning. Xanthippos and the Athenians were left to settle accounts in the eastern Aegean.

Leotychidas, however, was no isolationist. He nursed a strong grievance against those Greeks who had sided with Xerxes and felt honour-bound to redress matters. In Spartan eyes the Greek 'medisers', that is, those who supported the Medes (another name for the Persians), were traitors, pure and simple. But as the career of Kleomenes I had shown, interventionism in a Spartan king was strewn with traps. It had been fourteen years since Leotychidas' abortive attempt to arrest the friends of Persia at Aigina. He seems to have failed to learn the lesson from it, which was that the Ephors were ever ready to pounce on any sign of extraordinary royal power. First on Leotychidas' hit list was the Aleuadai clan which ruled Thessaly on a feudal basis and had supplied the Persian army with a good deal of its provisions and horses.

Leotychidas had given an indication of his character during the episode at the theatre in Sparta where he had publicly humiliated the newly-deposed Demaratos. He had a rude as well as a sharp tongue, as when he upbraided a poor priest who said there would be true happiness only in the afterlife. 'Then die as soon as you can, you idiot, to stop moaning about your poverty!' was Leotychidas' reply. He had no time for the sons of Demaratos who, not surprisingly, were in the habit of bad-mouthing him. 'No wonder,' was the king's riposte, 'for none of them could ever speak a good word.' Similarly, he scoffed at a soothsayer who saw a snake coiling around the key to a gate and pronounced it a portent. 'Now if the key had coiled around the snake, *that* would be a portent!' he quipped.[8]

His callousness turned out to be his undoing. In 477, he was sent to settle accounts with the Thessalians. He lost his first clash with them, arousing the Ephors' suspicions that he had been bribed to lose. The Spartan government was told how the king had been surprised in his tent sitting on a sack of bribe money. After a trial he was banished to exile in Tegea, which was now becoming a refuge for disaffected high-born Spartans. His house was demolished. The Spartan establishment clearly desired to pull in its horns; more foreign adventures would deplete Sparta of manpower and make it more vulnerable to potential revolt by subject peoples and Helots. And farther north, the rising power of Athens would not let the Spartan establishment rest for long.

# Chapter 6

# The Cold War Kings

**Pleistarchos**
**Pleistoanax**
**Archidamos II**

## Pleistarchos (480–459)

What it is customary to call Greece's Golden Age was not an overly peaceful one. The clamour of armies in conflict sounded a constant counterpoint to the great accomplishments of the Greek mind. One of the recurring themes of history is the speed with which allies in a general war can turn against one another once the external threat is removed. The Cold War pitting the democratic West against the Russian-dominated communist bloc after the Second World War provides an almost exact parallel with fifth century Athens, with its navy and democracy, facing down Sparta, with its army and authoritarian regime. Ancient Greece's cold war lasted without a break, often turning hot, from 479 to 431.

Sparta was increasingly suspicious of the Athenian leader Themistokles, who basked in the glory of Salamis and used his popularity to build up an Aegean empire and powerful navy to defend it with. When Themistokles began building a newer and stronger wall around Athens the Spartans' suspicions turned to dark certainty – why would Athens need a wall unless it was plotting war against other Greek states? Themistokles journeyed to Sparta to personally calm the fears. There he stalled for time as the whole Athenian population, including women and children, laboured night and day to complete about seven kilometres of city wall. When it was finished, Themistokles had a *fait accompli* to present to the Spartans, which only enraged them the more. Athenian perfidy became a byword in Lakedaimon.

In 475 some Spartan hotheads urged a pre-emptive attack on Athens. Coming just four years after the successful Spartan-Athenian cooperation at Plataia, the proposal shows just how afraid the Ephors were that Sparta might lose whatever military advantage it had. The attack never took place thanks to a far-seeing member of the Gerousia named Hetoimaridas who argued persuasively against it.

Leonidas' widow Gorgo remained in high regard in Sparta. When an Athenian woman asked her how Spartan women had characters strong enough to rule men (whereas in Athens women were kept completely out of social affairs), she replied: 'Because we are the only ones who give birth to real men.'

In light of this quote, which gives us an insight into the mind of the average Spartan woman, it is a pity that we have next to no information on Gorgo's son Pleistarchos, who was a minor when Leonidas died. Herodotus provides a tantalizing half-clue. Shortly after Leonidas was killed a Spartan delegation arrived at Xerxes' headquarters in Thessaly, solemnly demanding financial reparations for his death. It's not certain what such a move was intended to achieve. Xerxes laughed loud and long at the quaint demand, quipping that the Greeks would soon get adequate recompense, but not of the financial kind. Was the naive mission the work of young Pleistarchos, or his guardian Kleombrotos, Leonidas' younger brother, from whom such an emotional reaction might be expected?

There is, in fact, a question mark over who exactly wielded actual power in Sparta in the 470s. After the flight of Leotychidas II a veil of ignorance descends over the royal houses. Very little is known of Pleistarchos or his short reign which he began under the guardianship of his uncle Pausanias, the acclaimed victor of Plataia. The situation in the Eurypontid house is even murkier; that throne seems to have been left open until Leotychidas' death in 469, when he was formally succeeded by his grandson Archidamos II, a minor. Someone had to fill the power vacuum, and Pausanias felt he was the one to do it. Still young and vigorous, and one of the most popular men in all Greece, Pausanias had seen what the Greeks could do when united and had the idea of dragging Sparta out of its traditional isolation.

At the conclusion of the Persian wars Pausanias was in command of twenty Peloponnesian ships charged with mopping up odd Persian outposts in and around the Aegean. First a joint Spartan-Athenian force neutralized Persian bases in Cyprus, moving on to Byzantion (Byzantium, later Constantinople, and later Istanbul) at the mouth of the Bosporus – a key position on the Greek grain route from the Black Sea colonies. But Byzantion was where the Spartans, though they could win battles, demonstrated that they were poor administrators of occupied territories. And Pausanias fell into the trap. If we are to credit his enemies, his character did not match his ambitions. He was known as a blunt and often harsh man, one might think a typical product of the Spartan *agoge*. Like many others brought up austerely before being exposed to wealth, the Oriental luxuries available to him in Byzantion turned his mind. He took on the ways of an Oriental despot, gorging himself on huge meals and wearing Persian garb. Thucydides reports that when he became angry 'his fury was such that no-one could stand before him.'

The Spartans serving under Pausanias could hardly be expected to put up with such behaviour which, moreover, was turning large numbers of Ionian Greeks against Sparta and into the arms of Athens whose local commander, Aristides (known as the Just for his fairness in public affairs), was a model of good manners and sense. Pausanias accordingly was recalled to Sparta under a darkening cloud, which by now included strident claims that he was plotting to subdue all Greece with Persian help. None of this could be proven, and it is admittedly hard to imagine the victor of Plataia turning into a Persian stooge within a few short years. The Ephors would have thought so, too, which is probably why he was convicted on the relatively minor count of 'injustice against private persons'. He was, however, stripped of his naval command. His irresponsible conduct at Byzantion had been a serious blow to Spartan prestige in the region, handing another geopolitical advantage to Athens.

After receiving his rap on the knuckles at home, Pausanias sailed back to Asia Minor, settling in the area around Troy. What exactly he did there is not known. There is no evidence, again, that he plotted anything with the Persians. He most likely used the interval to think of ways to change the hidebound Spartan regime. His experiences of the world outside Sparta might have corrupted him, but they had also broadened his mind. More-over, he was related to the Agiad house, on the basis of which he had been assigned the regency in place of Pleistarchos, and could well have shared the Agiads' anti-Ephor sentiments. Pausanias, in short, regarded the 470s Ephorate as an obsolete institution in dire need of change. He wanted Sparta to be as Athens was becoming – dynamic and outward-looking, with a strong presence in the islands and the Greek cities of Asia Minor.

After a brief period in the region of Troy, Pausanias was once more recalled to Sparta. There seems to have been no lack of people to report adversely on his doings. On the way home he probably felt he had little to fear, as the old charge of plotting with Persia had been dropped. But now it was being bandied about that he was planning to enlist the Helots and other members of the underclass in a peasants' revolt. Pausanias duly disembarked at Lakedaimon, and while on the road to Sparta met a group of Ephors coming the other way. As Thucydides recounts the incident, the expressions on the Ephors' faces told Pausanias what he could expect. He ran for the nearest holy place, a shrine to Poseidon, and took refuge in its sanctuary. The Ephors took off the shrine roof, walled up the doors, placed a guard and left him there to starve. When Pausanias was on the point of expiring the

Ephors took him out, as it would be a sin to allow him to die in a sacred place, and buried him nearby. Such was the end of the victor of Plataia.

The year 470 marks a nadir in the power of the Spartan royal houses. Pausanias had just been disposed of. His protégé Pleistarchos had probably reached his majority, as Pausanias' regency had ended in 476. If we assume that Leonidas I and Gorgo had a son soon after Leonidas' accession (at the latest), then Pleistarchos would have been at least in his mid-teens. As for the Eurypontid house, it was on the verge of installing the teenage Archidamos II, the grandson of Leotychidas II. Neither king would have been old enough to exercise any real influence over political events. This was now exclusively the Ephors' show, and just in time, as Argos, under a new democratic regime, had decided to measure swords with Sparta once more. Barely had that conflict begun than in 469, probably encouraged by the political turmoil involving Pausanias, Sparta's Messenian subjects rose up to begin the Third Messenian War.

Many Messenians and other *perioikoi* had fought and died alongside the Spartans from Thermopylai to Salamis and Plataia. Men who had contributed to the struggle and risked their lives for Greek liberty could naturally expect to be rewarded with a bit of political liberty themselves. Information about the Third Messenian war is scant. The rebel attacks, and the Spartan expeditions to contain them, centred about Mount Ithome. Arimnestos, an officer who had distinguished himself at Plataia, led a force to seize Stenyklaros but was slain with all his men. Five years into the revolt a devastating earthquake levelled Sparta, killing some 20,000 people in Lakedaimon, including a gymnasium full of youths exercising. Only five houses in Sparta remained standing. Plutarch reports that even the crags of Mount Taygetos were split open.

In 460 the anti-Persian grand alliance was finally scrapped. The Argives had been giving trouble on Lakedaimon's northeast frontier and Pleistarchos was given the chance to walk in his father's footsteps and lead a punitive expedition. Not much is known about this operation. Pleistarchos met a combined force of Argives and Athenians at Oinoe west of Argos, and here the lack of Spartan soldiers, depleted by the Messenian revolt and the earthquake, told against him and his outnumbered army was driven from the field. Pleistarchos himself died the following year aged about thirty; perhaps he had been wounded in the field, perhaps he had become ill; our sources tell us nothing.

Pleistarchos, despite his being the son of Leonidas I, is one of those Spartan kings curiously passed over by the annalists. Whatever is known about him personally comes from Plutarch, who himself is sparing with details. He appears to have had a dour sense of humour, as when he was told he was being praised by a notorious bad-mouther. 'I wonder if anyone told him I was dead,' was Pleistarchos' reaction, 'for the man can never say a good word about anyone who is alive.' But he was careful not to overdo his wittiness, remarking of one comic performer that he was in danger of becoming a joke himself, 'like those who wrestle all the time and become wrestlers.' And he dismissed an entertainer who could imitate a nightingale, saying he could get more pleasure from listening to the bird itself.[1]

## Pleistoanax (459–409)

Pleistoanax, a cousin of Pleistarchos, succeeded to the Agiad throne in 459, when Sparta still hadn't fully recovered from the earthquake. The first we see of him is at the head of a Peloponnesian expedition sent to ravage the western approaches to Athens. The five-year truce with Athens had been allowed to expire and the Ephors were in a bellicose mood once more.

From the little we know, Pleistoanax was not a warlike king, and Perikles, the Athenian leader, may very well have known it. The young king's first stab at command in the field in 446 ended ignominiously. Kleandridas, the Ephor sent along to keep an eye on him, accepted a large bribe from the Athenian state treasury to withdraw. There is no way of knowing whether Pleistoanax himself took any of the money, but the Spartan government believed that he had and he was exiled. Kleandridas fled to Italy to escape the death sentence. The following year, a humiliated Sparta agreed to a thirty-year peace with Athens.

Pleistoanax spent a quarter of a century in the political wilderness, an exile in Arkadia. It wasn't until about 425, when Sparta was ten years into the life-and-death struggle with Athens known as the Peloponnesian War, that he was recalled to the throne as part of a new effort to make peace with Athens. Pleistoanax was known as a pacifist – perhaps the first pacifist king of Sparta – and his reinstatement was expected to buttress a precious breathing space in which Sparta could replenish its manhood. The attempt fell through because of Athenian intransigence. Pleistoanax himself had no love lost for Athens. In the only known anecdote about him, he bristled when an Athenian orator called the Spartans unlearned. 'You're right,' Pleistoanax replied, 'for we alone of the Greeks have not learned evil from you.'[2] He continued to play an obligatory but small military part in the war until shortly before his death in 409. (See Agis II below.)

## Archidamos II (469–427)

While young and weak kings occupied the Agiad throne, the Eurypontid house dramatically picked up the sceptre of leadership after the earthquake of

464. The disaster had triggered a general peasants' revolt. Columns of armed Helots marched on the ruined city in a *jacquerie* the likes of which had never before been seen. Long years of hatred of the Spartan ruling class and its methods now bore their bitter fruit. Yet it was not the Ephors or the Gerousia who confronted the peasant army but young King Archidamos II, five years on the Eurypontid throne. As the Spartan citizenry panicked, trying to save what could be saved from the ruins of their homes before the vengeful peasantry could loot them; Archidamos had the bugles sounded to muster all the surviving soldiers whom he lined up in formation on the outskirts of the city. When the serfs saw the firm line with the king at its head they called off their attack and fled to join the Messenian rebels at Mount Ithome. (One wonders where the young Agiad king Pleistarchos was during this upheaval, and whether he was in a position to do anything.) The quake and its sequel shook the Ephors' power to the core. Their humiliation was such that they had no qualms about appealing to Athens for military help against the Messenians under the terms of the 481 grand alliance that had not lapsed. The rebels were finally brought to heel again about 462.

All over the Greek world states jostled for power and resources, some appealing to Athens for aid and others looking to Sparta. Megara wanted to expand its southern lands at the expense of Corinth and called in Athenian help. Athens needed employment for its naval rowers and trounced the Corinthians. For a new and extremely capable leader had come to power in Athens. This was Perikles, the head of the democratic faction, who was a genius at manipulating the Athenian citizenry that had a distinct economic interest in building up the city's empire. In 457 Perikles ordered an eleven-kilometre double wall, known as the Long Walls, built to connect Athens with its vital port of Piraeus. Unlike his more conservative predecessors, Perikles made no secret of his distaste for Sparta and its institutions. This was too much for the Spartan establishment which now feared that Athens as a foe would be invincible. Might not a swift military blow topple Perikles before he could become too powerful? The Athenians' aid in suppressing the Messenians was already forgotten. In July 457 Sparta sent Nikomedes, the guardian of young Pleistoanax, into Boiotia with 12,000 men. The aim was to bypass Athens and attack the city from its northern approaches. Meeting them on the field of Tanagra were 14,000 Athenians under Perikles himself and a force of Thessalian horsemen. The Thessalians had become allies of Athens ever since Leotychidas II's abortive invasion of their territory.

For two days at Tanagra both sides butchered each other at close quarters, neither giving an inch. Some of the bitterness of the fight is attributed to the fact that the differences between Sparta and Athens had now become ideological – autocracy versus democracy. Perikles himself fought in the

Athenian front line with admirable valour. A typical devious politician he might be, but at Tanagra he proved himself a fearless general as well, adding to his laurels. On the evening of the second day the Thessalian horsemen – never democrats by conviction – decided the issue by defecting to the Spartans. Sparta thus claimed a tactical victory, but at the cost of very heavy casualties that it could ill afford to sustain after the Third Messenian War and earthquake. Athenian losses, too, were grievous, enough to make the philosopher Aristotle much later conclude that this and other battles left Athens deprived of noble young men with character enough to rule, leaving statecraft at the mercy of demagogues and lightweights.

The result of the battle of Tanagra worsened the Spartan population crisis. The cream of its military-age Spartiates had perished. The whole domain of Lakedaimon, in fact, now numbered something less than 20,000 citizens. Sparta had desperate need of a breathing-space. The response of the Ephors and the Gerousia was to turn the state in on itself, imagining that by continuing the old *agoge* and Lykourgean discipline, Sparta could turn its back on the rest of Greece. But the lack of fighting men was never quite made good. The most that Sparta could do was intrigue with the aristocratic factions of city-states around Greece in a policy of sniping at Athenian power wherever it could be found. And the kings were expected to fall in with this policy.

About 451 the Ephors agreed to a five-year truce with Athens. Perikles recalled Kimon, his main pro-Spartan political opponent, from exile. Kimon travelled to Sparta for the negotiations and formed a cordial relationship with King Archidamos, who wanted to know more about this Perikles, of whom so much was heard. According to Plutarch, when the king found occasion to ask Kimon whether Perikles was a good wrestler, the Athenian replied: 'When I throw him, he claims he hasn't fallen, then convinces the spectators that he has won.'

Athens may have lost the battle at Tanagra, but Perikles' personal courage and leadership in that encounter caused his star to soar ever higher. He ordered punitive military and naval expeditions against Sparta and its allies. One of these reached Gytheion, the port of Sparta, and burned the ship-yards. With money extorted from Athens' island empire he erected the great Parthenon on the Acropolis of Athens. Inside the Parthenon's precincts stood a giant golden statue of the goddess Athena, Athens' protectress deity; her plumed helmet and shining spear point were visible from far out to sea, an unmistakable message to Athens' foes. As Perikles' citizens cheered, Athenian sailors gladly crewed the triremes that sailed against Persian out-posts as far as Cyprus and Egypt. Xerxes' successor as Persian Great King, Artaxerxes I, sued for peace with the Greeks in 449. By the Peace of Kallias,

Artaxerxes pledged to keep all his provincial governors no less than three days' journey from the Ionian coast, restrict his warships to neutral areas and, most importantly, recognize the liberty of the Ionian Greek states. Athens, for its part, pledged not to attack Persian possessions. The great thirty-year conflict with Asia, it appeared, was over. The bones under the grass at Marathon, Thermopylai and Plataia could rest in peace.

While the Athenian fleet ruled the Greek waves, Sparta felt it had to make some gesture to show the Greeks that it was still a force to be reckoned with. In central Greece the Phokians had just taken over sacred Delphi, the site of the untouchable Oracle, and Sparta declared a 'holy war' against the Phokians to get it back. The attempt – known as the Second Sacred War – was an uncertain affair which ended with the Athenians stepping in and keeping Delphi in Phokian hands. Stalemates such as this moved cooler minds in Athens and Sparta in 445 to agree on a thirty-year peace. Everyone, it seems, was in need of a rest and re-fit.

As happens many times in history, truces in times of armed balance of power are actually breathing spaces to enable the major opponents to limber up for full-scale war. The truce that was to last for thirty years struggled on for less than half that. Athens by now had abandoned all pretence of administering a voluntary alliance of Aegean states and had hardened its alliance into a proper empire. Sparta perceived this and was determined to resist it. The two city-states were like boxers circling one another warily, looking for a chance to deliver a decisive blow. At stake was nothing less than the domination of all Greece. Smaller conflicts around Greece were seized upon by both cities – by Athens to expand its power and reach, and by Sparta to block such moves. The Athenians' aggressive conduct in the Aegean, and their open ambition to become the superpower of the Mediterranean, enabled Spartan propaganda to paint them as worse tyrants than the Persians had been.

Barely a year would pass in which some Athenian squadron was not sailing to put down some rebellion or prop up some threatened ally, anywhere in the Greek world from Korkyra (Corfu) in the west, to Thrake in the north and Samos in the east, where a revolt was crushed in 440. For the states of the Peloponnese, the activity of Athens represented a particular danger. Corinth had been a pioneer in establishing colonies in the west, all the way to Korkyra and across the sea to Sicily and southern Italy. The sea route through the Gulf of Corinth, up the west coast to Korkyra and then across the sea to Sicily, had become vital for the trade of Corinth, and by extension the whole Peloponnese, including Sparta and its allies. Athens was now muscling in on this area where it was seen to have no business.

Menelaion. (*Author's photograph*)

Bronze Age remains near the Menelaion, possibly of Menelaos' palace complex.
*photograph*)

3. Enthroned archaic male figure, possibly a king, on 6th century BC stele base. (*Sparta Archaeological Museum*)

4. Menelaos stabbing Helen, on 6th centur stele base. (*Sparta Archaeological Museum*)

5. Kastor and Polydeukes (the Dioskouri), on late 6th century BC stele base. (*Sparta Archaeological l*

nt Taygetos as seen from central Sparta. (*Author's photograph*)

Eurotas River today. (*Author's photograph*)

8. Remains of the Acropolis of Sparta. (*Author's photograph*)

9. Remains of the theatre of Sparta. (*Author's photograph*)

A Spartan warrior often believed to be Leonidas I, 470s BC.
(Sparta Archaeological Museum)

(bottom left) Lysandros, general, Roman copy of a bust. (Ekdotiki Athinon)

(bottom right) Archidamos III – the only likeness of a Spartan (Ekdotiki Athinon)

13. The Leuktra ba[...]
and the restored T[...]
monument today.
(*Ekdotiki Athinon*)

14. Remains of the
temple near Aulis where
Agesilaos' sacrifices were
abruptly halted in 396 BC.
(*Ekdotiki Athinon*)

15. Modern Sparta[...]
environs as seen fr[...]
Menelaion.
(*Author's photograph*)

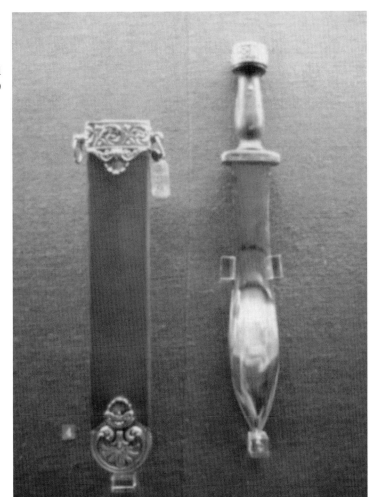

Spartan short sword and scabbard. (*Hellenic War Museum*)

Troops in formation with the sarissa pike, adopted by Cleomenes III from the Macedonians. (*Hellenic War Museum*)

18. The modern statue of Leonidas I in Sparta. (*Author's photograph*)

19. A high school student places a wreath Cenotaph of Leonidas in central Sparta, 27 October 2011. (*Author's photograph*)

# Sparta and Athens bury the hatchet

### FROM JOHN CARR IN ATHENS

NO LONGER will Athenians and Spartans spear each other on the field of battle. The Peloponnesian War is formally at an end, 24 centuries after it started.

The Mayor of Athens, Dimitris Avramopoulos, and the Mayor of Sparta, Demosthenis Matalas, buried the hatchet in Sparta on Sunday — exactly 2,400 years after Athens surrendered — by signing a 200-word declaration pledging "unbreakable bonds" between the two cities whose rivalry dominated classical Greece.

The climax of that rivalry was the 27-year Peloponnesian War, which marked the start of Athens's decline as a leading Greek power. The historian Xenophon, who recorded the last years of the war, does not mention any treaty.

Nobody gave this a thought until the conservative Sparta city council, as a gesture to a fellow conservative, made Mr Avramopoulos an honorary citizen. Mr Avramopoulos saw the chance to make official something that most Athenians would probably have liked to forget.

20. Author's news sto from *The Times*, 13 M 1996.

King Archidamos during this period walked a diplomatic tightrope. As patriotic a Spartan as anyone, he nonetheless tried to steer his city away from war with Athens as deftly as he could. He knew that an all-out conflict with Athens would be long and ruinous for all concerned – a prescience all too well borne out by subsequent events. He maintained personal friendships with opponents of Perikles, such as Thucydides of Melesias (not to be confused with Thucydides of Oloros, the historian), the head of the Athenian aristocratic faction. Thucydides was alarmed at the dominance of the democrats under Perikles, a dominance that had turned to grasping tyranny at the expense of Athens' subjects, and he admired Sparta as a sober state that could manage its power less offensively.

Despite Archidamos' good intentions, Spartan distrust of the Athenian establishment grew. In 435 Korkyra declared its independence from its mother-city Corinth. Obsessively concerned about the safety of its trade routes to Sicily and the west, Corinth sent seventy-five ships beefed up by units from Megara, Ambrakia and Leukas, to restore order. A Korkyraian fleet of eighty ships lined up to stop them at Aktion (near modern Preveza) across the strait from Leukas and defeated them in pitched battle. The Korkyraians massacred their prisoners and then appealed to Athens to decide the issue. The Athenians saw their chance to seize Korkyra, a vital stop on the sea route to Sicily and Magna Graecia, not to mention the possessor of the biggest navy in the west. Corinth retaliated by launching a crash ship-building programme, turning out ninety state-of-the-art triremes in two years. In 433, after a vast and chaotic naval encounter with the Corinthians off Sybota opposite Korkyra, the Athenians sailed in triumph to occupy the island. Perikles had won again.

Furious, the Corinthians appealed to Archidamos for Sparta to step in and uphold Peloponnesian interests. (Pleistoanax was in exile and the Agiad royal house appeared, to all intents and purposes, to be in suspension.) The king was in a quandary. He knew very well what was at stake but had a duty to stick to the thirty-year truce with Athens that was still in effect. By now he must have been well into middle age at least, with the wisdom that ordinarily would accompany the aging process. Yet he had to face down the bellicose Ephors, whose ears burned with bitter complaints from Corinth, Aigina and Megara, all uncomfortably close to Athens and feeling directly threatened. Megara in particular claimed that the Athenians were on the verge of gobbling up its prosperous colony Byzantion at the mouth of the Bosporus that controlled access to the Black Sea colonies.

Shortly after the naval encounter at Sybota, Athens grabbed Potidaia, a Corinthian colony on the Chalkidike peninsula (modern Halkidiki) in the north. Corinth, now the strongest commercial state in Greece, issued an appeal to all the Greek states having some grudge against Athens to send delegates to a general conference at Sparta. There was no lack of takers. At Sparta, before the Apella, the Corinthians did most of the talking. The Athenians, they said, had long since erased the glory of Marathon by becoming aggressive, unscrupulous and grasping, never missing a chance at advancing their interests by fair means or foul. The Spartans, too, came in for a Corinthian tongue-lashing as dull, unimaginative and hidebound, inward-looking and willing to let Athens run rings round them. Where, sneered the Corinthians, were the great traditions of Tyrtaios and Leonidas?

This crass attempt to shame Sparta into action did not go unchallenged. An Athenian delegation that happened to be in Sparta on unrelated business was admitted to the Apella to state the Athenian case. It was blunt and hardly diplomatic, essentially an affirmation of the idea that in international politics, might makes right. They duly reminded their hearers of the glories of Marathon and Salamis, but the reference fell flat. Tempers began to fray, and at this point Archidamos rose to speak.

'At my age,' Thucydides reports him as beginning his address, 'I've had experience of many wars ...' He went on to voice a fear that Athens and Sparta were edging towards a collision greater than any that had gone before. He knew the Athenian navy to be unbeatable. But – and this was probably a sop to the Ephors who were listening – if Sparta and its allies felt they needed to make war on Athens they should wait until they built up the necessary military power and economic clout. 'Do not take up arms yet,' Archidamos counselled his fellow-Spartans. 'For if we allow ourselves to be stung into premature action ... we shall only involve the Peloponnese in more difficulty and disgrace.'[3] The Ephors were unconvinced. They wanted war with Athens now. One of their number, Sthenelaidas, rose and called for a vote; the decision for war was carried by a large majority. The most Archidamos could do in the face of the war fever was advise patience until the state was up to strength.

With Sparta now headed for a major clash with Athens, Sparta's allies fell into line, with the apparent blessing of the Oracle at Delphi. Athens ordered a general mobilization and marshalled its own allies, including the Aegean islands and Korkyra in the west. Argos remained strictly neutral. In the early spring of 431, 'when Chrysis the high priestess of Argos was in the forty-eighth year of her priesthood, [and] Ainesias being Ephor at Sparta,' as Thucydides puts it, a force of 300 Thebans entered Plataia under cover of a rainy night to enlist that traditional Athenian ally on the Spartan side. When morning came the Plataian people attacked the Theban invaders with anything they could find, including roof tiles, and drove them out of their city.

The news of the affray at Plataia hit Sparta like a bolt of lightning. King Archidamos placed himself at the head of the army and led it to the Isthmus to be ready to invade Attica. Here he hesitated. It seems he wanted to make one last try at avoiding a war he knew would be long and vicious. He sent a herald named Melesippos to Athens to suggest peace terms. But Perikles refused to negotiate, as he said, with an enemy already on the march. Melesippos was escorted back to the border. As Thucydides recounts the scene, at the frontier the Spartan turned to his escorts. 'Today is the beginning of great sorrows for the Greeks,' he said, and proceeded on his way. The great and suicidal Peloponnesian War was on.

Sparta entered the conflict with a standing army of not more than 6,000 men, of whom perhaps 2,500 were full-fledged Spartiate hoplites. But it could count on the bigger forces of its Peloponnesian allies such as Corinth, Thebes, Leukas and Ambrakia in the northwest that could field a combined army of anything up to 50,000 or so. Sparta also had its renowned 300-strong royal bodyguard cavalry. Athens had ready an expeditionary army of 13,000 hoplites and a 1,000-horse cavalry, plus a reserve of 13,000 men assigned to guard the city walls and country forts.

It was in the navy that Athens placed its trust. When hostilities began in 431 Athens had some 300 fully-commissioned triremes on hand, and a shipbuilding programme in full swing that would soon yield 100 more. Some 80,000 citizens were recruited as rowers and auxiliary naval personnel (assuming 200 men to man each trireme). These seamen were well-trained and had plenty of recent operational experience. The Spartan alliance, by contrast, was weak in ships. Thanks largely to Corinth, the Spartans could count on an allied naval force of some 180 warships at most, but the quality of the crews – mainly impressed serfs and Helots – left much to be desired. Sparta was keenly aware of this deficiency, and was about to take steps to rectify it.

Archidamos marched on Athens with 60,000 Spartan and allied troops, a very considerable force for the time. Its size shook even the unflappable Perikles, who moreover was in a dilemma. Archidamos was an open-minded king who liked to establish cordial relations even with enemy leaders, and Perikles was no exception. According to Plutarch, the Athenians knew of this friendship, which meant that Perikles had to walk a tightrope. There were rumours that Archidamos intended to spare Perikles' country estates from destruction. To maintain his image with the people, Perikles had to make a public admission that he didn't care what happened to his property. When Archidamos moved out from the Isthmus in the direction of Athens he avoided the usual western approach to the city via Megara and Eleusis, cutting inland to Oinoe, not far from the battlefield of Plataia. Even now he was hoping that this demonstration of force might bring the Athenians to their senses. Prodded perhaps by the Ephors with him, he swung back to the south, skirmishing with some Athenian horse to emerge from the hills at Acharnai, about fifteen kilometres north of Athens, where homes and farmsteads lay burned and abandoned.

Archidamos' appearance at Acharnai, within sight of Athens, threw the city into a panic. Perikles placed Athens under a state of siege, ordering the entire population of Attica to move within the city walls for their own protection. As a countermove he sent 100 triremes to raid the Peloponnesian coast, the vulnerable underbelly of the Spartan alliance. As Perikles had calculated, the raid forced Archidamos to withdraw. Perikles himself successfully led an Athenian force against hostile Megara, but the Athenians on the Peloponnesian raid were worsted at the fortress of Methone (near modern Kalamata) in Messenia. It was at Methone that a particularly able Spartan officer scored his first notable victory. His name was Brasidas, and much more would be heard from him.

Early in the summer of 430 Archidamos again led the Spartans into Attica. He had not been there long before his men saw palls of smoke rising from Athens. The smoke was from funeral pyres, as the city had been smitten by plague, probably a virulent form of typhus or malaria. When deserters arrived at Archidamos' camp with horror stories of mass death in the streets, he got smartly out. In the midst of the plague Perikles found it in him – perhaps as a morale-boosting measure – to man 300 triremes with 4,000 troops and 400 horsemen for another raid on the Peloponnesian coast. But the disease went with them; the raid had to be cancelled after a quarter of the men had died. Perikles himself was fined for allegedly misusing public funds and driven from office. His sister and two of his sons died of the plague; he would follow them not long afterwards.

In 429, with the worst of the epidemic over, Archidamos made his third march northwards. This time he moved on Plataia, hoping to detach that city from the Athenian alliance. The king offered the Plataians protection in return for their neutrality and temporary surrender of their properties. 'Go wherever you please while the war lasts,' he told them, 'and with the return of peace we will give it you all back.' He offered to pay them a rent for their sequestered property. The Plataians considered this, but allowed themselves to be swayed by Athens, which urged them to hold out. Furious that his reasonable proposals were rejected out of hand, Archidamos made a dramatic appeal to the gods as witnesses to the 'authors of iniquity' and proceeded to play hardball.

The Spartans got down to work erecting a huge earthen mound around the city. The Plataians, for their part, increased the height of their own wall in proportion. Then some bright Plataian had the idea of drawing in the earth from the Spartan mound through a hole in the wall. After wondering why their mound was shrinking rather than growing, the Spartans cottoned on to what was happening and blocked the offending hole. All the Plataian non-combatants were evacuated to Athens, leaving 400 Plataians and 80 Athenians, and 110 women to bake the bread.

Neither side spared any ingenuity in the siege. The Plataians tried a repeat of the earth-drawing trick, but without much success. The Spartans brought up battering rams. The Plataians began to build an inner wall to retire behind should the outer wall be breached. They brought up great wooden beams and dropped them onto the Spartans' rams, smashing them. The Spartans' next trick was to fill the space between their mound and the city wall with brushwood and set it on fire. Only a timely thunderstorm saved Plataia from immolation. Archidamos may well have seen the storm as a sign of divine displeasure, or many of his men were anxious to go home for the harvest. He demobilized his army, leaving a garrison to continue the siege.

That same summer a Spartan expedition came to grief near Ambrakia, while an Athenian naval squadron under Phormion smashed a Corinthian fleet in the Rhion narrows. This was the signal for Brasidas, a rising Spartan officer, to test his mettle on the unfamiliar element of the sea. He found the dispirited Peloponnesian fleet languishing on the southern shore of the Gulf of Corinth, gave the crews a pep talk and led them in a spirited attack on Phormion's Athenians anchored at Naupaktos on the north shore. Taken by surprise, the Athenian triremes fled to the shelter of the Naupaktos base. One trireme straggled and appeared to be doomed, until its skipper made an audacious turn around a stationary merchant ship and rammed its Leukadian pursuer broadside, in one of the most brilliant naval manoeuvres of all time. Panic suddenly seized Brasidas' fleet, soon to be shattered by the newly-exultant Athenians.

The Spartan reverses made the government look to a previously-unthink-able source for help – the Persians. The immediate motive was money. Wars in any age are expensive undertakings, as Archidamos himself had warned his fellow-Spartans on the eve of the war. The previous year, envoys from Lakedaimon had actually set out for Asia to solicit aid when they were captured by Thrakian tribesmen and sent in chains to Athens, where they were executed by being hurled into the infamous *barathron*, an abyss for condemned criminals.

We don't know what Archidamos thought of this approach. But it appears to have been forgotten as Brasidas marched his ship crews overland to the Isthmus, each man carrying his oar and cushion. At Megara they boarded forty Megarian ships to attack Piraeus. But at this point there was a change of strategy, and Brasidas decided to ravage Salamis instead. Panic seized Athens again, and all the while Archidamos continued his siege of Plataia.

As campaigning in Greece was mainly confined to the warmer months, the winter provided a breathing space for both camps. In Sparta the Ephors fumed at the lack of a proper navy. In the spring of 428 the island of Lesbos revolted from the Athenian empire. Lesbos was very important, a large and prosperous island lying very near Athens' grain route. A mission from Mytilene, the chief town of Lesbos, asked for Spartan help. During the eighty-eighth Olympic games of 428 the Spartans agreed to take Lesbos into their own alliance, and promised a new joint land and sea attack on Athens. A Spartan officer named Salaithos sailed secretly to Mytilene to organize a revolt, but he was eventually captured by the Athenians and put to death.

In these opening years of the Peloponnesian War a black curtain of cruelty and intolerance came down on Greece, closing the so-called Golden Age. Ideological fanaticism prepared the ground for some of the greatest war crimes in human history. In Athens, after the death of Perikles an uncouth demagogue named Kleon had taken control. One of his first acts was to pass a death sentence on all the adult males of Mytilene and order the enslavement of the women and children. In one of the great real-life cliff-hangers of history, the ship carrying the order was overtaken at the last minute by another ship racing behind it with a rescinding order, and a whole population was spared.

The Spartans were in no less ruthless a mood. Archidamos' wall around Plataia was doing its job well. The few hundred defenders in the city, close to starvation, thought up a plan of escape. Estimating the height of the Spartan wall by the number of layers of bricks in it, they built ladders of equal length and waited for a stormy night when they knew the Spartan guards would be huddled in their shelters. On the first such night 220 Plataians and Athenians carrying the ladders splashed across a five-metre-wide gap between the city and the Spartan walls. Each man had his right foot bare to better grasp the muddy ground. At this point eight men lost their nerve and turned back.

As the first of the escapers reached the top of the wall, one of them dislodged a brick that clattered to the ground. The guards, alerted by the noise, couldn't see much in the foul weather and ran about in confusion. The Plataians remaining in the city created a diversion by pretending to attack the wall at a point opposite to where the escape was in progress. The escapers killed the guards on the wall, fought off some more, tore a gap in the battlements and waded through a freezing water-filled ditch to freedom. One man was caught at the ditch. The pursuing Spartans assumed the escapers would head south towards Athens, but instead they went north. Signal fires which the Spartans lit to warn their units near Thebes were soon 'garbled' by other fires lit by the Plataians. Two hundred and twelve escapers eventually reached the safety of Athens.

The 225 remaining in Plataia must have known what was awaiting them. As each surrendered he was asked a question: 'Have you or have you not rendered Sparta any service during this war?' The captives protested at this: did not the Spartans remember the great battle against the Persians at this very spot fifty years before, one of the greatest moments in Greek history? The Spartans, though, were every bit as vicious and vindictive as the Athenian Kleon. They just repeated the question. Every man thus questioned answered a decisive no, and was executed forthwith. The women who had baked the bread were carried off to slavery. Plataia was razed. Today it's an insignificant little village.

In 427 King Archidamos II died, to be succeeded by his eldest son Agis II. Archidamos can be counted among Sparta's wiser and more competent kings, not as hard in character as most, but with definite limits to his patience. He believed in the interventionist tradition begun by the Agiads Kleomenes I and Leonidas I, and by his Eurypontid grandfather Leotychidas II. These kings were determined to claw back the royal influence gradually lost to the Ephors and the Gerousia over the seventh and sixth centuries. Archidamos combined a Spartan spirit with statesmanlike wisdom. He seems to have encouraged women's rights, as his daughter Kyniska was the first Greek woman to enter a team of chariot horses in the Olympic Games and win the first prize (though women themselves were barred, on pain of death, from competing or even showing their face in the Olympic precincts). In the political sphere Archidamos had tried to put a brake on Sparta's slide towards war with Athens, but in the end his sense of military duty won out. Yet the gratuitous massacre of the Plataians, whether he ordered it or merely acquiesced in it, must remain a disappointing and final black mark against him.

## Chapter 7

# Projecting Power

**Agis II**
**Pausanias**

### Agis II (427–399)

Agis' first move as commander-in-chief was to continue his father's established tactic of invading Attica and keeping the Athenians within their walls, depriving them of the chance to cultivate farms and raise livestock. He marched in that direction as soon as the campaigning season opened in the spring of 426, but a series of strong earthquakes that hit the Peloponnese put the fear of the gods in him and he returned home, his mission unaccomplished.

Thucydides the historian has no problem with the earthquake explanation for Agis' withdrawal. But there could be more than meets the Thucydidean eye. During that summer Aristophanes, the great Athenian comic playwright, was penning his *Acharnians*, in which some of his characters joyfully speak of impending peace with Sparta. It had been a year of Athenian victories on land and sea, and morale in Sparta was correspondingly low. There may have been some exploratory negotiations to that effect, as Pleistoanax, the exiled pacifist Agiad king, was recalled to Sparta about this time, probably as a conciliatory gesture to Athens. But Kleon and his war party, boosted by Athenian successes, dismissed all overtures.

The quakes struck as Athens was experiencing a second onslaught of the plague. But that didn't stop Kleon from keeping up the pressure to secure the trade route to the West and Sicily. Sicilian wheat had to be kept from the Spartans and their allies at all costs. But Demosthenes, the Athenian general sent to reduce Athens' enemies in northwest Greece, came to serious grief in those rough parts. The hardy Aitolian hillmen slaughtered Demosthenes' marines, and the strategic port of Naupaktos on the Gulf of Corinth was only just saved. A Spartan general, Eurylochos, now decided to move into the area. On a small, egg-shaped hillock near Amphilochian Argos (now Amphilochia) he was overwhelmed by an attack by Demosthenes' remaining Athenians and he himself slain. Menedaios, the Spartan second-in-command, agreed on an ordered withdrawal. But Sparta's main ally in the area, Ambrakia, was overwhelmed by the Athenians and knocked out of the war. In Athens Demosthenes became a hero.

In the following summer Agis made his usual foray to the area of Acharnai, establishing a camp at Dekeleia. He seems to have been a competent but not very imaginative soldier, a sort of latter-day Menelaos, as would presently be dramatically displayed. He and Demosthenes never met, but he was clearly out-generalled by the Athenian. For as Agis stolidly sat at his base at Dekeleia on what was little more than glorified guard duty, Demosthenes put into motion an audacious plan to occupy and fortify Pylos on the west Messenian coast. In propaganda terms Pylos was the legendary home of King Nestor of Homeric fame, whose descendants were believed to have provided the first kings of Athens. The practical strategic advantage of Pylos was that it could be made into an alternative station on the way to Sicily in case Korkyra fell to the Spartan alliance, which it was in danger of doing. Moreover, Pylos lay on Lakedaimon's western doorstep, and its occupation would confirm Athens' power in the Peloponnese. News of the seizure of Pylos came as a shock to the Spartan Ephors, who hurriedly recalled Agis from Dekeleia and the fleet from Korkyra.

Pylos is a fine natural harbour sheltered by a long island called Sphakteria. This island leaves two narrow entrances to the harbour, both easily defensible. As Demosthenes assessed the position, it was admirably placed to tie down Spartan forces that might otherwise threaten Athens. As the rest of the Athenian fleet sailed on to Korkyra, Demosthenes stayed behind with a mere five ships and their crews to continue the fortification work.

Sparta acted with alacrity. In short order Demosthenes and his handful of Athenians found themselves hemmed in. The Spartan general Epitadas landed 420 soldiers, plus auxiliaries, on Sphakteria. Demosthenes had only three ships drawn up on the beach; two had been sent to recall the rest of the Athenian fleet. The Spartan commander Epitadas, with the redoubtable Brasidas in command of one ship, sent his triremes towards the beach but the defenders there fought them off. Brasidas saw that wasn't working, so he ordered his helmsman to run the ship onto the rocks so that he could get at the Athenian fort. Brasidas led the charge down the gangplank, but he never made it to the other end, as Athenian spears sliced into him and he slumped grievously wounded into the ship's hull. His shield tumbled into the foaming waters and was later recovered by the Athenians as a prized trophy.

The outnumbered Athenians held the beach. After two days of fruitless assaults the Spartans retired for a breather. Then the Athenian fleet arrived; the Spartan ships put out to meet them, but were smashed in a vicious encounter. Epitadas' men on Sphakteria were now blockaded by the Athenian fleet. But it was a double encirclement, as on the mainland shore opposite, Demosthenes was surrounded by a large Peloponnesian land force. But the 14,000 Athenians, supplied by sea, could afford to wait. Epitadas' Spartans, cut off on Sphakteria, made up one-tenth of Sparta's elite hoplite manpower. If they were eliminated, there was the ever-present threat of a Helot revolt. Thus a cease-fire was arranged during which the beleaguered Spartans on Sphakteria would be supplied with provisions from home while a Spartan mission travelled to Athens to discuss possible terms for a more durable peace. If ever there was a chance for the Peloponnesian War to conclude in favour of Athens, this was it. But Kleon and his war party were on a roll. They sensed that Sparta was on the ropes and was ripe for a knockout blow, and dismissed the Spartan mission.

The double encirclement at Pylos dragged on for two months. Opinion in Athens was becoming edgy. In a tumultuous debate in the Athenian Assembly, Kleon boasted that if he were given command at Pylos he would either capture or kill all the Spartans on Sphakteria within twenty days. It was a mad boast, and the assemblymen roared with laughter. But Kleon had put his reputation on the line and had to keep his promise. Thus, in the garb of a general, he duly arrived at Pylos.

A fire meanwhile had burned all the trees on Sphakteria, leaving the Spartans exposed. Kleon offered the Spartans humiliating terms he knew they would reject. When they did reject them, Demosthenes landed 800 Athenians on Sphakteria by night. The Athenians swept the length of the island, forcing Epitadas to the northern end. At the break of dawn the Athenians charged over the layers of ash from the burned woods, raising a choking grey cloud that confused the defenders. Epitadas fell during the withdrawal. Kleon called a halt to the fighting, wanting to take his enemies alive. Styphon, the highest-ranking Spartan officer left, agreed to surrender. Well within Kleon's twenty-day deadline, 291 Spartan prisoners were on their way to Athens.

'Nothing which happened in the war,' notes the ordinarily stone-sober Thucydides, 'caused greater amazement in Greece; for it was universally imagined that the Spartans would never give up their arms ... but would fight to the last and die sword in hand.' Sphakteria was the first time in anyone's memory that a Spartan army had capitulated rather than be killed on the spot. Spartan and adversary alike were very conscious of this. As the Spartan prisoners were being led off to captivity, one Athenian sneered: 'Where are your brave men now?'[1]

Sphakteria showed to what degree the Spartan military establishment had been weakened by seven years of war. Agis temporarily halted his annual forays into Attica, after the Athenians threatened to slaughter their Spartan prisoners. Shortly afterwards, the Athenian general Nikias captured the island of Kythera off the south-eastern tip of the Peloponnese – in the very mouth of the sea approach to Lakonia – instituting an Athenian blockade. The Peloponnesian navies were confined to their ports. Worse still, the Helots of Lakedaimon could be trusted less than ever before. As a precautionary measure, hundreds of the more suspect Helots were killed on some pretext or other, while 700 of the loyal ones were enfranchised and incorporated into a regular Spartan army regiment, the Neodamodeis, or New Citizens.

The conflict between Sparta and Athens plunged almost all Greece into the ancient equivalent of a world war. In Thucydides' words, 'the whole Hellenic world was in commotion; in every city the chiefs of the democracy and the oligarchy were struggling, the one to bring in the Athenians, the other the Lakedaimonians.' Neither side spared any measure, however brutal, to attain its ends. The kings of Sparta – first Archidamos II and Pleistoanax, then Agis II and Pausanias (Pleistoanax's son and successor) – were mere military instruments in the hands of the Ephors and Gerousia. True, Pleistoanax's pacifism kept him away from the worst rigours of the war, while Archidamos was generally conciliatory where he could be. But their political influence throughout the Peloponnesian War can be said to be virtually nil.

The Spartan in the spotlight was now Brasidas, a general who was assuming the calibre of the famous Leonidas. Brasidas was well-nigh indestructible. He had recovered from the severe wounds he sustained while charging down the gangplank at Pylos in time to march to the defence of Megara, which had just been recaptured by Demosthenes. Brasidas repulsed the Athenians and marched into Megara, looking the other way while the city's pro-Athenian democrats were butchered. After that he marched all the way into Macedon, forging a chain of opposition to Athens, to be used at the first opportunity.

In 424 Athens decided to settle accounts with its direct neighbours to the north, the Boiotians, who were stoutly pro-Spartan. The general Hippokrates (not to be confused with the father of medicine) invaded Boiotia with about 7,000 green reservists in which philosophers marched alongside farmhands. One of the former was Sokrates, toting his spear and shield like everybody else. Hippokrates' plan went terribly wrong. At Delion the Thebans smashed his lines with a flying column of troops twenty-five men deep. This column, called the phalanx, was something new in Greek warfare, which so far had consisted of lines of men pushing against each other. The Theban phalanx was like a hammer, sending the Athenians flying in all directions. Sokrates acquitted himself very well, giving the lie to the common notion that intellectuals don't make good soldiers. One of the last to retreat, he stared down his enemies in stunning defiance. The Thebans completed the destruction by bringing up a primitive flame-thrower to burn the remaining Athenians out of a temple where they had holed up. Athens lost 1,200 hoplites, including Hippokrates.

In the north, Brasidas was carrying the main Spartan war effort on his own brawny shoulders. He probably didn't realize it at the time, but Athens had committed a major strategic error by trying to fight Sparta's allies on land instead of sticking to naval operations. The disaster at Delion had unnecessarily depleted Athenian manpower, especially after two waves of plague. Before the Athenians knew it, Brasidas was at the gates of Amphipolis, their most important colony in the north, the main Athenian source of vital ship timber and precious metals. Thucydides, the historian who was also a general, sailed to relieve Amphipolis but was too late. He was cashiered for his pains, leaving him time to research and pen his monumental *The Peloponnesian War*.

Brasidas, on the point of seizing Amphipolis, was understandably disappointed when news reached him that Sparta and Athens had signed another truce. He was not only a brave soldier, but also a sharp mind. Once he caught a mouse that had got into the store of figs, and it bit him. Brasidas let it go with the calm reflection that even a mouse, small as it was, had the courage to defend itself to save its life. On one campaign a spear pierced his shield and wounded him. In the middle of the fight he calmly plucked the spear out and killed the nearest enemy soldier with it. Later he quipped that his shield had 'turned traitor.'[2]

War-weariness in Athens had turned Kleon out of office, replacing him with Nikias, an aristocratic moderate with no ill-feeling towards Sparta. Brasidas simply ignored the development, seizing a couple more coastal towns in the Chalkidike peninsula. Kleon's war party, as a result, came back into power, and Kleon himself – his military confidence puffed up by his recent success at Pylos – sailed personally to relieve Amphipolis at the head of 1,200 hoplites, 300 horsemen and a few thousand allied troops.

Kleon soon found himself face to face with Brasidas' 5,000 mixed troops on heights on opposite sides of Amphipolis. With 150 picked men Brasidas entered Amphipolis to join the beleaguered Spartan commander, Klearidas. Kleon marched his army up to the closed city gate. Some of his men, peeping under the gate, saw much movement of feet and horses' hooves. Kleon, correctly assuming that a counterattack was imminent, turned to withdraw. As his front ranks wheeled left, the gate opened and Brasidas and his squads hurtled out, slamming into the exposed Athenian right flank. The Athenians broke and ran. Kleon fell with a javelin in him, one of about 600 Athenians killed. But the rear of the Athenian line held fast, and Klearidas asked Brasidas to help him push it back. As Brasidas came running up a spear got him. This time his extraordinary luck ran out – he died after being carried into the city and knowing that his Spartans had again been victorious.

The shock in Athens and Sparta from the loss of those cities' most famous men quickly concentrated minds. With Kleon gone the Athenian moderates under Nikias lost little time in establishing contact with Pleistoanax in Sparta. The Spartan people were demanding the return of their prisoners-of-war, needed for bringing in the crops. In the spring of 421, after several months of negotiations, what is called the Peace of Nikias was worked out. The peace was, somewhat overambitiously, stipulated to last for fifty years. It enshrined the independence and autonomy of the Oracle at Delphi and contained an impossibly idealistic provision that future territorial and other disputes should be settled diplomatically rather than by recourse to arms. It was not the first time, and certainly not the last, that such pious intentions were to prove flimsier than the material they were written on.

If it was too much to expect inveterate foes to suddenly become friends on the say-so of Nikias and Pleistoanax, politics in Greece soon gave everyone a reality check. Other powers such as Corinth, Argos, Megara and Thebes never considered themselves bound by the truce. Argos in particular now saw its chance to become the prime power in the Peloponnese in place of the temporarily exhausted Sparta. Warfare in the north was continuing as if nothing had happened. Amphipolis remained in Spartan hands, a constant threat to Athens' timber and ore supplies. The bad feeling over this was exploited expertly by a talented young noble who had fought alongside Sokrates at Delion and had sat at the philosopher's feet. Alkibiades, a nephew of Perikles, in his mid-thirties was already an Athenian byword for controversial celebrity. He now took it upon himself to lead Athens' radical democrats and renew the war with Sparta for purposes of nothing more or less than personal glory.

In 419 Alkibiades talked the Argives into making an attempt on Epidauros (modern Epidavros), a flourishing community that had become very wealthy as a healing centre. King Agis mobilized a force to defend Epidauros but turned back after his army's diviners pronounced the omens bad. That this happened twice makes it quite likely that Agis learned that Alkibiades and 1,000 Athenians had joined the Argives, outnumbering the Spartans. Thanks, however, to revolving-door politics in Athens, Nikias' moderate party was returned to power in 418. The Athenian force was pulled back, Argos was now left without protection, and so Agis collected some 20,000 men – 4,200 Spartan hoplites, 500 picked light-armed infantry of the Brasidas Regiment, 11,000 Boiotians including cavalry, and 2,000 Corinthians and other Peloponnesians. Blocking his path were 16,000 Argives, Mantineans and Eleans. Agis surrounded the enemy near Phlious, within marching distance of Argos. The Argive generals suggested a truce, which Agis accepted. The battlefield truce, though, was loudly condemned in Sparta and Argos, whose leaderships had been spoiling for a fight.

Agis' sudden conciliatory stand has never been adequately explained. Many Spartans blamed him for giving up a heaven-sent opportunity to trample the old Argive foe once and for all. The Ephors came within an ace of ordering his house demolished and saddling him with a heavy fine. Agis pleaded with them to give him another chance, which they did. He was given to understand that tactical wisdom had to take a back seat to political necessity. He was promptly ordered back to Argos and told not to come back without a victory. To make sure he complied, the Ephors attached ten senior commissars to his staff.

When Agis caught sight of the Argives and their allies waiting for him on higher ground, he advanced on them. He had come within a spear-throw of the enemy lines when one of the commissars asked him what he thought he was doing. Advancing uphill against a strong enemy that outnumbered the Spartans would be suicidal. Uncomfortably aware of being assessed every moment, the king seemed to be overcompensating for boldness. When he received the advice to halt, says Plutarch, he chafed. 'He who would rule over many must fight with many,' he said, defining his idea of the duties of a wartime king – and perhaps to make himself sound good.[3] But the commissars had other ideas, and Agis about-faced, leading the army back the way it had come. His next, more reasonable, idea was to lure the enemy into an attack by setting sappers to divert a local watercourse. The next day the Argives and their allies, 10,000 in number and anxious to get in their blow, got into formation and charged down the slope.

'Never within their recorded history,' writes Thucydides, 'were the Lakedaimonians more dismayed than at that instant.' Agis was caught off guard but recovered quickly, barking orders to switch from marching to battle order. The switch was a brilliant example of Spartan skill and discipline, carried out to the rousing battle songs of Tyrtaios. The king and his Spartiates held the centre, the Brasidas regiment of Neodamodeis and the Skiritai regiment the left, and a mixed Spartan-Tegeate force the right. The solidified Spartan line, eight men deep and shield to shield, marching in step to the flute, began its slow and deliberate advance to meet the enemy. Just before the lines clashed, the Spartan line shifted rightward as each man automatically sought the protection of his comrade's shield. It was, as we have seen, a common hoplite phenomenon, which it seems no amount of training could thoroughly eradicate. The same was happening on the other side, and the two lines began to resemble a giant revolving door. Agis fretted that his line might be taken in its left flank by the Mantineians on the enemy right.

He ordered the Skiritai and the Brasidas Neodamodeis on his far left to extend their line. To fill the resulting gap in the middle he ordered Aristokles and Hipponoidas, two of his unit commanders, to bring up troops from the right.

At that moment the opposing lines clashed, and Aristokles and Hipponoidas judged it better to stay in place rather than obey the king's order. Agis ordered the Skiritai back to their former position, but it was too late. The Argives poured into the breach, routing the Skiritai and Neodamodeis, and surging right up to the wagons in the rear. In the centre Agis and his unstoppable Spartans steamrolled the enemy and threatened to outflank the Athenian contingent; the two Athenian officers in command of the contingent were killed. Victorious on his front, Agis turned to help the broken left of his line. The rout of the Argives and their allies became general; they lost some 700 men to the Spartans' 300. Agis had the smashing victory he had been ordered to bring home in time to celebrate the Karneia festival. He may well have saved his own Eurypontid throne in the process. Pleistoanax, who had been on the way with a reinforcement of reservists, turned back on news of the victory. Aristokles and Hipponoidas, the two officers who disobeyed the king's battlefield orders, were convicted and banished.

That winter Agis made a punitive expedition to Argos, razed its walls and massacred a number of its men. The army was partly made up of allied troops who quailed when they saw an Argive force drawn up to meet them. 'Don't worry, men,' Agis said, 'if we who are victorious are scared, imagine those whom we have in the past defeated.'[4] Pleistoanax, more out of obligation than anything else, led the full Spartan army against an unruly Peloponnesian tribe called the Parrhasians who had been causing trouble on the border with Arkadia. He had little trouble pacifying the area and demolishing a fort that could have threatened the main road northwards out of Lakedaimon.

Athens shocked the Greek world in 416 when it put to death all the male citizens of the island of Melos, and sold the women and children as slaves, merely because that island's government wished to mind its own business and stay neutral in the war. The instigator of this atrocity was Alkibiades, who was morphing into the most formidable and unscrupulous foe of Sparta since Perikles. Agis would soon have occasion to take a good deal of notice of him. But Alkibiades wasn't satisfied with subduing the Aegean area. Carrying the enthusiastic democratic faction with him – a faction that was making quite a bit of money out of the war – he hatched an ambitious plan to extend Athens' power to the west. The poorer Athenians were ready to vote for anything that would keep their pockets filled and slake their chauvinistic thirst. That's when the vision of a big and fertile island in west was dangled before them. Sicily! If Athens could grab Sicily, it would have resources enough to rule the Mediterranean and make its citizens the wealthiest in the world. Alkibiades had little trouble persuading the Athenian democratic majority to fall in with the plan, and thus one bright morning in the middle of June 415, some 2,000 and 7,000 allied troops marched down to Piraeus to embark on sixty flag-bedecked triremes and forty transports for the great send-off to Sicily. In command were the Spartophobe Alkibiades, the Spartophile Nikias, and Lamachos, a bluff regular soldier whose views on Sparta, if he had any, are not known.

Barely had the Athenian fleet arrived off Sicily than Alkibiades was recalled to Athens to face trial on charges of disrespect for religion. He had been notorious as a riotous partier, carouser and mocker of convention, and not above some late-night delinquency, and there was no lack of ammunition for his political enemies to use against him. The arrest warrant reached him as his ship was moored off Katana (modern Catania). He pretended to comply, and had sailed for Athens when he jumped ship at Thourioi on the Italian coast. Eventually, what a modern Spartan academic calls 'this most miserable of all traitors'[5] ended up in Sparta, determined to work with Athens' worst foe in order to assuage his bruised ego.

The dour Spartans, for their part, were fascinated by the charismatic young Athenian with the magnetic personality who until recently had been their most feared adversary. He was an immediate social success. The Spartans' admiration for him grew yet more when he happily took to their austere way of life, including bathing in the cold Eurotas every morning and subsisting on barley bread and black broth. Writes Plutarch:

> Alkibiades possessed one special gift ... which surpassed all the rest and served to attach men to him, namely that he could assimilate and adapt himself to the pursuits and the manner of living of others and submit himself to more startling transformations than a chameleon.[6]

Small wonder, then, that Alkibiades would make an enormous impression on a certain leading member of Spartan womanhood. In a replay of Helen's fascination for the smooth-tongued young prince from Troy, Agis' wife Timaia fell for Alkibiades. At the time Agis was away at Dekeleia keeping a watch on Athens – on the advice of Alkibiades, no less, whose motives were as much erotic as strategic.

Part of Agis' furious energy in devastating the Athenian countryside could have reflected his hatred of Alkibiades. Spies had reported to him about Timaia's affair, which she made no attempt to keep secret. Reports of it had even reached Athens, where it was a subject for comic playwrights, the ancient equivalent of the tabloid press. Alkibiades himself openly boasted that he had sex with Timaia (whose name, ironically, means 'Honour Woman') not because he was attracted to her but because that way he could raise descendants who would one day take over Sparta. To give Timaia her due, according to Plutarch, Agis hadn't been sleeping with his wife for ten months, ever since an earthquake one night had sent him flying out of bed in fright, apparently dousing his sex drive in no small measure.[7] In state affairs Alkibiades rendered signal service to the Spartan cause by recommending a general, Gylippos, to boost the war effort against the Athenians in Sicily. But he kept his wits about him as he was canny enough to know that love and war cannot mix for long, and that his affair with Timaia would eventually bring down royal wrath.

That was not all. While cavorting with the Spartan queen, Alkibiades was also playing footsie with the Persians. The ears of Darius II, the Great King, had perked up at the Athenian difficulties in Sicily, awakening hopes that he might swallow up the Ionian Greek cities of Asia Minor once more. Tissaphernes, the Persian satrap (regional governor) based at Sardis, sent an envoy to Sparta suggesting an alliance. The Ephors were in a quandary. To stoop to receive aid from the old foe of Greek liberty, to negate the great moral victories of Thermopylai and Plataia, was no light consideration. Their dilemma intensified when more envoys, this time from Pharnabazus, another Persian satrap, called at Sparta with the proposal that Sparta help Pharnabazus topple Darius II.

Alkibiades argued in favour of Tissaphernes' offer, but he sensed that his days of usefulness to the Spartans had come to an end. It was one thing to cuckold King Agis; it was quite another to suggest an alliance with the Persians. The Spartans began to recall old Athenian suspicions of his erratic character. Timaia probably warned him that her husband was plotting to have him murdered. He talked the Ephors into giving him five ships which he took to Chios to aid that island's revolt. From there he slipped across to Asia Minor and promptly found refuge in Tissaphernes' court. The Ephors sentenced him to death *in absentia*.

In September 413 the grand Athenian army, poorly led and low in morale, was annihilated by the Sicilian Greeks coordinated by the Spartan Gylippos. It was a stunning blow that might have crushed a weaker state. But Athens still had some fight left in it. A committee including the tragic playwright Sophokles was set up to work out how to carry on the war with a reduced budget. The lavish gold adorning the Acropolis statues and monuments was stripped off and melted down for coinage. Agis judged that Athens was weakened enough for him to be able to leave his base at Dekeleia to ravage parts of eastern Greece and seize money to send home. Rid of the man who had cuckolded him, he found a new energy, moving on to Euboia – so far a solidly pro-Athenian island – to organize revolts in some of the communities there. Plans were made to lay 100 new Spartan keels to challenge Athens on the sea.

In 412 the Ephors overcame their scruples and signed a pact with Persia, giving Darius II hegemony over the Ionian Greek cities, in effect selling them down the river. Sparta and Persia agreed to join forces to fight Athens, with neither party entitled to make a separate peace. Such was the need for war money in Sparta that the city's old ideology of upholding Greek freedoms was completely eclipsed. Gold, not honour, was the Ephors' new watchword. True, there was a good deal of righteous fury among the Spartan citizenry at this new turn of affairs. But we don't know if the kings shared it. Pleistoanax, one gets the impression from Thucydides, merely went through the motions of being a military king, while Agis returned to Dekeleia, destroying the countryside, keeping Athens' reserve troops manning the walls around the clock, and taking in escaped slaves. In short, doing what he was told.

Athens' disaster in Sicily discredited that city's democratic faction, which in 411 was overthrown by the oligarchs. The new government sent a mission to Agis at Dekeleia with feelers for a peace on the basis of *uti possidetis* – that the warring parties keep whatever territory they had acquired so far. Agis insisted that Athens give up its control of the sea. The reply indicates that either Agis shared the war aims of the Ephors or had no choice but to follow their orders like a glorified ambassador. The demand was stoutly refused, so Agis confidently marched out from his base at Dekeleia to deliver what he hoped might be the knockout blow to Athens. Instead, he found a line of Athenian reservists waiting for him outside the walls, and he had to fall back.

Sparta soon had another chance to end the war when it transpired that Alkibiades was back on the scene, this time on Samos, liberally employing Tissaphernes' gold to build up an Athenian democratic navy to seize back power from the oligarchic regime. A Spartan fleet under Agesandridas appeared within sight of Athens. There was a general rush to man the walls, but Agesandridas bypassed Piraeus and headed to Euboia to reduce Athens' allies there. An Athenian fleet sent to chase him was decimated, but he unaccountably failed to follow up the victory. Had Agesandridas promptly invested Athens by sea, the war would easily have been over.

The Spartan navy, bolstered by Persian gold, was beginning to show a good account of itself. It defeated an Athenian fleet at Kynossema in the Hellespont, but the Athenians again proved the better sailors. The year 410 was taken up with a series of naval battles for control of the Hellespont trade route, where Alkibiades personally proved his worth as a naval commander. The following year, Agis made another foray up to the walls of Athens. Adding to his ranks were many slaves who had escaped from the silver mines at Laurion. But as before, had found a line of determined reservists ready to receive him; in his precipitate retreat he lost some of his rearguard to Athenian skirmishers. That same year, gentle King Pleistoanax of the Agiad house died, to be succeeded by his son Pausanias.

One glorious midsummer day in 407 Alkibiades returned to a grand welcome in Athens and talked the citizen body into appointing him general-in-chief of Athens' armed forces. He didn't have much time to rest. Three months later Sparta sent an extremely able officer named Lysandros to direct operations in the Aegean theatre – flush, of course, with Darius II's limitless funding. Lysandros made himself popular with his men by raising their pay and bringing Darius' younger brother Cyrus on side. When Alkibiades learned of it, he sailed to Samos with 100 triremes and 1,500 hoplites. At Notion, just north of Ephesos (modern Kusadasi), an Athenian squadron commander rashly got himself into an unnecessary scrap, costing his side fifteen ships and his own life. The ruling democratic faction at Athens blamed Alkibiades for the setback, and thus the wily Athenian again got smartly out, this time ensconcing himself in a private castle on the north shore of the Hellespont.

When Lysandros' one-year term as admiral expired, he was replaced in the eastern Aegean by Kallikratidas, one of those simple soldiers whose sterling character shines through the fog of centuries. On orders from home, Kallikratidas journeyed cap in hand to Cyrus, who controlled the campaign purse-strings. As the sympathetic Xenophon tells it, the Persian prince – 'busy drinking,' according to a servant – kept the Spartan waiting in an ante-room for a long time. Plutarch says that Cyrus never bothered to see Kallikratidas; Xenophon, more sympathetic to Cyrus, says Cyrus told Kallikratidas to wait two days for the money. Both authors agree, however, that disgust over-flowed in Kallikratidas' noble soul at the debased spectacle of Sparta stooping to beg from the despised barbarian whom the united Greeks had vanquished not too many decades before. 'If I return alive to Sparta,' he is reported as saying, perhaps to Cyrus himself, before leaving for his base at Miletos, 'I will do all in my power to reconcile the Spartans with the Athenians.'

But, for the present, duty was duty. Taking the pro-Athenian town of Methymna on the island of Lesbos, Kallikratidas displayed another facet of his sterling character by refusing to follow the usual custom of selling any of his free-born Greek prisoners into slavery. 'No Greek will be a slave as long as I'm in charge here,' he said. Shortly afterwards Kallikratidas sailed out to intercept an Athenian fleet at Arginousai, on the Asia Minor coast opposite Lesbos. The sight of the fleet was daunting enough for the commander of the Megarian squadron in the Peloponnesian fleet to counsel withdrawal. Kallikratidas wouldn't hear of it. 'My own death will not be as great a loss to

Sparta as a retreat,' he said. Those brave words were among his last. Early in
the encounter, his flagship rammed an Athenian trireme. The shock of the
collision hurled Kallikratidas, who appears to have been precariously clinging
to a bulwark, into the sea. He never returned to Sparta to make his peace
with Athens. The great battle was inconclusive, as a storm blew up, scattering
the surviving vessels of both sides and drowning thousands of men. (The six
Athenian commanders at Arginousai, including Perikles, the son of the late
statesman, were tried for criminal incompetence and executed.)

Across the Aegean the Spartans were not having an easy time of it.
Eteonikos, the new Spartan commander in the Aegean theatre, like so many
of his countrymen thrust to high office in foreign parts, courted unpopularity
by his high-handed behaviour to the locals. After ordering the murder of a
blind old man on Chios who was mistakenly believed to be part of a mutiny,
Eteonikos was recalled. This was the cue for the far abler Lysandros to take
over, and in early 404 he made the now *de rigueur* cap-in-hand trip to Cyrus.
The Persian prince grumbled – he was becoming tired of the quarrelsome
Greeks endlessly badgering him for cash – but duly paid up. Flush with
Persian gold, Lysandros led 200 triremes north to Lampsakos on the southern
shore of the Hellespont, directly threatening the Athenian grain route.
Athens sent 180 ships under Konon to re-take Lampsakos. Konon anchored
the fleet at Aigos Potamoi on the north shore of the Hellespont, a few
kilometres downstream from the Spartans.

Aigos Potamoi was a bad place to stay. There was no town or large
community nearby, so every evening the Athenian crews had to leave their
ships undefended and forage inland for supplies. The Athenians apparently
expected to lure Lysandros to the attack, but the wily Spartan refused to
play ball. For four days Konon held his ships ready in battle formation, and
for four days Lysandros stayed put. To all this there was a witness. From
his castle in the vicinity Alkibiades could see how vulnerable the Athenian
fleet was. One day he rode into the Greek camp with sound advice to move
downstream to a more secure base at Sestos. The Athenian commanders
brusquely advised Alkibiades to mind his own business and sent him away.

All this time Lysandros had been sending daily spy boat patrols out from
Lampsakos to see what the Athenians were up to. He noted their invariable
habit of leaving the beached ships each evening to seek supplies. Towards
the end of the fifth day he struck. At the right moment one of his spy boats
hoisted a burnished shield as a signal for the Spartan fleet to advance. The
attack caught the Athenians totally by surprise; only Konon's squadron was
even half-ready and a mere nine ships could be manned in time. These were
overrun with ease, as was the whole Athenian fleet in one fell swoop. After

the action the Athenian state trireme *Paralos* plied its lonely way to Athens with the news that the great war was finally lost.

Now the Athenians' past atrocities and war crimes came back to haunt them. The Corinthian allies of Sparta spewed the most hate. One Athenian officer in particular, Philokles, was accused of having thrown the crews of two captured Peloponnesian ships into the sea to drown. Provoked by charges such as these, Lysandros ordered him and 3,000 other prisoners killed. Philokles' body suffered the added indignity of remaining unburied. An Athenian officer named Adeimantos was spared on the grounds that he had displayed humane conduct in the past.

After the first burst of despair and panic, the Athenian assembly voted to brace for what was expected to be a long siege. In Sparta, on the news of the victory at Aigos Potamoi, King Pausanias of the Agiad house, the son of Pleistoanax, called up the Spartan reserves and led them to join Agis at Dekeleia. Lysandros eventually turned up with 180 ships to blockade the port of Piraeus. The Ephors demanded that the Athenians pull down the Long Walls to Piraeus. The Athenian government refused. For three months ordinary Athenians died of hunger in the streets until Theramenes, a moderate Athenian, agreed to the Ephors' demands. Athens, finally accepting defeat, was forbidden from having more than twelve warships in commission and compelled to do Sparta's bidding everywhere. In the early summer of 404 the Long Walls were razed to the ground, to the accompaniment of young girls playing flutes. And on that weird note, the great and terrible Peloponnesian War sputtered out.

Sparta was at the peak of its prestige and power throughout Greece. Lysandros made a triumphal entry into the city with the bows of scores of Athenian warships and enormous amounts of silver booty. For King Agis, however, a considerable bit of unfinished business was waiting in the north-west, specifically in Elis, the home of the Olympic Games. Back in 420 Elis had been an ally of Athens and consequently had barred Sparta from participating in the games. During the ninety-first Olympiad in 416 one Spartan who had competed under another state's name was struck in the face by the judges when he went up to receive his prize.

Agis took advantage of a border dispute to invade Elis in 401. His forces got to Olympia but an earthquake stopped him in his tracks – Sparta's kings were nothing if not respectful of such elemental messages. Nonetheless, enough booty was carried off to make the expedition worthwhile. Agis resumed the campaign, probably the following year, with a stronger force that overwhelmed the Elean resistance. For the first time in nearly twenty years the Spartans again had legal access to the Olympic Games.

Either on this expedition or some other in the same region, Agis travelled to Delphi to deposit one-tenth of that year's war booty as a dedication to the gods. He was getting on in years now, and as he and his party were approaching the Isthmus on their way home, he fell ill. Xenophon, our source for these events, doesn't say what the ailment was. But Agis expired soon after he was carried into Sparta. He was buried, according to Xenophon, 'with more than usually great honours.'[8]

The twenty-eight-year reign of Agis II had coincided with some of the most tumultuous events in Spartan history. He saw his city emerge victorious in the Peloponnesian War, having personally contributed to its military operations in no small way. Pausanias the historian credits him with 'remarkable military achievements.' Yet in hindsight he remains curiously two-dimensional, given a trace of character only in a few situations, including the tactical alertness he displayed at the battle of Mantineia. Of his personal life we know nothing except the rather demeaning fact of his wife Timaia's affair with Alkibiades, an event not calculated to raise his prestige. Yet he had a lofty view of the value of Sparta and its institutions, and was a good soldier, with a soldier's blunt logic. When someone asked him how many Spartan fighting men there were, he replied, 'Enough to keep all bad men away.' When asked, in the typical Greek way, how one could be a free man, he replied, 'By feeling contempt for death.' During one battle, when someone suggested allowing the fleeing foe to escape, he retorted, 'If we don't fight the cowards, how are we going to fight the braver ones who stand their ground?'[9]

In the best Lakonian tradition Agis was not one to waste words. More than once he responded to long-winded appeals from envoys from other Greek states with complete silence, the most eloquent response of all. In his old age he saw the old Spartan disciplined ideal become corrupted with money and ease, but he took it philosophically. 'When I was a boy,' he told an elderly curmudgeon:

> I used to hear from my father that everything was topsy-turvy among [the Spartans]; and my father said that, when he was a boy, his father had said this to him; so nobody ought to be surprised if conditions later are worse than those earlier.'[10]

## Pausanias (409–395)

Pausanias seems to have inherited his father Pleistoanax's dislike of aggression as a national policy. In the closing stages of the Peloponnesian War he dutifully led the Spartan reserves to Dekeleia to join Agis in ravaging the Athenian countryside. When the Long Walls fell and Athens was consumed in a civil war between the so-called Thirty Tyrants and the democrats, he supported the Thirty which defeated the democrats in a hard fight near the port.

Xenophon credits Pausanias with being a democrat at heart and reports that he secretly communicated with the Athenian democrats, urging that both factions make peace and become friends of the Spartans. This sounded good to the commissars accompanying the king, and after some negotiations the Thirty Tyrants agreed to step down and go into exile. Pausanias was seriously concerned that Sparta should maintain its image as the liberator of Greece. But when he looked on his general Lysandros he saw a man busy preparing a Spartan despotism to replace the Athenian one. He dissolved his army and returned to Sparta.

For a young king, this could have been a diplomatic triumph of the first magnitude. But the Spartan establishment didn't see it that way. In their eyes Pausanias was merely continuing the pro-populist traditions of his Agiad royal house. Had he not restored to power the Athenian democrats – the very people who had made war on Sparta in the first place and had tried to enslave the whole Greek world? He was put on trial before a special assizes of the Gerousia and Ephors, presided over by Agis. In the Gerousia the verdict was split equally – fourteen to fourteen – with Agis adding his vote in favour of conviction. The whole body of Ephors, however, some of whom had accompanied Pausanias to Athens, swung the vote for an acquittal and he was let off.

Pausanias' reign may have seen Sparta at the pinnacle of its power. But already forces were in motion that would seriously erode that power from within, deriving as they did from Sparta's very position as the strongest state in Greece. The now-defunct Athenian empire had built itself up, as all empires do, on money that could buy armed force. Sparta had plenty of the latter but very little of the former. It had no large commercial and business class, as at Athens, to familiarize people with trade and encourage innovation, and to raise state revenues. So far Sparta's main currency had been iron! It was all very well while Lakedaimon remained a conservative inland power, but when the city began receiving copious amounts of Persian gold to win the war with Athens, the old order was overturned. Corruption tempted everyone, high and low.

Lysandros was one of those who easily gave in to it. Though reported to have been descended from the Herakleidai, he wasn't a member of either Spartan royal house. In fact, he grew up in poverty. His personality was typically Spartan in discipline and sense of honour, though Plutarch reveals what could have been a well-concealed inferiority complex that emerged as a tendency to fawn over the rich and powerful, as well as mental depressive traits.[11]

Lysandros had sent to Sparta a considerable fortune in Athenian gold and silver. The man entrusted with transporting this treasure was Gylippos, the hero of the Sicilian campaign. On the way, however, it was found that Gylippos had purloined a goodly portion of the loot by unstitching the base of the bags in which it was carried, leaving the seals untouched. Gylippos fled before he could be apprehended. Lysandros was blamed for allegedly encouraging the personal enrichment of his subordinates. It was suspected, probably rightly, that some high-ranking Spartans had deposited their ill-gotten gains at Delphi – the ancient equivalent of a Swiss bank. The damage was done: Sparta had begun to fall in love with money, with incalculable consequences. In the words of one modern commentator, 'the Spartans were astounded to find how hard it was to fight the temptation of silver.'[12]

Not only the Spartan economy, but also its society was undergoing profound pressures. At war's end Sparta could field no more than about 4,000 Spartiate hoplites, among whom were an undetermined number of Neodamodeis. The brittle Spartiates class was slowly breaking apart. A family's land, for example, could not be broken up or sold. This rule left a lot of young men landless and thus unable to contribute to the city's upkeep, resulting in their disfranchisement to second-class citizens. Such a person was officially an Inferior (*hypomeion*, meaning literally 'under-minus,') a pejorative term that cannot have made them feel any better. By the beginning of the fourth century about one-third of the citizen class had been downgraded to Inferior status, and in 399 one of them decided to do something about it.

For some time various holy men had been going about Sparta warning of a 'dire conspiracy' against the state. Perhaps they were tipped off that an Inferior named Kinadon was trying to convert many of his co-Inferiors and serfs to class revolution. Betrayed by an informer, Kinadon was arrested in 398. When hauled before the Ephors, the brave and burly Spartan readily admitted that he was fighting for social equality. His punishment was to be paraded through the city in a neck-shackle and flogged. Some source claim he was executed, but that seems unlikely, as Kinadon's potential following in Lakedaimon outnumbered the privileged Spartiates class by about twenty to one. Making him into a martyr would almost certainly have triggered a mass revolt that Sparta did not need at that time.[13]

Lysandros, meanwhile, had been getting ideas beyond his station. Disappointed by the indifferent performance of Pausanias (and probably his father Pleistoanax) and the tendency of at least one royal house to fail to provide vigorous leadership in time of crisis, he began to imagine himself king in their place. Evidence was soon to emerge that Lysandros plotted to have the dual kingship done away with as obsolete and replaced by an elective monarchy – with himself as first elected monarch. He had a manifesto drawn up and sometime between 400 and 396 he consulted three oracles in Greece, including that of Delphi. All endorsed his plan. But the priests of a fourth oracle, this time in Libya, tipped off the Spartan authorities. Lysandros was interrogated, but talked himself out of an arrest.

Pausanias had to play second fiddle to the new Eurypontid king, Agesilaos II, the younger brother of Agis II, who seems to have died without much issue. Agesilaos almost at once embarked on an ambitious plan to conquer as much as he could of Asia Minor (see Agesilaos II below). The Persians retaliated by bribing various Greek cities to rebel against Spartan suzerainty. Thebes was one of these cities. The Thebans soon found ways to engineer Spartan hostility, with the result that a Peloponnesian force under Lysandros, followed by another led by King Pausanias, marched on Thebes in 395. (Agesilaos was already on the other side of the Aegean Sea tackling Persia.)

Before Pausanias could come within sight of Thebes, Lysandros encamped at Haliartos, a small town in Boiotia. The Thebans decided to halt the Spartans there and staged a surprise attack on them under the walls of Haliartos, where Lysandros was killed. The Spartans retired to higher ground, stopping the Thebans by rolling boulders onto them. At that point Pausanias appeared with his army, plunging the Thebans into gloom. But the king was unsure of what to do. He heard that an Athenian force might be coming up to aid the Thebans, and rightly feared being caught between two fires. He knew, according to Pausanias his namesake historian, that 'the disasters of the Lakedaimonians always took place when they had been caught between two enemy forces.' The memories of Thermopylai and Sphakteria were still vivid.[14] After a conference with his commanders he decided that the situation was too risky: the Peloponnesians hadn't enough cavalry, Lysandros was dead, and about 1,000 other Spartan dead were still strewn unburied about the countryside around Haliartos. Pausanias asked for a truce to collect the dead. Pressing their advantage, the Thebans agreed on condition that Pausanias forthwith quit their territory. Jeered at and even assaulted by the local peasantry, Pausanias and his Peloponnesians marched away in disgrace.

Pausanias must have known what would await him in Sparta, and sure enough, he found himself on trial for his life. The charges against him were weighty. He had failed to turn up for a coordinated rendezvous with Lysandros at Haliartos and had preferred to collect his army's dead under a truce when it would have been nobler to fight to get them. The older charge of his favours to Athenian democrats was also brought up. Unsurprisingly, Pausanias didn't present himself to be formally arraigned. He slipped away to Tegea, that refuge of disaffected Spartans.

It may not be inaccurate to attribute Pausanias' hesitant habits to a form of hypochondria. Words attributed to him suggest that he was obsessed with medical matters. He certainly didn't trust doctors. When once a doctor checked him out and found nothing wrong with him, Pausanias retorted that it was because the man wasn't his regular physician. 'The best doctor,' he opined once, 'is he who doesn't let his patients rot but buries them quickly.' Commenting to a friend on the shortcomings of a certain physician, he averred that if he had allowed the man to come anywhere near him he (Pausanias) wouldn't be alive. Even in exile in Tegea he was fond of employing medical metaphors. At one point, while he was praising his home city, he was asked why he hadn't elected to stay there. 'Because a doctor spends his time not among the healthy but the sick,' he said.[15] Shortly afterwards he died of an unknown ailment.

# Chapter 8

# Domination and Decline

Agesilaos II
Agesipolis I
Kleombrotos I

## Agesilaos II (399–360)

Hardly was Agis' body cold than his son Leotychidas and brother Agesilaos clashed over the succession. Leotychidas, though, was seriously hampered by that old bane of the Spartan royal houses, doubts about his legitimacy. In Leotychidas' case the doubts were one degree below certainty, as Agis had never acknowledged the boy, believing him – probably correctly – to be the son of the irresistible Athenian Alkibiades. His mother Timaia certainly did nothing to dispel any doubts. She had been indiscreet enough to whisper to her chambermaids that the boy's real name was Alkibiades. The usual recourse was had to the Oracle of Delphi, which delivered itself of the sinister verdict that Sparta, 'of sound limbs, should never give birth to a lame kingdom.' Like most such pronouncements, this was capable of several interpretations, and thus only obscured the issue. Just what did 'lame' mean? The obvious conclusion would have been Agesilaos' actual lameness, as he was born with one leg shorter than the other. Leotychidas naturally felt vindicated. But, others argued, the term 'lame' could be a metaphor for the alleged illegitimacy of Leotychidas. On his deathbed Agis had been talked into acknowledging Leotychidas but the Ephors, probably knowing better, dismissed the statement as untrustworthy. The clincher was that Lysandros, the influential general, backed Agesilaos, who became king.

Like Leonidas I before him, Agesilaos ('Leader of the People') as a younger brother was not expected to become a king. Thus, like his famous Agiad forbear, he was subjected to the full *agoge* which shaped his character to become, in the words of the admiring Plutarch, 'the better fitted for government ... He proved the most popular-tempered of the Spartan kings, his early life having added to his natural kingly and commanding qualities the gentle and humane feelings of a citizen.'[1] Still a youth, he attracted the attention of Lysandros as impetuous and courageous in training, yet obedient to his superiors and 'more hurt by the least rebuke or disgrace than ... by any toil or hardship.'[2]

Agesilaos was somewhat short of stature, and not well built. His only really obvious flaw was his slight lameness. Someone doubtless must have brought to mind the fine imposed upon Archidamos I in the seventh century for marrying a diminutive wife, and wondered whether the shortness gene had emerged in the latest occupant of the Eurypontid throne. Probably in compensation for his lack of physical presence, he early in life developed an urge to excel in everything.

On his accession his first act was to donate half of Leotychidas' estate to the desperately poor family of his mother Eupolia – a telling commentary on the decline of many noble Spartan families at this time. Then, if we are to believe Plutarch, he consciously became a yes-man for the Gerousia and Ephors, overturning generations of rivalry between the royal houses and the government. When the Ephors said jump to it, he jumped. He rose respectfully from his own royal seat whenever an Ephor entered. To his friends he was loyal to a fault, handing out pardons left and right. Naturally this increased his popularity, and equally naturally, this popularity triggered the Ephors' suspicions.

Agesilaos' assiduous courting of public opinion masked a massive ambition. Of all the kings of either house at the turn of the fourth century he was the one who most keenly believed in Spartan supremacy. Ignoring the city's economic and social limitations, he believed Sparta was in a position not only to lead Greece but to take revenge for the Persian conquest of the Ionian Greek seaboard in the past century. Helping shape this ambition was his love of the Homeric epics, especially the *Iliad*, and he dreamed of becoming another Agamemnon who would lead a great Greek army back to the shores of Troy and take back the Greek lands now under alien subjugation.

When he assumed the throne Agesilaos was in his forties. He would therefore have had plenty of time in his younger days to nurture his fantasies, and so it was not difficult for Lysandros to talk him into heading a force of 2,000 Neodamodeis and 6,000 Peloponnesian allies, to be commanded by thirty Spartiates officers under himself, for an expedition across the Aegean. He jumped at the chance. He imagined he was Agamemnon to such a degree that, following in the Achaian king's precise footsteps, he arranged a ritual sacrifice on the coast at Aulis on the Boiotian coast, where Agamemnon had sailed from. But he didn't count on the local Boiotian authorities, who had banned the rites and sent horsemen to fling the charred offerings from the altar and bring the proceedings to an undignified halt. Calling angrily on the gods as witnesses to this impiety, Agesilaos boarded his ship, 'very much discouraged in mind at this omen.'[3]

He landed on the Asian coast at Ephesos in the summer of 396 to back up a longstanding Spartan demand that Artaxerxes II Mnemon, the Persian Great King, restore the Ionian Greeks' independence. Tissaphernes, the Persian satrap who once had received Alkibiades, pretended to accept the Greek demand and asked for time to consult the Great King, all the while secretly calling for reinforcements. Then Lysandros turned up in the Greek camp, discomfiting Agesilaos, whose scrawny appearance and genial character paled before the big, bluff general. In the throes of a severe inferiority complex, the king obstructed Lysandros' every initiative. In public he half-jokingly referred to Lysandros as his 'meat-carver.' When Lysandros had had enough of this he confronted Agesilaos. 'You certainly know how to humiliate your friends,' he chided the king, according to Plutarch.

'I humiliate those who pretend to have more power than I do,' Agesilaos replied.

Lysandros thereupon asked the king for a reassignment to a place where he could serve 'without incurring [royal] displeasure.' Agesilaos gladly obliged, and sent Lysandros to fight for Spartan interests in the Hellespont. Plutarch thinks that this encounter sparked Lysandros' plot to do away with the Spartan dual monarchy.[4] As soon as Tissaphernes received enough reinforcements, he issued an ultimatum to Agesilaos, who had far from enough men with him. Tissaphernes expected the Greeks to attack him in the south, but instead Agesilaos turned northwards and made a long forced march to Daskyleion, the headquarters of the Persian satrap Pharnabazus. The Spartan king in the meantime had amassed 4,000 more troops, but his cavalry was far inferior to that of the Persians. A stalemated battle resulted in Agesilaos retreating to the coast to raise a better cavalry corps. The Persians, for their part, resumed deliveries of cash to Sparta's rivals in Greece.

In the spring of 395, with his men specially trained and drilled and a stronger cavalry, Agesilaos was ready to try again. He had spent the winter subjecting not only his army but also himself to the rigours of camp life. A physical fitness fanatic, he slept on a hard bed and inured himself to extremes of heat and cold. Captured slaves were ordered to exhibit themselves naked in the slave market so the Greeks could see how other races neglected their bodies. 'In a place where the men revere the gods, exercise themselves in the art of war and submit to discipline,' Xenophon writes admiringly, 'is it not natural that optimism should shine?' With plenty of food and provisions supplied by Ephesos, Agesilaos started anew on the march into Asia. 'We do not fear the wealth of the enemy,' sang the enthusiastic troops. Some of his men were experienced veterans of the Ten Thousand, who under Xenophon himself had made an epic march through the wilds of Iraq and what is now Turkey a few years before. If those fellows weren't afraid, what was there to worry about?

From his base at Ephesos Agesilaos moved with 20,000 men on Sardis, harassed all the way by Tissaphernes' cavalry. After reducing the city and burning the satrap's palace he cleverly outfought a Persian force by driving it into an ambush where 1,400 Greeks waited in a wood. Caught between two fires, the Persians were routed, many drowning in the Paktolos River. A number of camels were seized as booty. Tissaphernes and the remnant of his force were besieged in Sardis while Agesilaos led the main force on a raid of devastation in the hinterland. The Great King rewarded Tissaphernes for his failure by executing him. The satrap's successor, Tithraustes, promised on behalf of Artaxerxes to respect the Ionian Greeks' independence if Agesilaos quit Asia. Agesilaos requested a six-month truce to consult his government and Tithraustes agreed.

The Ephors, pleased with these successes, assigned Agesilaos command of the Spartan navy as well as the army. The king delegated the navy to his brother-in-law Peisandros, an ambitious but inexperienced officer, and led the army on a long overland march of some 500 miles into what is now northern Turkey in search of local allies who could provide men, horses and provisions for what he was sure would be another showdown with the Persians. Then he doubled back and marched to Daskyleion on the south coast of the Propontis (Sea of Marmara) where he could winter. His men didn't have much time to rest, however, as Pharnabazus attacked as the Greek troops were out foraging for supplies, killing some Greeks. Herippidas, a Spartan senior officer sent by the Ephors in place of the king's usual thirty-strong guard, led a detachment of hoplites, light-armed infantry and horsemen in a spirited charge against Pharnabazus' camp and captured it.

The Persian satrap had it out with Agesilaos in a tense meeting. Xenophon, who may have been present, describes how Pharnabazus turned up in his elaborate official apparel and realized he was overdressed when he saw Agesilaos in a simple tunic sitting informally on the grass with his thirty Spartiates escorts. The Persian was about to tell his servants to put down soft and luxurious blankets, but out of shame he, too, consented to sit on the hard ground. Pharnabazus began with a plaintive lecture on how the Spartans were being quite ungrateful to the power which a short time before had helped it win the war against Athens. Agesilaos retorted that Pharnabazus wasn't his enemy; his boss the Great King was, and he suggested that Pharnabazus defect. 'If the king sends another general in my place, I'll join you,' the Persian replied. 'If he keeps me in my post, I will fight you with all means at my command.'

Agesilaos shook hands with the Persian in rueful admiration at his resolve. 'I wish such a brave man were my friend and not my enemy,' he said.[5]

By this time Agesilaos had become renowned throughout Asia Minor as the very model of soldierly virtue. Writes Plutarch:

> The Greeks that inhabited Asia were much pleased to see the great lords and governors of Persia, with all their pride, cruelty, and luxury in which they lived, trembling and bowing before a man in a poor thread-bare cloak, and, at one laconic word out of his mouth, obsequiously deferring and changing their wishes and purposes.

A finer example of the contrast between the values of the West and the East can hardly be found in history.

Agesilaos had little time in which to bask in his renown, as an order came recalling him home. A conflict which history knows as the Corinthian War had just broken out, and Sparta was heavily involved in it. Persian money, not to mention a growing anti-Spartan feeling bubbling under the surface of Greek affairs, had changed minds not only in Thebes but also in that erstwhile ally of Sparta, Corinth. While Agesilaos was busy in Asia Minor the Corinthians, Thebans, Argives and Athenians had banded together in an anti-Spartan coalition. Agesilaos was saddened at the news and frustrated that in the midst of his grand revenge against the Persians the quarrelsome Greeks at home were undermining his effort. 'Woe to Greece which has destroyed so many of her men,' he sighed. 'If they had lived to fight with us, they could have vanquished all the barbarians.'

While he was marching down through Macedon and Thessaly he learned of the death of Peisandros his brother-in-law in a sea battle with the Athenians off Knidos in Asia Minor. In the Peloponnese Spartan forces under the command of Aristodamos, the guardian of Pausanias' young son Agesipolis, had been routed by a mixed army of Athenians, Thebans, Corinthians and Argives. Agesilaos' march south through Thessaly was an ordeal. Thessalian cavalry harassed his every move, forcing him to keep his columns as tight as possible. At Pharsalos, enraged by a particularly audacious attack on his rear guard, Agesilaos hurled his few horsemen against the Thessalians, catching them off their guard and decimating one of their squadrons in a daring manoeuvre.

In August 394 the Corinthians and their allies met Agesilaos at Koroneia in Boiotia. Each side had about 20,000 men. Agesilaos placed his Spartiates and Neodamodeis with him on the right. In the centre were Ionian Greek and Thracian units under Herippidas, and various allied contingents made up the left wing. The Thebans opened the battle with a howling charge against Agesilaos' left, which broke and ran. Heripiddas stoutly held the

Spartan centre, while Agesilaos' Spartans on the right charged the enemy left, which broke in its turn. The Thebans had reached Agesilaos' rear when he realized what was happening. He wheeled his own victorious wing around to shore up the left. At this point the Thebans moved to help their own defeated left. On the way they encountered Agesilaos' column bearing down on them like an express train.

The impact was shattering. Though his column was outnumbered Agesilaos stayed in the thick of the fight, surrounded by his fifty-strong volunteer bodyguard and receiving multiple wounds. He liked to say that the Spartans used short swords because 'we fight close to the enemy.'[6] But the Thebans were too strong and so either Agesilaos or some officer ordered the Spartans to open a gap in the ranks. The Thebans, believing themselves victorious, surged through but in the process scattered, which was the signal for the Spartans to counterattack and drive the Thebans off the field, leaving some 600 of their number dead to a cost of about 350 for the Peloponnesians. Agesilaos refused to be treated for his wounds until he had been carried around the field and seen to it that the dead were properly gathered up. At one point Androkleidas, an officer, walked up to him. 'Sire,' he said, 'those wounds were given to you by people you yourself had trained to fight.' Agesilaos knew what Androkleidas meant. The Thebans had been toughened up by years of fighting Spartan forces.

When Agesilaos recovered he appointed a general, Gylis, to lead the army while he journeyed to Delphi to dedicate his tithe of the booty collected from Asia Minor. Shortly afterwards Gylis and his second-in-command Pelles perished in guerrilla operations against the local Lokrians. Returning from Delphi, Agesilaos saw no further strategic use in remaining in central Greece. He disbanded the Peloponnesian army and sent it home by ferrying it across the Gulf of Corinth, as hostile Corinth blocked the usual route over the Isthmus.

At home he was careful not to ape the habits of other leading Spartans who had gone on foreign expeditions and come home changed in their ways. His food remained simple, he bathed like the others in the Eurotas River, and resisted the temptation to drape his wife Kleora in fancy clothes. He kept his old furniture and fittings to the extent that the gates of his house almost rotted away. In the political sphere he had a mind to expose the machinations of the late Lysandros, who still had a considerable following in Lakedaimon. He is believed to have come up with such damning evidence of Lysandros' supposed treachery that the Ephors strongly urged him to keep quiet about it. He took their advice, thus sparing Sparta what could have been a full-blown political upheaval.

Plutarch has preserved several instances that show up Agesilaos' character. He had no time for puffed-up personalities. When a famous tragic actor named Kallipides was brought to Agesilaos, the king appeared to take no notice of him. 'Sire, don't you know me?' Kallipides pressed.

'Sure, you're Kallipides the showman,' Agesilaos deadpanned, and that was all.

There was also a doctor named Menekrates who was so good at curing certain serious ailments that he was given the title 'Zeus' by admiring patients. Menekrates, taking his grand nickname a tad too seriously, had occasion to write to Agesilaos, addressing the letter: 'Zeus Menekrates to King Agesilaos.' The king's answering salutation: 'To Menekrates, health and a sound mind.'[7]

The new power of Corinth moved the Ephors to declare war on that city in 390. No-one could be allowed to block the Isthmus, not even the city nearest to it. Agesilaos duly led an army to seize the Corinthian flocks of sheep and goats, taking by surprise the city which was celebrating the Isthmian Games. Agesilaos was patient as the Corinthians barricaded themselves behind the walls and he lured Corinthian forces away from guarding their livestock. He then marched along the coast towards the hot springs at Therma (now Loutraki), while a detachment occupied the high ground above. It was a cold and rainy night with hail, Xenophon relates, and Agesilaos, concerned about his men on the mountain, sent up a dozen men with fire in braziers to help them cook their food. The next day the Spartans bottled up an enemy force on the Heraion promontory, taking many prisoners.

Well might Agesilaos be proud of this success. But he may not have heard of an especially capable Athenian general who had developed advanced tactical ideas and was about to put them into practice against the Spartans. This was Iphikrates, best described as the nearest thing to a military philosopher the Greeks produced. For some time Iphikrates had noticed that the flexible guerrilla-like tactics of mountain peoples such as the Arkadians and Aitolians had repeatedly worsted the traditional hoplite formations. These light-armed troops were called peltasts (*peltastai*), after the *peltai*, or light shields, which were their only protection. The peltasts depended more on their fast movement and offensive weaponry, such as short slashing swords and long spears.

Iphikrates liked to compare an ideal fighting force to the human body. The commanding general was, of course, the head. The light infantry were the hands, the versatile prime means of combat. The cavalry were the legs and feet, the instruments of mobility. The regular hoplites were the breast, a bulwark against attack. Iphikrates put his newly-formed peltast force to the test as Agesilaos was rounding up the enemy near Therma, and the Amyklaian *mora* of the Spartan army had just left Corinth to march home on leave.

As the swarm of peltasts came into view the *mora* did exactly what was expected of it: the hoplites fell into traditional battle formation and advanced to outflank the enemy left. It didn't work. Iphikrates' light-armed men got in the first blow with their long spears, darting back out of range before the Spartans could get at them. As the frustrated Spartans re-formed, the peltasts rushed at them again, cutting some down. Another attempt at a Spartan counterattack, and another, had the same maddening result, until most of the Amyklaian *mora*, about 250 men, lay dead. In this single encounter the myth of the fabled Spartan military superiority was finally debunked. Agesilaos, when informed of the defeat, jumped up and grabbed a spear and called a snap meeting of his staff. But nothing came of it except a rather gratuitous destruction of Corinth's fruit and olive trees, and a return to Sparta. Agesilaos passed through the towns on his way at night so that his demoralized troops would not see the wicked smiles of delight on the inhabitants' faces. The shock of the Amyklaian *mora* massacre reverberated through Lakedaimon.

The Corinthian War was over, but in its place several brush fires broke out. Sparta, which had a stake in keeping the Greek peace, was often forced to intervene to douse them. In 389 Agesilaos had to move against the Akarnanians in the northwest who were causing trouble for Sparta's allies in the region. The campaign was an oddly half-hearted one. Hampered by effective guerrilla opposition, the king was slow in ravaging the lands and failed to reduce a single Akarnanian town. He eventually pulled out and promised to return the following summer, which he did, while his young co-king Agesipolis I invaded Argive territory (see Agesipolis I below). Spartan naval forces also found themselves occupied against the Athenians in the Saronic Gulf.

By 386 Artaxerxes II judged correctly that the major Greek powers for the second time in two decades had fought themselves to an exhausted standstill. A Spartan admiral named Antalkidas – possibly hungry for Persian money – travelled to Sardis to sound out the Great King on a cessation of hostilities. He began a stampede of Greek envoys to Sardis, where they heard Artaxerxes' terms: Persia would cease meddling in Greek affairs and secure peace in the Aegean, in return for complete domination over the Greek cities of Asia Minor. Moreover, each Greek city would retain its freedom from domination by another. At a conference in Sparta the Greeks agreed to the terms of what is known as the Peace of Antalkidas. Agesilaos wasn't happy about it, as it appeared to negate all he had recently fought for. The bitter truth was that the Greeks of Asia Minor lost their last hope of political liberty, for which the Persian Wars had been fought, sold down the river by Persian hard gold.

For the next few years Agesilaos had to put up with his domestic opponents' efforts to influence foreign policy. One of them was Sphodrias, a Spartan governor in Boiotia, who dreamed up a plan to help the Thebans attack Athens. Sphodrias, though, lost his nerve as the force came within sight of the city. On top of that, he was recalled to Sparta to be tried for his life for endangering the peace. But Sphodrias had a handsome son named Kleonymos who had formed an attachment to Agesilaos' son Archidamos (the future Archidamos III). On the day scheduled for Sphodrias' sentencing, Archidamos got up the courage to ask his father for clemency for his friend's father.

Agesilaos' reply was non-committal, but the reaction masked his genuine fondness for his children. When they were very young he would enjoy riding wooden toy horses with them. His second son Kleombrotos worshipped him. Once when a visitor got into a heated debate with Agesilaos about what constituted excellence, Kleombrotos spoke up. 'My father is a better man than you,' he told the visitor, 'until you, too, have become a father.'[8] Agesilaos in the end prevailed on the court to acquit Sphodrias. But this act of kindness alienated him from the citizens who correctly perceived it as a perversion of justice from purely personal motives.

Tensions with Thebes continued. In 382 Agesilaos took the field again as his new co-king in the Agiad house, Kleombrotos I, was unwilling to risk Spartan manpower (see Kleombrotos I below). Being over sixty now, he had every reason to retire and leave the campaigning to younger men. But like many soldiers he found it impossible to just fade into the background. He was still healthy and vigorous, and felt he had a great deal more to contribute; a glorious battle death may have been what he was seeking. In fact, personal rather than strategic considerations were now dominating Spartan warfare. It was not to the slightest advantage to Sparta to fight Thebes, which was growing in power and military expertise. It wasn't long before a few battles – in which the king received more wounds – showed up the futility of the Theban campaign. It was said that Agesilaos, realizing this, tried to save face in the field by sitting down his Lakedaimonians on one side and the enemy on the other, and calling on all the artisans and craftsmen on each side to fall out. None of the Spartans moved, as they were all professional soldiers. 'You see, friends,' Agesilaos chuckled to his foes, 'how many more soldiers we have than you.'

As the Spartans were marching back home, outside Megara, Agesilaos had a sudden severe pain in his sound leg, with inflammation and swelling. It was probably phlebitis, which his doctor tried to cure by bleeding him below the ankle. As a result he very nearly bled to death, and was carried into Sparta in a very weak condition. It took him months to recover.

His illness, and the vagaries of advancing age, embittered Agesilaos. It was obvious now to everyone in Sparta that the city had passed its apex of power and that Thebes now had the upper hand in Greece. Therefore there was general relief when ambassadors from Thebes came to Sparta to sound out the Ephors and Agesilaos about a peace treaty. Heading the Theban mission was Epaminondas, a man distinguished for his learning and proud spirit. Epaminondas was the only one who refused to kowtow to Agesilaos, instead delivering a stern lecture on past Spartan misdeeds and the 'distress and suffering' visited on Sparta's neighbours. This arrogance infuriated Agesilaos so much that he dismissed the Thebans out of hand and renewed his war on them. In 371 Kleombrotos, the younger king, was despatched northwards with an army.

Kleombrotos promptly met disaster at the hands of Epaminondas on the field of Leuktra (see Kleombrotos I below). Sparta again was plunged into mourning. Some minds harked back to the old Delphic warning against a 'lame kingdom.' Agesilaos did what he could to placate the grumblers. The battle at Leuktra had witnessed the unusual spectacle of a large number of Spartans running away. Ordinarily the penalty for cowardice in the field consisted of official public dishonour and, for single men, a ban on marrying any Lakedaimonian woman. An officially-designated coward could be assaulted in the street with impunity, was not allowed to enter the public baths, and was obliged to wear ragged and patched clothes as well as only half his beard – to make him as conspicuous and contemptible as possible. The problem was that after Leuktra there would be a rather large number of such men (including members of distinguished families) about, so Agesilaos waived the rule for one day. He later led some of those 'cowards' on an expedition into Arkadia where he ravaged the countryside and made them feel like soldiers again.

After Leuktra, Lakedaimon lay at the mercy of Epaminondas. He invaded the area with 40,000 hoplites, augmented by some 30,000 allied peltasts and camp-followers. He marched unopposed into the Lakonian valley and forded the Eurotas River, arriving at the outskirts of Sparta. Agesilaos wisely declined to give battle, fortifying the main points of the city. 'Our young men are the walls of Sparta,' he would say, 'and the points of their spears are its boundaries.'[9] But panic reigned. Old men cursed the times, and women ran about wailing in despair, as the smoke of the Thebans' fires wafted overhead. The king was depressed. Writes Plutarch:

> He was afflicted by the sense of his lost glory. Having come to the throne of Sparta when it was in its most flourishing and powerful condition, he now lived to see it laid low in esteem, and all its great

boasts cut down, even that which he himself had been fond of using, that the women of Sparta had never seen the smoke of the enemy's fires.[10]

The Eurotas was flooded at the time and Epaminondas stood in front of his men observing it. He was seen by the Spartans who pointed him out to Agesilaos. 'Oh brave man!' were the only words the king uttered. Epaminondas sized up the Spartan defences and concluded that to winkle the defenders out would be too costly. It was a great relief when the Thebans marched off, burning as they went. Why they retreated is still something of a mystery. Winter may have been approaching. One ancient report claims that Agesilaos bribed Epaminondas to leave with ten talents.

There was only one state to turn to for help – Athens. Probably no Spartan mission ever entered Athens as humbly as that which sat before the assembly in 369. The envoys ran through all the time-worn reminders of the glory days when the united Greeks had stood up to Persia, and buttered up the Athenians by praising their naval tradition. It all rang rather hollow in Athenian ears – after all, it had been just thirty-five years since Spartan arrogance had laid Athens low. Yet when it came to a vote, the Athenian assembly displayed good sense by voting aid to Sparta. Iphikrates led a flying column to Corinth to try and catch Epaminondas as he marched home, but was too late.

The extremity of Sparta had nurtured a strong dissident movement at home. No sooner had Epaminondas withdrawn than about 200 Spartan malcontents seized the Temple of Artemis. It's not clear what their aims were, for Agesilaos with almost absurd ease managed to dupe them. We are told that he approached them and told them that their efforts would meet with more success in another part of town. Plutarch hints that he might have disguised himself to be able to carry it off. At any rate, fifteen of the dissidents were arrested and executed.

The incident points up the plummeting morale in Sparta. Barely was that mini-insurrection over than a more serious one erupted, involving serious Spartans plotting real revolution. There was no time for pussy-footing now. Acting in concert with the Ephors, Agesilaos had the ringleaders put to death without trial. Once more rule of law in Sparta – the authority more to be feared, in Demaratos' words, than any despot – had been cast by the wayside. The army was suffering a wave of desertions by Helots and other peasants, most of whom joined the ranks of the Thebans and their allies. The result was that a little more than 1,000 Spartiates were available for military duty, compared to some 9,000 sixty years before.

Agesilaos left off campaigning for a while, passing the baton to his son Archidamos who vanquished the Arkadians in an almost bloodless (for Sparta) encounter known as the Tearless Battle (see Archidamos III below). When Archidamos returned Agesilaos went out to meet him weeping with gratitude. Men and women formed a procession to the Eurotas, lifting up their arms and thanking the gods 'that Sparta was now cleared of disgrace and indignity.' Spartan men, Plutarch assures us, could look their wives in the face again.[11]

The decade of the 360s was one of confusion in Greece, as city-states aligned and re-aligned with one another with kaleidoscopic rapidity and Sparta wrestled to keep its alliance intact. The turmoil extended to the Greek states of Asia Minor under Persian control. Sparta saw a potential advantage in this by offering to send help to a rebellious Persian satrap named Ariobarzanes. The Spartan economy was in a parlous state, and urgent funding was required for the expected future showdown with the Thebans and their allies. Ariobarzanes promised whatever money Sparta desired, and thus Agesilaos, now pushing eighty, embarked again for a voyage across the Aegean at the head of a mercenary force, this time to help the Persians instead of fighting them. It seems his fame had lingered among the inhabitants of the Ionian seaboard, for as soon as he arrived Ariobarzanes' foes dissolved like the mist. Agesilaos occupied Phokaia and sailed back to Sparta flush with the promised funds.

In 362 Epaminondas came to the conclusion that one more decisive blow in the Peloponnese would crush Sparta for good, and led some 35,000 infantry and cavalry from Boiotia, Euboia and Thessaly into the Peloponnese. The indestructible old warrior Agesilaos now embarked on his last campaign. He had led the army out as far as Sellasia, north of Sparta, when he heard that Epaminondas was coming down the Lakonian valley like an avalanche. For the second time in seven years Agesilaos prudently fell back to entrench himself in the city. The Theban general this time avoided the mistake of 369 by occupying higher ground overlooking the Spartan citadel. A surprise attack by prince Archidamos with barely a hundred men drove the Thebans from the spot with considerable slaughter. Unnerved by the unexpected setback, Epaminondas retreated up the Lakonian valley to Tegea.

Before reaching Sparta Epaminondas had delayed at Nemea, intending to ambush an Athenian expedition he believed would pass that spot on its way to help Sparta. He waited in vain, as the navy-minded Athenians sent their force by sea. The consequence of the delay was that Sparta, Athens and Mantineia had time to put together 22,000 troops to confront him at Mantineia. Though his forces outnumbered those of the enemy, Epaminondas found himself in the position of Xerxes at Thermopylai – forced to attack on a narrow, well-defended front. But he had the Theban secret weapon up his sleeve – the battering-ram phalanx that had been so effective at Leuktra (see Kleombrotos I below).

To mask his position Epaminondas ordered his units to parade back and forth, raising clouds of dust. The Spartans and Athenians, not suspecting what was afoot, settled down to a leisurely lunch, in the middle of which the Theban phalanx came thundering onto the Spartan right. At the same time a squadron of Theban horsemen attacked the Athenians on the left. True to form, Epaminondas and the Theban phalanx smashed through the Spartan line, 'like a warship,' wrote Xenophon, 'with all the striking power in the bow.' The column was about to veer right to mop up the Athenians when the offensive without warning had the life taken out of it – news spread that Epaminondas had been mortally wounded. In a matter of minutes the Thebans lost their fighting spirit. The Athenians were able to drive back the enemy on their front. Xenophon's own son Gryllos, fighting in the Spartan ranks, was credited with personally striking the blow that killed Epaminondas. Both forces withdrew from the field, though both the Thebans and the Athenians, who bore the brunt of the fighting, claimed a victory of sorts on the grounds that they had not actually retreated. (Here Xenophon concludes his history of Greek affairs with the pessimistic sentence that yet greater troubles were in store for Greece: 'I'll stop writing here, and let someone else deal with what happened afterwards.'[12])

Agesilaos' main foe was dead. But Sparta was still under threat, this time from Messenia, which had thrown off long-term Spartan suzerainty. After the battle at Mantineia most Greek states had agreed on a period of peace. But as long as the Messenian issue remained unresolved Sparta could not let its guard down. One of those who had backed Messenian independence was Artaxerxes II Mnemon, obviously in the hope of weakening Sparta. And when in 361 Artaxerxes' regional satraps in the Middle East and Egypt rose in revolt against him, rugged old Agesilaos was there in the line-up, leading 1,000 Spartan hoplites over the sea to Egypt to help Pharaoh Tacho shake off Persian rule.

The old king's fame had certainly preceded him, as Egyptian officials lined up eagerly to catch a glimpse of this grand figure when he landed on Egyptian shores. Instead they saw a small and withered old man, dressed in a poor man's simple cloak, resting on the grass. Amazement turned to sarcasm as Agesilaos refused all gifts handed to him except some flour, calves and geese; he waved away the sweets and perfumes which he sent on to the Helots in his army. But Agesilaos, too, was disillusioned with what he found. He found Pharaoh Tacho to be a haughty and shallow man, insisting on keeping command of the rebel army and relegating the Spartan king to commander of the 10,000 Greek mercenaries in Egyptian service.

Tacho's rebellion came quickly to grief. A nephew of his named Nectanebo refused to accept Tacho's orders and carried most of the Egyptian army with him. The Athenian commander of the navy, Chabrias, backed Tacho and urged Agesilaos to do likewise. Agesilaos, on the contrary, favoured Nectanebo and consulted the Ephors, who replied that the king should exercise his judgement in the best interests of Sparta. When Agesilaos led his men to join Nectanebo's camp Tacho fled to Persia.

But Nectanebo soon found another foe in Acoris, a pharaoh-pretender who had strong forces at his command. Nectanebo urged Agesilaos to attack Acoris but the king hesitated. Perhaps age had finally eroded his resolve and dash. Agesilaos, his army and Nectanebo found themselves besieged in a town on the Nile Delta, cut off by a moat that Acoris' forces were digging. Nectanebo and the Greek soldiers urged an immediate breakout before their food could run out, but still Agesilaos refused. His aim, he said, was to wait until the moat was almost complete, and then line up the defence on the narrow unexcavated portion to repulse the attackers. It was an inversion of the Thermopylai trick, and it worked. Time and again Acoris' troops counterattacked, only to be driven back with heavy loss.

When Acoris gave up the attempt a grateful Nectanebo showered Agesilaos with gifts and a huge sum of money for Sparta. Agesilaos was waiting to embark at a Libyan port to take the money home when he died, aged eighty-four. His men preserved his body in honey and carried him to Sparta where he was buried 'with greater honours than they had given to any other king.'[13]

Agesilaos II looms larger in history than any other Spartan king, mainly because so much was written about him. He reigned at a time when Greek historiography was getting into its stride after Thucydides. He was one of just three Spartan kings whom Plutarch deemed important enough to write a short biography of. It is to Plutarch that we owe the many human details about his character and lifestyle that are missing in so many sources for earlier kings. Agesilaos' thirty-nine-year reign spanned the apex of Spartan power to the beginning of its decline. He was the second Spartan king after Leotychidas II to set foot in Asia for the express purpose of defeating Persia. At least one modern commentator has seen in Agesilaos a precursor of Alexander the Great.[14] It can be argued that his adherence to the Spartan disciplinary ideal and healthy lifestyle gave him such a long and energetic life. He had a talent for bringing self-important characters down a peg or two, as seen in his deflation of Lysandros. To him, bravery in the field was but a means to a greater end – justice among human beings. 'If all the world were just,' he liked to say, 'there would be no need of valour.'[15]

## Agesipolis I (395–380)

In the first half of the fourth century fate decreed that the Agiad house of Spartan kings would be put utterly in the shade by the Eurypontid Agesilaos II. No fewer than five Agiad kings reigned alongside Agesilaos, starting with Pausanias and ending with Kleomenes II. The reigns of three of these kings lasted fifteen years or less. When Pausanias fled into exile in 395, his delicate young son Agesipolis took on the burden of his father's bad publicity.

Plutarch describes the youth as quiet and retiring, not overly conforming to the rugged Spartan ideal. Agesilaos, himself just four years on the Eurypontid throne and pushing fifty, took his young co-king under his benevolent wing. It was a longstanding custom in Sparta that whenever the two kings were in the city they dined together. The rule was an effective way of nipping in the bud any uncontrollable rivalry that might arise. Indeed, it could be urged that the dual Spartan monarchy, politically outmoded since the sixth century, survived as long as it did precisely because of customs such as this.

By such convivial means Agesilaos made a firm friend of Agesipolis. The boy was also openly gay, which wasn't frowned on in Greece as long as the resulting relationships were conducted in a spirit of public modesty and genuine concern for the other.[16] There is no evidence that Agesilaos himself formed any kind of homosexual attachment to Agesipolis, though he never hesitated to advise him on affairs of the heart and be his confidant in all matters. It may be thought that Agesilaos this way cynically sought to gain influence over his co-king, but from the evidence available it's more probable that Agesilaos sincerely had the well-being of the diffident youth at heart.

Agesilaos must have played some part in training Agesipolis for his hereditary role of general in the field, however unsuited the young man's character may have been to soldiering and hardship. For in 384, in the eleventh year of Agesipolis' reign, we have a picture rather different from the tender-heart painted by Plutarch: Xenophon reports him as leading a Spartan army to Mantineia after that city refused a Spartan demand to raze its walls. The choice to lead the army had at first been Agesilaos, but the older king declined on the grounds that the Mantineians had helped his father Agis II against the Messenians, and he could not thus show ingratitude. It may well have been an excuse to give Agesipolis the opportunity to test his mettle in the field, as any Spartan king worth his salt was required to do.

Agesipolis' tactics in front of Mantineia suggests that his abilities had been built up considerably in the space of less than ten years. At that time he would have been in his mid-twenties. As the Mantineians still refused to dismantle their walls Agesipolis ordered a trench dug around the city, employing half his troops to do the digging and the other half to cover them. He was about to build an investing wall along the trench when it occurred to him that he could shorten his soldiers' hardships by a stratagem. The river running through Mantineia was in full spate in that season, so he ordered the river blocked where it exited the city. Mantineia was soon flooded. The rising water lapped against the brick foundations of the Mantineians' wall until it began to crack and lean. The defenders' efforts to shore up the wall came to nothing; eventually they agreed to let it fall down.

At this point, Xenophon reports, 'Agesipolis' father' advised his son not to push his luck, suggesting that it would be diplomatic to allow the Mantineian democrats and their Argive allies to leave the city under a safe-conduct. The father can only have been Pausanias, who thus was still alive eleven years after his flight, and in a position to advise his son. The democrats and Argives walked out between files of muttering Spartan troops, itchy fingers on their spears, lined up on either side of the road. Agesipolis had the triumph he needed to legitimate himself in the eyes of the Spartans.

Soon afterwards Agesipolis was sent to chastise Sparta's old foe Argos over some unknown grievance. At the frontier he dismissed the Argive envoys who came with a proposal for a truce; perhaps the accompanying Ephors were the real decision-makers here. According to Pausanias the historian, a series of earthquakes and storms struck while the Lakedaimonian army was encamped under the walls of Argos; lightning killed some soldiers and the general grimness of the situation awoke divine dread in others. Reluctantly, possibly at the Ephors' advice, Agesipolis withdrew.

At about this time a call came from some small Thrakian towns in the north, alarmed by the growing power of Olynthos (near modern Nea Moudania in the Halkidiki peninsula). Two Spartan brothers, Eudamidas and Phoibidas, marched an army northwards. On the way Phoibidas was persuaded by the Thebans to stay in their city and rule as Spartan military governor. Eudamidas proceeded alone to Olynthos and besieged it, but found the siege hard going as attacks by Thrakian light-armed peltasts were a constant nuisance. In the summer of 381 King Agesipolis took over. Arriving in the territory of the Olynthians, he laid it waste and took Torone by assault. But in the oppressive heat he sickened of a fever. He asked to be carried into the shade of a shrine to Dionysos, and there he lay for a week until he died. His body was encased in honey and taken home for burial. He was barely thirty years old.

We have a composite picture of Agesipolis. One half, in the lines of Plutarch, is that of a shy young man who early in life appeared to display hardly any talent for leadership in the tough Spartan world. The other, painted by Xenophon and Pausanias, shows a rather stronger character who acquitted himself well in the field and could have achieved much had he lived longer. Unlike many Spartans, he maintained a sensitive respect for Athens as a onetime bearer of the torch of Greek liberty and justice. Plutarch tells us that when he heard that Athens had agreed that its neighbour Megara should mediate a diplomatic dispute, he said it was a shame that the Athenians, 'who have held the hegemony of the Greeks,' should stoop to being judged by less capable people.[7]

Agesilaos wept when Agesipolis' body was brought home. He had formed a genuine attachment to his young co-king, something rare in Spartan annals. Perhaps he looked forward to a day when he could join both royal houses in a drive for continued Spartan greatness. For this, one feels, he had gradually formed Agesipolis' character. As for Agesipolis himself, his death on campaign more than compensated for his unpromising beginnings.

## Kleombrotos I (380–371)

By the middle of the 370s, as we have seen, Sparta's supremacy in the Greek world was coming under serious challenge by Thebes. To counter this trend Sparta sent envoys to stiffen the Spartan alliance and regulate the military contributions of each in case of war. In 378 the exiled democrats of Thebes staged a coup against the city's Spartan-controlled government. The attempt was made during a gala evening, when a group of armed exiles slipped into Thebes amidst the peasants trudging back after a day in the fields. Once inside, they made straight for the festivities while other dissidents urged the people to rise up. Seven of the assailants are said to have crashed the party disguised as prostitutes. Daggers flashed, and in very short time Thebes' dictators were dead. Dawn broke to find a mob of Theban rebels besieging the Spartan garrison in the citadel. The Spartans and their local supporters were allowed to depart under a safe-conduct that was immediately and shamefully violated. Even the children of the Theban oligarchs were slaughtered like lambs. Kleombrotos I was sent to lead a punitive expedition.

Kleombrotos was Agesipolis' brother and successor, as Agesipolis died without children. He seems to have been somewhat more of a soldier, as on his first military mission he annihilated some Theban skirmishers in the passes of Mount Kithairon near the old battlefield of Plataia. The mass of Thebans stayed holed up within their walls, and Kleombrotos, unwilling to press a siege for which his army was unprepared, lingered for a couple of weeks and then withdrew with two-thirds of his force. The other third, under Sphodrias, was left there to recruit mercenaries.

Two years later the Spartans made another attempt to chastise Thebes. Agesilaos was still in bed recovering from the phlebitis attack he had suffered at Megara and so the assignment fell on Kleombrotos. This time, as he approached Mount Kithairon he found Thebans and Athenians on high ground over the main pass, ready to ambush him. A few dozen Spartans who attempted to dislodge the enemy from the heights were killed. Kleombrotos decided that the position was impossible to take by assault and led the army back home. The decision may have been strategically wise, but in hindsight it was the first concrete sign of the imminent decline of Sparta. Gone, it seemed, were the days when a Spartan king and his army would not hesitate to throw themselves against any foe, however numerically superior, simply because Spartan honour demanded nothing less. We don't know if this was Kleombrotos' specific fault; he was still very young, and the influence of the Ephors with the army should never be underestimated. But to many, the lack of resolution at Mount Kithairon signified a new hesitation among Sparta's leaders, a lack of confidence in the city's traditional strengths. Worse was to come.

It was at this juncture that the ever-watchful Artaxerxes II Mnemon, concerned at the wastage of good Greek fighting men, issued a call for mercenaries to help him quell the revolt in Egypt. Persian envoys entered Sparta in the summer of 371 and talked the Spartans and Athenians into a general disarmament, known as the King's Peace, that hopefully would free up professional Greek soldiers-of-fortune for the Great King's use. Thebes, though, balked. It was just coming into its own as a significant Greek power and was not going to be deprived of its ambitions. At the Sparta conference the Thebans insisted that the Boiotian League, which they led, be recognized as a unified power. But the Spartans and Athenians argued that such a move would be unfair to Plataia, with which both cities sympathized. The Thebans walked off in a huff, and the Spartan Apella ordered a pre-emptive strike against Thebes to bring it into line.

Kleombrotos was already in Phokis, in the area of Delphi, when he received orders to invade Boiotia with 11,000 infantry and cavalry. His friends warned him in no uncertain terms that his reputation at home as a warrior was already very shaky, given his previous lack of resolution in the same area. There were dark mutterings, they said, that Kleombrotos might even be a Theban sympathizer. 'If you want to see your homeland again,' they told him, 'you must order an attack.' Whatever his original plan, Kleombrotos now had no choice in the matter.

The Thebans were waiting for him to cross the mountainous frontier east of Delphi, but he gave them the slip and marched by a little-known route to Kreusis on the coast, where he captured twelve Theban warships, and then struck inland. Thebes was full of foreboding. It was said that temple doors had mysteriously swung open of their own accord and that the arms of the legendary hero Herakles had vanished. Soothsayers assured all who would listen that Herakles himself had donned his armour to defend Thebes. But the mass of people, including the soldiers, were not so sure. Epaminondas, the Theban commanding general, dismissed the tale. 'There is only one good omen, and that is to defend your country,' he said as he marched out to meet Kleombrotos with just 6,000 troops and 1,000 cavalrymen – a little over half the Spartan strength.

Both armies met on the dry plain of Leuktra, about fifteen kilometres southeast of Thebes. Kleombrotos called a final war council. The commanders convened just after lunch, when the wine had brightened everyone's outlook, and worked out their positions. The Spartan cavalry would be in the front line, with the *morai* behind them twelve men deep. On the other side Epaminondas also placed his cavalry in front, but his Theban infantry was massed at least fifty men deep on a shorter front. The Spartan line was little more than half as long as the Theban.

The Theban formation represented a revolution of sorts in land warfare. For some time the Thebans had been experimenting with a new infantry formation, the phalanx, made up of a column of men aimed lengthwise at the enemy line. The effectiveness of the phalanx had first been seen at Delion in 424, when the Thebans had routed the Athenians with it. Epaminondas in the meantime had perfected it, from a thirty-two man deep column to a solid rectangular hammerhead, fifty men deep and seventy wide. In it he placed Thebes' elite outfit, the 300-strong Sacred Band, composed of pairs of men so tightly bound that homosexual relationships were encouraged as a means of cementing cohesion. Thebes also had a distinct advantage in its cavalry. The plains of Boiotia were ideal for raising and training war horses and the horsemen were kept in shape through constant skirmishing with unruly neighbours. The Spartan cavalry, by contrast, was made up of sorry, ill-nourished nags raised by the wealthier families. The Spartan horsemen, also, were second-rate troops, quite inferior to their opponents in endurance and loyalty.

The rolling plain at Leuktra seemed ideal for traditional Spartan infantry tactics, so Kleombrotos deployed his forces five or six men deep, taking his place on the right, where a Spartan king had to be, and sending a screen of cavalry ahead. As he set his line in motion his cavalry hastily got to grips with the Theban horse and came off worsted. As the horsemen retired in confusion Epaminondas' second-in-command, Pelopidas, ordered the Sacred Band forward in a highly-disciplined left oblique direction. The Band hit the Spartan line like a tree trunk going through a window, catching

Kleombrotos as he was trying to outflank the Thebans to the right – the only possible manoeuvre that might stall the Theban advance. He never made it. Deinon, a senior Spartan officer, was killed, to be followed by the king's aide Sphodrias and his son Kleonymos, the youth who had formed an attachment to Agesilaos' son Archidamos. At some point – perhaps before, perhaps later – Kleombrotos himself fell mortally wounded.

'In great disasters,' Pausanias the historian opined, 'Providence is peculiarly apt to cut off early the general.'[18] If the leader falls early in the action, morale plummets and chances of victory dramatically decline. That's what happened at Leuktra. News of Kleombrotos' death shook the cohesion and resolve of the Spartan left wing which fell back in disorder. When about 1,000 Lakedaimonians and their allies had fallen, including 400 of the 700 Spartiates forming the core of the force, the commanders called a halt and gathered up the bodies under a truce. Xenophon hints that some Spartans were glad that the battle had turned out so badly for them; if that is true, then a germ of defeatism must already have been eating away at the army. The Thebans, for their part, erected a trophy on the battlefield. The monument, partly rebuilt, can be seen today.

News of the heavy defeat arrived in Sparta in the middle of a youth festival. The Ephors dared not release it to the public, but ordered the festival to continue while privately notifying the families of each of the 1,000 slain Spartans. The full realization hit the next morning, when, in a telling display of Spartan military-mindedness, the relatives of the dead rejoiced in the streets and squares while those whose sons survived skulked at home in shame. The Spartans would have to wait nine years until Kleombrotos was avenged, as we have seen, at Mantineia in 362 when Epaminondas perished (see Agesilaos II above).

The brothers Agesipolis I and Kleombrotos I deserve a special place in the annals of Sparta. Not nearly as much was written about them as about their contemporary Agesilaos II. Partly, of course, that is because both were struck down on campaign, one after the other, before they were thirty. Yet such poignant events tend to arouse a people's emotional response in the form of renewed pride in their sovereigns and state. The brothers' sacrifice could well have helped keep the Spartan dual kingship in place long after it ceased to be practically necessary.

*Chapter 9*

# Retreat

**Agesipolis II and Kleomenes II**
**Archidamos III**
**Agis III**
**Eudamidas I**

## Agesipolis II (371–370) and Kleomenes II (370–309)

Upon Kleombrotos I's death in action at Leuktra, Agesipolis, the elder of his two young sons, assumed the Agiad throne. We know little of the boy except from a throwaway phrase of Pausanias the historian, who dismisses Agesipolis II as 'not a striking figure in history.' Plutarch is a tiny bit more forthcoming, preserving a tradition that Agesipolis liked to breed dogs. On some foreign trip he asked that Sparta's export ban on dogs be waived for his own convenience. As his reign lasted just a year or less, it might normally be assumed that he died of illness or accident. Yet Plutarch hints that he may have been alive as late as 348, when Philip II of Macedon razed Olynthos in northern Greece. 'By heaven,' Agesipolis is said to have remarked on that occasion. 'He won't build another like it in many years!' It sounds a simplistic, almost childish statement, and raises the possibility that Agesipolis could have been retarded and was on those grounds deposed after a brief reign. But this is pure speculation.

Agesipolis' younger brother succeeded to the Agiad throne as Kleomenes II, reigning for an extraordinary sixty-one years. Yet even more extraordinary is Kleomenes II's utter invisibility in the annals. If there ever was a mystery man in Spartan history, it is he. Even Plutarch gives him just one brief appearance, as an aficionado of fighting cocks. When someone offered him some of the fowls, saying they would die fighting for victory, Kleomenes said he preferred having some that would win.[1] Such an anecdote, of course, is nothing to hang a biographical sketch on. Yet, to stretch a string of speculation, if we posit that his brother Agesipolis was in some way retarded, might not the same have applied to Kleomenes II, though in lesser degree?

Undeniably, one reason for his place deep in the shadows is that in the period 370–340 an exhausted Sparta took a back seat in Greek affairs. But even then one might suppose he would rate more than a couple of lines in Pausanias or Plutarch. If he was a weak-witted king, possibly the Ephors preferred to keep him at home as a ceremonial figure in the interests of unity, or to keep the weak Agiad house out of danger, while the energetic Eurypontid Archidamos III did the real work.

## Archidamos III (360–338)

The Battle of Mantineia of 362, and the death of Agesilaos II two years later, forms a watershed in Spartan history. Sparta's alliance, so powerful thirty years before, had shrunk to the southern half of the Peloponnese. Democratic, and hence anti-Spartan, revolts had been breaking out on all points of the horizon – Argos in 370, then Arkadia, Elis and Corinth. All that was left was Messenia to the west, and even that was none too secure. By the end of the 360s Sparta found itself diplomatically isolated by a so-called 'League of City-States' that claimed to be willing to include Sparta as well, but on condition that Messenia be freed. The Ephors refused, and so Sparta remained the odd one out.

The League of City-States was the most striking demonstration yet that Greece was exhausted, and that the Greeks longed to be allowed to pursue the paths of peace. The League even turned down an invitation by the Persian satraps to move against their Great King Artaxerxes II Mnemon. Athens was in the strongest position to do so, yet public opinion there was very much against costly adventurism. Memories of Marathon and Salamis were now fading, and the futility of Greek intervention in Asia Minor had been demonstrated more than once.

Of course, Greeks being Greeks, it was not long before the League of City-States came under strain from the conflicting tendencies within. By 357 tensions had risen to the breaking point known as the Allied War (sometimes called the Social War). This was almost entirely an Athenian affair, involving a futile attempt to re-establish dominion in the eastern Aegean, which Athens finally had to give up in 355. Sparta, technically an ally of Athens, could offer no help in the Allied War as the Messenians and Arkadians were continually harassing Lakedaimon with guerrilla warfare, tying down the army. This was the prime concern of Archidamos III, the son of Agesilaos, the ranking king.

While the Allied War was in progress, a rather nastier business blew up in central Greece, centring on Delphi and its sacred status. Since the First Sacred War almost three hundred years before, the states around Delphi had united in what was called an Amphiktyony, or mutual sacred bond, to safe-guard the site where Greek states had deposited untold wealth. Craggy and fabulously wealthy Delphi was the Switzerland of ancient Greece. Anything that happened to it was everyone's concern. By the middle of the fourth century the Amphiktyony had deteriorated into a plaything of whichever Greek state was dominant at a particular time. Religion barely figured in the considerations, except for propaganda purposes. When in 356 the Phokians, in whose territory Delphi was situated, rebelled from Theban control and reasserted their ancient claim to Delphi, war was certain. Tied down as he was in the Peloponnese, Archidamos sent money to the Phokians, but no troops. The Thebans gained an advantage and eventually took 3,000 prisoners whom they put to death by hanging or drowning. The Third Sacred War, as this conflict was known, lasted ten years and left yet more scars on Greece.

Archidamos III inherited much of his father's resolute nature. The day after the news from Leuktra reached Sparta he had stood in for his ailing father and marched north, gathering allied contingents as he went. At Aigosthena (modern Porto Germeno) on the coast he met the survivors of Leuktra and learned from them the true extent of the disaster. Appalled, he had turned for home.

We know nothing of Archidamos' childhood or youth, except for this march in 371, while he was still a prince. Pausanias rather sniffily credits him with having a share of the vast funds accumulated at Delphi, which might account for his interest in keeping the Thebans' hands off the place. Pausanias adds that Archidamos' wife Deinicha actually received bribes from the Phokians who controlled Delphi. Such a claim is quite credible, given the general decline in economic morality in Sparta since the end of the Peloponnesian War. By now the old ban on a Spartan citizen holding gold or silver was universally ignored. The richer families, to maintain their lifestyle and prevent a much-feared slide into Inferior status, would stop at nothing to acquire any form of wealth, however dubiously. Soon after Leuktra Archidamos led successful expeditions against Arkadia, though he later remarked that he would have preferred to subdue the Arkadians by diplomacy rather than force.[2] He probably misjudged the Arkadians, as he lost a battle against them in 364.

Pausanias the historian writes that when the Phokians during the Third Sacred War considered massacring all the males of Delphi, selling its women and children into slavery and razing the town to the ground, Archidamos interceded. An ancient Greek sacred war was the most vicious of wars. As it was assumed that it was triggered by disrespect to some deity, ordinary human rules of conduct did not apply and the way was open to atrocities of every kind. We don't know why the Phokians contemplated such a frightful action or how it would help their cause. But thanks to Archidamos, it didn't occur.

By this time, however, all Greek eyes were trained on the north, where a vigorous and ambitious king, Philip II of Macedon, had by fair means and foul managed to extend Macedonian influence over the mainland as far as Delphi and Boiotia. Philip had spent some of his early years as a hostage at Epaminondas' household in Thebes, where he imbibed Greek culture and military science, including the Theban invention of the phalanx. When he was twenty-three his elder brother, King Perdikkas III, was killed in battle against the Illyrians in the northwest, leaving him as regent for Perdikkas' infant son Amyntas. Within a few years the regency had become a regular kingship, as Philip neutralized the other claimants to the throne of Macedon, leaving him in sole undisputed power.

The Macedonian kingship resembled the Spartan one in that it cultivated the idea of political supremacy underpinned by military excellence. But Philip went one better in that he had a hearty contempt for the eternal squabbling of the Greek states and a driving ambition to forge them into a unified force which, seasoned by Greek culture, could in his view conquer the world. He knew he would encounter plenty of opposition from the Greeks themselves. Many did not even consider him a Greek at all. The Macedonian elite heartily reciprocated the sentiment, despising the southern Greeks as effete, immature and untrustworthy. To employ a recent analogy, the Macedonian attitude to the other Greeks can be compared to that of the proud Scots highlanders towards the English 'Sassenachs' in the eighteenth century.

With amazing energy Philip lost no time in organizing the Macedonian military into the most efficient fighting force the world had ever seen. The army was organized along essentially feudal lines. The infantry and cavalry were distinct and separate arms, the former including the Foot Companions that were to form the heart of the feared Macedonian phalanx. The cavalry, led by an elite body of nobles called the Companions, was formed into squadrons. Special Guards units were set up to guard the flanks of the infantry and cavalry, light-armed troops were recruited from the surrounding provinces, and advances were made in the design of catapults and other siege engines. The infantry had the newly-developed *sarissa*, a pike twice as long as a man. The points of the massed *sarissai* would thus protrude far in front of the lead soldiers of the phalanx like a series of staggered knife blades.

The Macedonian hills were rich in gold and silver ores, and thus of all the Greek states Macedon was by far the best-equipped with the financial and material means to wage a long war. To Philip, this long war was to be one of liberating the Asia Minor Greeks from Persian rule. But before he could accomplish this, he had to kick the recalcitrant southern Greeks into line.

Philip tested his new model army against the hostile Illyrians and Thrakians pressing in on Macedon's frontiers, receiving an arrow in one eye for his pains. Then, with the Third Sacred War, he saw his chance.

By 352 Philip was steamrolling down through Thessaly. On a piece of flat ground called the Crocus Field he hurled 20,000 Macedonians against the Phokians and all but annihilated them. To stop him, 1,000 Spartans plus some 9,400 Athenians and Achaians, took up Leonidas' old position at Thermopylai. But Philip was no Xerxes – he had no intention of sacrificing his well-trained Macedonians against an impregnable position – and turned his army around for home. Archidamos, if he had any doubts before, now knew who the main foe was, and for the rest of his life would pursue the aim of stopping Philip.

In 346, after Philip had spent some years whittling away the power of Athens in the north, he made plans for a new invasion of southern Greece. The Third Sacred War had been sputtering on for years as Thebes had been soliciting Macedonian aid against the Phokians. For the second time in six years 1,000 Spartans marched to the pass at Thermopylai, this time with Archidamos at their head. Fifty Athenian ships sailed up in support of a planned Phokian attack on Thebes. Then the regime changed in Phokis and Archidamos had no choice but to withdraw.

The fiasco at Thermopylai convinced Archidamos that the way to deal with Philip was to wait for him to come south. 'Here,' he told his advisers in Sparta, 'is where we shall be superior to the enemy.' He was a military realist, realizing that Sparta in the end controlled only as much land 'as could be reached with the spear.'[3] When his allies demanded to know how much their war contributions would come to, he fobbed them off with the observation that 'war does not feed on fixed rations.'

In hindsight, as Philip took over Thessaly and helped himself to its good horses in 344, it seems strange that Archidamos had let himself be drawn into a sideshow in Crete called the Foreign War. This blew up in 346 when Phalaikos, the vanquished leader of the Phokian forces in the Third Sacred War, fled to Knossos in Crete to help that ancient city extend its control over the island. The immediate target of the Knossians was Lyttos, where the Spartans' own system of governance had first taken root, and which as a consequence had a valid emotional claim to Spartan aid.

Little is known of the Foreign War except that Archidamos and his Spartans helped Lyttos defeat the Knossians. Of greater interest is that Archidamos saw his role now less as a defender of his state and more as a mercenary captain. It may be that at a time when Sparta was pulling in its horns, Archidamos entertained sentimental thoughts of imitating his father Agesilaos who had made such a name for himself projecting Spartan power far and wide. But since Leuktra the Spartan empire was no more, and it was futile to try and revive it in the face of Macedon.

Perhaps Archidamos had a pressing need for money, which could only come from outside. This might explain why in 342 he responded to an appeal from Taras, Sparta's colony on the heel of Italy, which was under attack from the Lucanians, a southern Italian tribe. Archidamos arrived at Taras with a fleet and army, and appears to have spent the next four years fighting the Lucanians. We do know for sure that he fell in battle against them in 338. No-one knows what happened to his body. Pausanias the historian blames 'the anger of Apollo' for the fact that Archidamos II failed to get a decent burial. The phrase conveniently covers a multitude of possibilities, though it connotes that Archidamos might have done something to bring the gods' anger down upon him.

### Agis III (338–331)

It was said that Archidamos III fell on the same day of the momentous battle of Chaironea near Thebes. True or not, the year 338 was another watershed in the history of Greece in general and Sparta in particular. It was the year in which Philip II extended his control over all of Greece except Athens and the Peloponnese. He had been seriously wounded in a Balkan campaign and, recuperating in his palace at Aigai, had plenty of time to work out his moves to take the rest of Greece.

A convenient excuse came with the outbreak of the Fourth Sacred War which, as its name implies, erupted among the states surrounding Delphi. Amphissa, a town lying among the olive groves beneath the heights of Delphi, tried to throw off Macedonian domination. Philip led another army southwards, bypassed Thermopylai, and before the Thebans and Athenians knew it, had come within striking distance of their cities. In the spring of 338 some 32,000 Athenians and Thebans and 1,400 cavalry moved north to halt Philip. Half of this force guarded the Amphissa pass in Phokis, west of Delphi; the other half plugged another gap in the hills about twenty-five kilometres farther north, to hopefully block Philip and his 32,000 Macedonians. But Philip bamboozled the opposing generals with a clever bit of disinformation, surged through the pass and ended up at Naupaktos on the north shore of the Gulf of Corinth, with the Peloponnese just across the water. The defenders were forced to fall back to the north Boiotian plain, precisely where Philip wanted them to be, near the town of Chaironeia.

He arrived to find his enemies lined up across a narrow section of plain a few kilometres wide. The Athenians were on the left; the Achaians, Megarians, Corinthians and other allies in the centre; and the Thebans on the right, as it was their homeland they were defending and thus they were entitled to the position of honour. But against Philip's superb generalship the Athenians deployed mediocre officers at best, and moreover were highly dependent on unreliable mercenaries. Philip placed Alexander, his impetuous and extremely capable eighteen-year-old son, at the head of the Companion cavalry on the right, and opened the action by thrusting forward with his infantry. When the lines clashed the Macedonians carried out a tactical withdrawal, a manoeuvre calling for great skill and discipline. Stratokles, the Athenian general, naively ordered a charge, opening a fatal gap on the right of the Athenian formation. That was the breach that Philip needed. He shot orders to Alexander, whose Companions rushed into the gap, smashing the Boiotian line and wiping out the Theban Sacred Band, which stood its ground to the last man.

Subduing Athens on easy terms – he came as a chastiser, he said, not a conqueror – Philip now headed for the Peloponnese. He received a hero's welcome everywhere except Sparta, which determined to resist him to the end. Besides the ineffectual Kleomenes II, the responsible king was Agis III, the elder son of Archidamos III. Agis kept up a staunchly independent stand when Philip called together representatives of all the other Greek states for a grand conference at Corinth to forge what was called the Greek League. The aim was to pull Greece together for a decisive invasion of the Persian Empire to finally free the Ionian Greeks and bring them at last into the political fold.

The Spartans wanted no part of being the subjects of a half-barbarian monarch, and so their diplomatic isolation was complete. What kings and Ephors alike apparently failed to realize was that the Greek city-state system was finally showing signs of age. The system had suited Sparta fine as long as its aims and ideology helped the city defend the Lakedaimonian homeland and uphold the independence of other Greek states. But when Philip demonstrated that an extensive and centralized state like Macedon could achieve a higher degree of political integration and military power, the writing was on the wall. Philip placed his capstone on the Greek League by styling himself Hegemon, or Leader, of the Greeks. Apart from the Spartans, most Greeks counted themselves lucky to get away with Philip's leniency and willingly let him have the title.

In the summer of 336 Philip II of Macedon, at forty-six, had every right to consider himself one of the luckiest men in the world. Then without warning, an assassin cut him down during his daughter's wedding. The reins of Macedonian power passed to Alexander, a mere twenty years old, who became Alexander III, or the Great.

To consolidate his power among the shocked Greeks, Alexander moved with terrifying speed, force-marching southward through Thessaly and

Boiotia and turning up at Corinth where he got himself confirmed as the new Hegemon of the Greeks and reminded them of their pledge to his father to help subdue Asia. As he had probably calculated, his sudden presence at Corinth intimidated the Greeks enough for him to turn his attention to unfinished military business in what is now Romania, to clear his left flank for the planned Asian invasion. On that campaign a report arose that Alexander had been killed, and the rumour spread through Greece. The Thebans believed it and kicked out the Macedonian garrison. But Alexander, far from dead, led his army on a two-week forced march to Thebes and razed that ancient city to the ground, slaughtering 6,000 people in the process. Thirty thousand more were sold into slavery.

The fall of Thebes was a cold shower for the Greeks. There was no doubt now about who was boss, and how he went about tackling opposition. It became blindingly obvious that the Greek League had degenerated into an instrument held together by raw fear. If Alexander had any hopes of obtaining the moral support of the Greeks for his planned invasion of Persia, he had to abandon them. When he began his ambitious expedition into Asia in 335, he knew he was leaving a good deal of resentment behind in Greece. He appointed a general, Antipatros, to hold the fort at Macedon with 15,000 troops ready to pacify southern Greece should the need arise.

In Sparta, Agis III waited for his chance. In 333, with Alexander absent for more than a year, he made his bid to recover as much of Greek independence as he could. He needed money, of course, and duly received some from a Persian admiral named Pharnabazus (not to be confused with the satrap who had aided Sparta in the Peloponnesian War) who was active in the Aegean Sea. Alexander had just fought and won the battle of Issus (near modern Iskenderun in Turkey), and there were plenty of Greek mercenaries who had fought on the Persian side and were now looking for another job. They found employment with Agis, who sent a force to invade Crete, bringing the ferociously independent Cretans over to his cause and forcing Alexander to detach some of his ships to the Aegean theatre.

Agis' success in Crete encouraged other Peloponnesians to come over to the Spartan side, such as the Achaians and Arkadians. An appeal to Athens for aid fell on deaf ears, as Athens had been completely cowed by Alexander. Megalopolis, too, held out. Agis laid siege to that city with 22,000 Spartans and other allies in 331, defeating the Macedonian general Korrhagos sent to block his way. Antipatros, the Macedonian boss of Greece, was away at the time fighting Thrakian tribes. He had just sent considerable reinforcements to Alexander, and much of the home army was tied down in the Thrakian revolt. On news of the siege of Megalopolis it took Antipatros several months to raise 40,000 troops with which he marched to relieve the siege. In the autumn of 331 or summer of 330 Antipatros threw his phalanx columns against the Spartans, who fought furiously, inflicting heavy casualties on the Macedonians. There in the front line was Agis, who fell grievously wounded. The historian Diodoros of Sicily describes his last stand:

> As he was being carried by his soldiers back to Sparta, he found himself surrounded by the enemy. Despairing of his own life, he ordered the rest to make their escape with all speed and to save themselves for the service of their country, but he himself armed and rising to his knees defended himself, killed some of the enemy and was himself slain by a javelin cast.[4]

Five thousand three hundred Spartans fell at Megalopolis. Fifty leading Spartans were taken as hostage to Macedon, while Sparta was ordered to join the Greek League, giving up under duress its vaunted independence.

## Eudamidas I (331–305)

On Agis III's death the succession in the Eurypontid house passed to his eldest surviving son, Eudamidas I. Pausanias the historian and others describe Eudamidas' twenty-six-year reign as one of peace for Sparta. This is no doubt because the state was quiescent under the Macedonian thumb through compulsory membership in the rubber-stamp Greek League. Though Alexander was now far away conquering as much as he could of Asia, with no-one knowing when or if he would return, few in Greece felt like rocking the boat.

But in Sparta there were those impetuous voices urging another war on the Macedonian suzerains. Eudamidas was aware of them and distrusted them as mere bluster. When asked why he insisted on keeping the peace he replied that he was convinced that the majority of Lakedaimonians wanted it. He was no warmonger. On hearing an orator expound that the wise man is the only good general, he quipped that the speaker could say that because 'he has never been amid the blare of trumpets.' He knew that the Macedonians, especially under the conqueror Alexander, were a tougher proposition than the Persians had ever been. To one critic who urged war he replied that to take on the Macedonians after having fought the Persians in the past would be like 'fighting fifty wolves after overcoming a thousand sheep.'[5]

Sparta desperately needed a rest. The supply of Spartiates now had dwindled to perhaps below four figures. The old rigorous ideals of Lykourgos were now history. Ever since the end of the Peloponnesian War corruption had followed the introduction of money and mobile wealth into Sparta. But there was still a modicum of pride left in the city. A man from Argos remarked to Eudamidas on the matter, accusing the Spartans of abandoning their long-established principles after going abroad. The king replied calmly that even though that might be the case, the man from Argos had become better merely by visiting Sparta. Eudamidas himself seemed to prefer a life of contemplation to fighting. He listened to visiting philosophers and was caustic about some of them. When the elderly Xenokrates came to visit and said he was seeking after virtue, Eudamidas wondered aloud that if the philosopher still hadn't found virtue at his advanced age, would he ever have time to use it if he did?[6]

Alexander the Great died in Babylon in 323 of a fever partly brought on by a bout of binge drinking. At the news mainland Greece reared up in rebellion like a wild horse. There were joyous outpourings in Athens, which only recently had been ordered to worship Alexander as a god – so far had the Macedonian conqueror strayed from his Greek upbringing. The Spartans had treated the order with the contempt it deserved – Damis, an influential Spartan, had deadpanned: 'If Alexander wants to be a god, let him be a god.' Leosthenes, an Athenian general, went to Sparta to recruit mercenaries which he lined up at the old reliable pass of Thermopylai. Antipatros hurried down from Macedon but failed to dislodge the defenders or carry the pass. There was no Ephialtes, it seems, to provide another route.

Sparta under Eudamidas declined to join the defending coalition, despite strident voices calling on him to do so. His decision turned out to be a wise one. The so-called Lamian War was now underway, and a large portion of the late Alexander's forces in Asia were crossing back to Greece to beef up Antipatros. Krateros, one of Alexander's top generals, met the Greek defenders at Krannon in Thessaly in the summer of 321 and routed them.

Antipatros dissolved the shell of the Greek League and turned the whole of Greece into a Macedonian province, what one modern historian has likened to a 'United States of Greece.'[7] The other side of the coin was that, in the words of another leading authority, Antipatros' move 'marked the end of the freedom which the Greeks as a race had enjoyed for more than a thousand years.'[8] The only semi-free city left – and even that in a formal rather than literal sense – was Sparta, which from now was condemned to slowly sink into backwater status, from which it has only partly recovered today.

# Chapter 10

# The Hooded Flame

**Areus I to Leonidas II (including Kleombrotos II)**
**Archidamos IV and Eudamidas II**

## Areus I (309–265) to Leonidas II (254–236), including Kleombrotos II (242–241)

Sparta at the end of the fourth century was like a tired boxer far past his prime, sullenly accepting forced retirement but never abandoning a spark of hope of a comeback. After Alexander the Macedonians could never fully keep their Greek subjects quiet. But neither were the Macedonians united in their purpose. Two of Alexander's generals, Antigonos and Kassandros, vied for influence in the Greek heartland. In 307 Antigonos' son Demetrios of Phaleron occupied Athens and ruled as a benevolent dictator until he tried to implement his vision of adding Sparta to his domains.

The curiously invisible Kleomenes II had died in 309, leaving two sons (an eldest son named Akrotatos had predeceased him). The stage was thus set for a struggle for the Agiad throne between Kleomenes' second son Kleonymos and his grandson Areus, the son of Akrotatos. The Gerousia, called on to arbitrate the dispute, decided that Kleonymos was too emotionally unstable and a violent man to boot – could this have been another sign of a presumed mental deficiency running through this section of the Agiad line since Agesipolis II? The Gerousia's accolade fell on Areus, who began his reign as Areus I. Kleonymos never forgave the Gerousia for this, even though the senators tried to mollify him with various honours, including the right to lead the army. It wasn't enough. From that time Kleonymos became a sworn foe of Sparta; Pausanias the historian says that 'committed many hostile acts against his fatherland,' without specifying them.[1]

Areus saw his chance to revive Spartan power against the dominant Macedonians, whose garrisons throughout Greece were earning them contempt. In 280 he tested the mettle of his army by attacking and plundering the town of Kirrha on the north shore of the Gulf of Corinth on a pretext having to do with the old quarrel of who controlled nearby Delphi. Observing the sack of Kirrha were some hardy Aitolian shepherds on the surrounding mountainsides. The shepherds called others, and before long they had formed into a body of about 500 who threw themselves on Areus' troops, killing a great many of them. The discomfiture deprived Sparta of more manpower just at the time it needed strength to raise its head against Macedon.

Meanwhile the pretender Kleonymos had not been idle. For about twenty years he made a living as a soldier of fortune in Italy. There he had got to know Pyrrhos I, the King of Epiros in northwest Greece, who was also campaigning there. He talked Pyrrhos into invading Lakedaimon to unseat Areus. The Epirote king was an excitable and superficial character, believing himself to be a conqueror of the calibre of a Philip or Alexander. He might have been a good campaigner but lacked patience and staying power. When Kleonymos approached him in 272, Pyrrhos had got himself into something of a mess in Macedon, where he tried unsuccessfully to topple the Macedonian king, Antigonos II Gonatas. Leaving many soldiers dead in Macedon, Pyrrhos cheerfully marched south, gathering forces from anti-Spartan states as he went. Smoothing his way also were those states who longed to throw off Macedonian rule, such as Elis and Achaia. Megalopolis and Messenia, too, boosted his ranks.

There could have been personal motives behind Kleonymos' treachery. It was rumoured that Areus' son Akrotatos was having an affair with Kleonymos' attractive wife Chilonis. Pyrrhos had already lulled the Spartans into a false sense of security by giving out that he had come to free the Peloponnese from the Macedonians. One evening Pyrrhos, accompanied by several elephants he had brought from Italy, reached the outskirts of Sparta. Kleonymos was all for bursting into the city at once but Pyrrhos preferred to wait until the morning, when his men were rested. The delay was fatal. During the night the Spartan women took matters in hand and upheld their formidable reputation. Scoffing at suggestions that they be evacuated, they took tools out of the men's hands and dug a circle of trenches, planting wagons on the earthworks up to their axles as a barrier. The men, they said, needed to rest before the battle to come.

Some of the 'men' were hardly old enough to merit the term. Areus at the time was in Crete with many soldiers on a mercenary mission – the need for money was always acute – and was hardly in a position to help. When day broke Pyrrhos sent his men against the Spartan defences and made a breach. Then Akrotatos – the royal youth accused of seducing Kleonymos' wife – with a flying column sped to the breach and sealed it. Fighting continued through the day and into the next, with the Spartan women and boys still holding. The women acted as rear-echelon units behind the lines, bringing up weapons, food and water. At the end of each day the women would calmly go home to bake the bread. On the second day a Corinthian unit managed to get through to boost the Spartan defence and enable it to hold out until Areus returned from Crete.

When Pyrrhos' third assault failed he gave up. Perseverance was never his strong suit. By now Areus had hurried back from Crete in time for him to pursue Pyrrhos northwards past Mantineia to Argos, where Pyrrhos found not only Areus' Spartans but also Antigonos Gonatas' Macedonians waiting for him. Pyrrhos took refuge in Argos but an angry Argive woman on a roof-top proved to be his undoing. She threw a roof tile at him, which stunned him long enough for a Macedonian soldier to slice his head off. What happened to Kleonymos is not recorded, but the Spartans had plenty of cause to be proud of their martial traditions. The old Spartan virtues, among men and women alike, had given their city another half-century's reprieve.

Greece around 270, in the words of a noted authority on the period, gives the impression of 'endless and meaningless collisions between self-seeking adventurers, who had no aim but their own aggrandizement.'[2] This situation arose in part because Macedon proved unable to keep the lid on Greece for very long. It had been more than a half century since Alexander the Great's death and most of his marshals had now left the scene as well, leaving to their sons and successors the increasingly difficult task of trying to keep the Macedonian empire together. Growing anarchy among the Greek states stymied economic development and stunted intellectual and cultural pursuits.

With Pyrrhos out of the way Antigonos II Gonatas of Macedon was quick to assert control of Argos and Megalopolis as a check on the revived ambitions of Sparta. He also secured the vital Isthmus of Corinth. More-over, Antigonos was keeping a wary eye on Ptolemy II of Egypt, the son of one of Alexander's generals, who feared Macedon's expansion of sea power in the eastern Mediterranean. It was this Ptolemy who appeared as a champion of Sparta and Athens. In 267 he brought them together in common cause for the first time since the great days of the Persian Wars. Areus accepted without hesitation, motivated not only by dreams of renewed Spartan glory but also by the money that he hoped to obtain from Ptolemy's Egyptian coffers. An Athenian politician named Chremonides voted for a revolt against Macedonian rule.

The Chremonidean War, named after its instigator, was a sorry affair from start to finish. Sparta and Athens, though both were eager to bring back an echo of their glory days, had to depend on Ptolemy's navy, which did not prove up to the responsibility placed on it. The plan was for the Egyptian fleet commander, Patroklos, to land on the Corinthian coast and help Areus' Spartan force detour around the Isthmus and engage Antigonos Gonatas near Athens. Patroklos, either out of timidity or on secret orders from Ptolemy, failed to make the landing. In 265, after two years of manoeuvring, Areus, 'with every available man of the Lakedaimonians,' was compelled to attempt a breach of the strong Macedonian line at the Isthmus.[3] It was a mad gamble which Areus duly lost, paying for it with his life.

Areus' death marked the end of Sparta as a leading power in Greece. With Sparta temporarily knocked out, Antigonos Gonatas was able to bring Athens to heel, installing a ten-year army of occupation in the city. From then on Athens sank into the status of a quiet university town, to remain so for the next thousand years under the Roman and Byzantine empires. In Sparta Areus I was succeeded by his son Akrotatos as Agiad king. Akrotatos, young and spirited, had an independence of mind which might have stood him in good stead in an earlier age, but made little sense in the time of Sparta's prostration under superior powers. Plutarch reports him as a youth as having clashed with his father on various moral issues, asserting that 'what is just is best for both a private citizen and a ruler.'[4] Not for him was the distinction between private and public morality. Akrotatos tested his independence in 362, three years into his reign, with an incautious attack on Megalopolis. The attack was decisively repulsed, and Akrotatos killed. The body of yet another Spartan king was carried home.

The structural weakness, as it were, of the Agiad house did not improve. Akrotatos left behind a wife well advanced in pregnancy, who gave birth to a boy who took the throne as Areus II. When he was eight years old he died of disease. The succession then fell on the nearest kinsman, Kleomenes II's grandson Leonidas, who took the title Leonidas II; though he was getting on in years and in character the very antithesis of his earlier illustrious namesake. The succession was, of course, disputed, in this case by Leonidas' son-in-law Kleombrotos, who had the backing of powerful factions. A number of negative rumours about Leonidas began to swirl around in the city, such as a story that as a boy he had 'vowed to ruin Sparta.'[5] The basis of such a tale is hard to assess. As an Agiad he could have been expected to share that house's traditional dislike of what was left of the aristocracy. According to the rumour he had made the vow to his father Kleonymos, the second son of Kleomenes II. It would make sense if we followed our previous line of speculation that Kleomenes was mentally unfit to rule in fact rather than in name, and as a result had earned the contempt of the Spartan elite for the Agiad line.

Kleombrotos didn't give up his scheming. The story of young Leonidas' alleged rash vow gained wide credence. Plutarch pronounced Leonidas 'not particularly suitable to his people.' He had spent some years among the luxuries of Persia – we are not sure why. Very likely, as a member of the Agiad house who had normally no expectation of becoming king, he had decided to live it up where he could. Like many a Spartan before him, Leonidas was dazzled by the elaborate delights of Oriental courts, especially among those of Alexander's old generals who had set themselves up as kings in their own right to ape the Asians. He took a Persian wife and had two children with her, but he appears to have abused her to the point at which she left him. He returned to Sparta, where his dissolute habits tarnished his image. His unpopularity grew when his young co-king Agis IV got the Apella to approve a radical programme of economic and social reform (see Agis IV below).

The wave of support for Agis forced Leonidas into exile in Arkadia. Formally deposed by the government, he was replaced by Kleombrotos. But Kleombrotos II enjoyed his royal status for less than a year. Such were the confusing processes of Spartan politics that before a year had passed the chief anti-Leonidas ephor was rotated out of office and Leonidas reinstated with the agreement of Agis. Meanwhile, misrule by the Ephors had heated popular discontent to fever pitch. Leonidas stirred up the Ephors and Apella against Kleombrotos and Agis, who had to seek sanctuary in temples (see Agis IV below). Leonidas, of course, had a score to settle with Kleombrotos. He called on him in the Temple of Poseidon, planning to have him murdered. There he upbraided Kleombrotos for usurping the Agiad throne in an underhand manner. Chilonis, Kleombrotos' wife and Leonidas' daughter, had joined him in the sanctuary. Plutarch paints a touching picture of Chilonis, unkempt and in dirty clothes, sitting embracing her husband with her two young children, eyeing her accusing father.

'I condoled with you in your banishment,' Plutarch reports her as telling Leonidas, 'and now you are restored, must I still remain in grief and misery?' She knew she was arguing for her husband's life. In scenes reminiscent of a Euripidean tragedy, Chilonis chided her father in dramatic terms for even considering killing his son-in-law just to keep his throne. When she finished, she 'rested her face on her husband's head, and looked round with her weeping eyes on those who stood before her.'

Chilonis' tears saved Kleombrotos' life. Leonidas ordered him banished from Sparta, but asked Chilonis to stay with her father in return for his sparing her husband's life. The 'excellent woman' would have none of it. 'She rose up immediately, and taking one of her children in her arms, gave the other to her husband; and making reverence to the altar of the goddess, went out and followed him.'[6]

Leonidas now took his revenge in earnest. Shortly after regaining the throne he had Agis murdered in the foulest circumstances (see Agis IV below). Yet when he died in 236 he left behind a son who was destined to vindicate the idealism of Agis, revive the power and influence of the Agiad house in ways no-one could have foreseen, and bring about its demise in a blaze of activity.

## Archidamos IV (305–275) and Eudamidas II (275–244)

When the mild-mannered Eudamidas I died in 305, his son succeeded him as Archidamos IV of the Eurypontids. In those years the Agiad house was consumed in a dispute over succession issues that absorbed the attention of Areus I. Therefore it fell to Archidamos to try and stem a determined attempt by the Macedonians under Demetrios Poliorketes (the Besieger) to subdue the entire Peloponnese including Sparta. Archidamos met Demetrios on the old battleground of Mantineia, failed to halt his advance and lost 500 prisoners, 200 of whom were slaughtered. When Demetrios invaded Lakedaimon the Spartans were in the process of building the first city wall in their history. Far gone were the days when a Spartan's spear-throw was his best defence. The walls were still incomplete, and the city quite ill-defended, when an emergency in Asia compelled Demetrios to suddenly pull his forces out.

Little is known about the rest of Archidamos' reign. His wife Archidamia was wealthy, and no doubt this contributed somewhat to oiling the wheels of rule. Foreign and military policy was in the capable hands of his Agiad co-king Areus I. On Archidamos' death in 275 he was succeeded by his son Eudamidas II, of whom, again, very little has been written. Pausanias ends his account of the Agiad kings with Eudamidas, remarking only that during his thirty-one-year reign Sparta knew peace. That probably meant in practical terms that Sparta was recuperating from its hard knocks at Macedonian hands. Eudamidas II overlapped the brief Agiad reigns of Akrotatos and Areus II, ending in the middle of that of Leonidas II.

In the middle of the third century it appeared that one by one, the great powers of Greece had had their day. Athens' greatness had collapsed with the end of the Peloponnesian War in 404. The subsequent Spartan ascendancy had fallen abruptly with the death of the wide-ranging Agesilaos II. Then the battle of Leuktra had propelled Thebes to top-dog status before that city knuckled under to the overwhelming power of Macedon. Now Macedonian power in Greece was crumbling. Which new Greek power would now rise as the arbiter of the mainland's fortunes?

The answer came in the person of a nobly-born, handsome and serious youth from the north Peloponnesian town of Sikyon named Aratos. Sikyon had maintained its Dorian character and institutions through the centuries, and some of this tradition survived in Aratos. As a boy he had narrowly escaped being murdered along with his father in a bloody coup d'etat. Aratos grew to maturity in Argos, where his tall stature, athletic prowess, sober speech and handsome face drew notice in all the right places. Yet inside him, ignited probably by the frightening experience of his childhood, there burned an implacable hatred for dictators of any sort. In 251 he hatched a plan to topple Nikokles, the tyrant of his home town. Young as he was, his plot was a clever one. One night Aratos and his confederates scaled the walls of Sikyon on shaky ladders, the sound of the climb covered by the barking of dogs. Once inside the city they killed the mercenary guards. Nikokles fled and the grateful crowd burned his house in a conflagration 'visible as far as Corinth.'[7]

Aratos' next move was to enrol Sikyon in the Achaian League, the up-and-coming power in Greece. So far nothing much had been heard from Achaia, which comprised a string of towns on the north Peloponnesian coast including Patrai and Aigion. These communities had never bonded together into a unified political entity. They had been a passive stage across which Greek armies marched back and forth over the centuries. The Achaians claimed to be descendants of the Achaians of Agamemnon, driven from the lands around Mykenai by the Dorians. Now, with the other states of Greece worn out and the Macedonian presence still considerable, the Achaian League took up the banner of leadership.

Aratos soon got himself elected *strategos*, or general-in-chief, of the Achaian League. For the admiring Plutarch it was an example of 'how Greek prowess was invincible, whenever it enjoyed good order, discipline, and a sensible leader.'[8] Aratos' character suited him for his larger responsibilities in ridding Greece of autocrats, though it was tempered with a cautiousness that could sometimes be excessive. His enemies claimed that he was also a highly nervous man, prone to emptying his bowels before a battle; if that is true, then his respectable military career in the face of such a disability would argue for exceptional determination. Be that as it may, Aratos took his successes modestly and was extremely popular with the Achaians.

Antigonos Gonatas, naturally, eyed this Peloponnesian newcomer warily. One of his first counter-moves was to fortify the Acrocorinth, the citadel of Corinth that soars 2,000 feet just southwest of the city and Isthmus. The Acrocorinth was the key to controlling the sole land passage from the Peloponnese to the rest of Greece. Operating from inside Corinth, Aratos got together a small guerrilla force that captured the Acrocorinth in a spectacular night assault in 243. Aratos then set about liberating the Peloponnesian towns from their tyrants, later moving on the wild tribes of Aitolia in the northwest. Aratos' successes drew the attention of Sparta, which yet again saw the chance to strike a blow against the despised Macedonians.

# Chapter 11

# The Reformers

Agis IV
Eudamidas III and Archidamos V
Kleomenes III
Eukleidas

## Agis IV (244–241)

When Eudamidas II died in 244 he was succeeded by his son Agis, who, as Agis IV, would inaugurate an unexpected new era in the Spartan kingship, diverting its energies from conquest and preserving the status quo into something resembling social revolution. Sixth in line of the Eurypontid house after the activist Agesilaos II, Agis IV entertained similar dreams of glory and had the ability to put them into action, but in an entirely different political direction.

Sparta in the middle of the third century was vastly different city from what it had been a hundred years before. Plutarch places the start of the decline in 404, when Sparta prostrated Athens and seized its silver and gold reserves.[1] As long as Sparta preserved the land-ownership system enacted by Lykourgos in the eighth century, social stability was assured. But at some point an arrogant Ephor named Epitadeus had quarrelled with his son, and to keep from having to bequeath his property to his son he enacted a decree that any Spartan had the right to sell his holdings to whomever he wished. The law triggered a frenzy of property acquisitions by the rich, who thus became richer, while the number of landless exploded. In consequence the elite citizenry represented by the Spartiates class shrank rapidly. At Agis' accession it numbered no more than about 700, of whom only about 100 actually owned any land or estate. The rest had become disfranchised to Inferior status or lower, not far above the *perioikoi* or Helots, whose ranks were constantly swelling as the status boundaries shifted downwards. The top layer of the Spartan elite had maintained its position by an influx of wealth gained often by dishonest means and flaunted selfishly and provocatively.

The luxury and decadence of a few households stood in stark contrast to the rest of the population, among whom thoughts of revolt simmered ever more intensely.

As in all ages when a civilization is on the decline, thinkers began spinning radical social theories. In the third century the school of Sceptics, for example, gave a philosophical tint to the general social and political disillusionment by proclaiming that nothing could ever really be known. Fascinating characters such as Diogenes the Cynic were all for casting off the artifices of civilization and returning to nature. He had a large following. The outer world being a disappointment, the inner world was now sought. Epikouros, the founder of the Epicurean school, urged a withdrawal from worldly affairs and an inward preoccupation with the contemplative life. The Stoics tried to find a basic virtue in spare living and indifference to material goods and power. In the religious sphere the old faith in the Olympian gods had been corrupted by exposure to Oriental deities. The Macedonians attempted to substitute king-worship, but this was abhorrent to the Greeks. Centuries of politics and its violent component, war, had apparently not done much to improve the Greeks' destiny. Therefore it followed that something must be wrong with the society itself. It fell to Sparta, where the contrast between rich and poor was most pronounced, to start the ancient Greek experiment in social revolution.

Part of the reason why the chronicle of Sparta's kings of both houses between about 370 and 240 is so lean of detail, and why with few exceptions they ceased to play important roles in war or politics, is that the old Spartan virtues were abandoned under the growing economic corruption and inequality. The days when a king of either house would automatically march abroad to do his duty, whether he was inclined to do so or not (such as Pleistoanax or Agesipolis I), were over. The kings of the later fourth and earlier third centuries – if they reigned long enough – tended to be stay-at-homes either out of mental incapacity (Kleomenes II, perhaps) or philosophical discouragement. Agis III and Areus I, it is true, fought valiantly, but their efforts were exceptions to the general rule. Above all, belonging to the ceremonial top layer of Spartiates, they seemed oblivious of the worsening social situation around them.

The old, austere standards of Lykourgos were very much on Agis' mind as he began to sound out the other elite young men of Sparta and found them, too, conscience-stricken at the economic inequality around them and idealistically committed to some action. He could have been influenced by the communist-type theories then in vogue among some schools of philosophy.[2] In the public squares Agis made no secret of his disgust with the state of the city. He despised his Agiad co-king, Leonidas II, who flaunted his decadence while retaining the allegiance of older Spartiates clinging to the status quo. Some in Sparta may have noted that the old ideological difference between the 'democratic' Agiad house and 'conservative' Eurypontid house had now been stood on its head: it was the Eurypontid Agis who was now the man of the people, and far more fervently than any Agiad king had been.

Agis had unexpected success in canvassing his friends. One who pledged to help him was Lysandros the son of Libys, a direct descendant of the Lysandros who had defeated Athens more than a century and a half before. Another was Mandroklidas, an influential man with a talent for organization. Of course, there were the inevitable questionable adherents motivated more by hoped-for power and wealth in the expected new order than by any concern for the poor. One of these was Agesilaos, his uncle from his mother Agesistrata's side, talked into joining the club by his son Hippomedon, of proven courage in battle – yet himself hoping to get his many debts cancelled by a regime change.

Viewing this mixed bag, Agis tried to get his mother 'on side'. At first Agesistrata was against the whole idea. She saw little sense in overturning the established order for an ideal, an operation with huge prospects of failure for such a young and inexperienced king as her son was. But Agis must have been a persuasive talker, for she slowly began to change her mind. 'I can't pretend to rival other kings in riches,' Agis told Agesistrata, in a not-so-veiled reference to his co-king Leonidas II, 'but if I can restore to the Spartans their former equality I'll be a great king.' Not many mothers would be able to resist such noble sentiments from a son. Agesistrata could have had a vision of the Eurypontid house attaining some of its old glory untainted by material wealth. She in turn converted her mother Archidamia, the wealthy widow of Archidamos IV, and both together spread the message among the other women of Spartan society.

The women of Sparta had lost nothing of their inner strength and influence over the centuries. But they used this influence overwhelmingly in support of the men, as witnessed by their brave efforts in the siege of Sparta by Pyrrhos in 272. Influential Spartiates would routinely confer with their wives on weighty political issues and seek their advice. Moreover, it was the women of the Spartiates who managed the money, and thus they had a vested interest in keeping things as they were. Few upper-class women, it turned out, were willing to part with their luxuries and status as Agesistrata and Archidamia were urging, and the complaints reached the ears of Leonidas.

By now Agis knew that a majority of Spartans and other Lakedaimonians were with him, but also that Leonidas was going to be a formidable adversary. Agis scored an early triumph by securing the election of Lysandros as Ephor. Lysandros then released Agis' political manifesto: first, a return to the rules and polity of Lykourgos; second, a general amnesty of debts (perhaps thanks to Hippomedon's influence); third, all land between Mount Taygetos and the Eurotas River up to Pellana and Sellasia in the north to be seized, divided into 4,500 equal lots and distributed among the native-born Spartan citizenry; and fourth, the rest of Lakedaimon to be divided into 15,000 allotments for those *perioikoi* and other country-dwellers who could furnish hoplites for the Spartan army.

It was as radical as anything ever seen in Greece, not to mention Sparta, and at once came up against howls of outrage from the old men in the Gerousia. Lysandros countered this by convening the Apella, where he proclaimed that Agis 'would not allow the majesty of Sparta to remain in contempt to gratify a few rich men.'[3] He and other orators reminded the Apella of old oracles warning the Spartans of the dangers of the love of money. A more recent oracle was recruited as urging that Sparta return to the pure days of Lykourgos. Agis himself then rose and promised to give up his landholdings and contribute a large sum of money from his own purse for the cause of social reform. He added that his mother and grandmother were fully behind him. The Apella cheered him to the rafters. Here at last was a king worthy of the name!

Leonidas listened to all this with growing alarm. His great fear was that Agis' cause would engulf himself and the Agiad house by forcing them to contribute their own riches now that Agis had set the noble example. Rising to speak, he seized on the reference to Lykourgos to make his own point. Plutarch reports the exchange this way:

'Was not Lykourgos a wise man and lover of his country?' Leonidas asked, as the whole Apella listened attentively.

'Yes, he was,' Agis said.

'Then when did he ever cancel debts or admit foreigners to citizenship, since he wanted to clear the city of all foreigners?'

Agis must have smiled bitterly at this. He hit back by disparaging Leonidas as one who had taken a Persian wife and spent much time in the East, and who therefore was the last person qualified to invoke Lykourgos' achievements.

Lykourgos took away debts and loans by taking away money itself [Agis said]. He objected to people of foreign ways in case they infected the city with their love of riches ... How can you blame us for wanting to cut off superfluity and luxury? All the harmony and order of our city have been destroyed.[4]

That was the signal for a face-off between the rich and the rest in Sparta. The former adhered to Leonidas, the latter to Agis. Though massively outnumbered in society, the former managed to get the barest majority in the Gerousia to reject Agis' plan. Lysandros took his revenge on the Leonidists by a crude but effective scheme. Every nine years, Plutarch reports, it was the custom of the Ephors to pick a moonless and cloudless night and sit and gaze at the stars. They would be on the lookout for a shooting star, and if they saw one they would interpret it as a sign that one of the kings had done something wrong and deserved suspension from office unless an oracle from Delphi or Olympia decreed otherwise.

Plutarch's assertion is eyebrow-raising, as on most clear nights in Greece, especially in the summer, shooting stars are common. Anyone watching the sky for any length of time can hardly miss one. Did that mean that every nine years one of Sparta's kings would have had to be booted out? The historical record, of course, does not support this, even assuming that Delphi could intervene each time. The rule might explain a few otherwise mysterious reign endings such as that of Agesipolis II. Most likely Plutarch's narrative misses out some detail. To make it more believable, there would have had to be some pre-existing royal issue at stake. Any rate, one of those nights duly fell in the middle of the crisis, and Lysandros duly reported that indeed the Ephors had seen a shooting star. The portent was seen as a reference to Leonidas' past abuse of his Persian wife. Lysandros prevailed on Kleombrotos to take Leonidas' place, and Leonidas fled, being formally deposed *in absentia* (see Leonidas II above).

Before the year was out, however, a new set of Ephors was rotated into office. These were more sympathetic to Leonidas than Lysandros and his followers had been. Lysandros perceived the potential danger he was in and suggested to Agis that he approach Kleombrotos to form a common front to keep the state together. The approach was successful; neither king looked favourably on the power of the Ephors. The clincher was a revival of the old rule that the Ephors were officially entitled to decide matters only when the two kings differed over an issue: when the kings were in agreement, the Ephors were compelled to go along with them. As a theoretical analysis of the royal powers it was not inaccurate, though everyone knew it had been ignored more than it had been observed. At any rate, it offered a face-saving way out for both factions.

In a public show of unity Agis and Kleombrotos walked together to the centre of the city, where they personally ushered the Ephors out of their seats and put others in their place. It's not clear whether Kleombrotos actually had come round to the radical ideas of Agis or had little choice, seeing that his Agiad house was at a disadvantage. Probably his motive was his personal hatred of Leonidas. When the Ephorate was replaced a number of young Spartans were armed to form a sort of people's militia. Some of Agis' more extreme followers plotted to assassinate Leonidas on his way into exile, but Agis scotched the plot in time.

One of the plotters had been Agis' uncle, the ex-Ephor Agesilaos. His motives in joining Agis' movement, as we have seen, were not of the purest. He apparently hoped that by doing away with Leonidas he might trigger a bout of unrest that would put the planned land redistribution on hold. 'While he gladly joined in the design to be quit of his debts,' writes Plutarch, 'he was not at all willing to part with his land.' Using the specious argument that the rich would be more willing to give up their lands if their debts were cancelled first, Agesilaos talked the authorities into organizing a great bonfire of debt documents in the central square. As the flames leaped upwards and the creditors grumbled, Agesilaos understandably exulted that he had never before seen 'so bright and pure a flame.'

The theatrics over with, Agis and the people prepared to put into effect the great land redistribution while Agesilaos dragged his feet, using one excuse after the other. At this point the outside world intervened. Aratos, the chief of the Achaian League, appealed to the Spartan Ephors for forces to help him repel a threatened attack on the Peloponnese by the Aitolians. As Sparta and the Achaians were bound by a mutual aid treaty, Agis had little choice but to lead the expedition. Frustrated as he might feel at leaving his labours hardly begun, he was pleased at the calibre of his soldiers, most of them poor but young Spartans happy to be freed from the burden of family debt and looking on their young king – perhaps the youngest man in the army – as a messiah. Those who watched the force marching in impeccable formation through the Peloponnese marvelled also at the sight of Agis who shared all the men's duties and dressed as simply.

Agis joined Aratos at Corinth. Aratos was uncertain of what to do. The Aitolians had massed north of the Isthmus, ready to force passage. But it was now well into autumn and many of the Achaian soldiers were anxious to return home to help with the harvest. Agis was all for attacking the enemy at once, but deferred to Aratos as the older and presumably wiser commander. Aratos decided against attacking, and so Agis marched his men back to Sparta, his honourable duty done. Aratos' hesitation has never been satisfactorily explained. Plutarch casts doubt on the harvest excuse. Did Aratos perhaps mistrust Agis, or did he simply lose his nerve in the way he was sometimes inclined to do? As for the Aitolians, they contented themselves with plundering a Peloponnesian town or two, and went home for the winter.

Agis returned to Sparta to find a city seething with discontent under the harsh economic measures his uncle Agesilaos had foisted on the people. Knowing he was despised by large numbers of people, Agesilaos kept an armed bodyguard about him. By now he made a point of contemptuously ignoring Kleombrotos, while maintaining outwardly polite relations with Agis simply because he was family. Shortly after Agis' return the people could take no more. The details of what happened are very vague. What appears to have been a wave of popular discontent ousted Agesilaos from office; his son Hippomedon had to literally tear him from the clutches of the mob who were intent on lynching him, and spirited him out of Sparta. Leonidas II was duly brought back and reinstated on the Agiad throne.

If Agis hoped that popular fury would be assuaged by Agesilaos' flight, he was mistaken. Passions were too high. Agis soon found that he, too, was in danger from the mob and with Kleombrotos sought sanctuary in temples. Kleombrotos and his young family, as we have seen, narrowly escaped death at the hands of Leonidas, who now turned to cultivating Agis, still holed up in the Temple of the Brazen House. Agis quite rightly refused to come out except to visit the nearby baths with three supposedly trusted friends. One of them, an Ephor named Amphares, was secretly in league with Leonidas, and moreover had borrowed a lot of valuable household items from Agesistrata, Agis' mother, without the slightest intention of giving them back. That was because he plotted to eliminate the whole family.

One day as Agis was returning from the baths Amphares accosted him in a hostile manner, ordering him to go before the Ephors 'to answer for [his] misdemeanours.' Before Agis could react, another of the three supposed friends, a powerfully-built character named Demochares, immobilized him by throwing his cloak around the king's neck and literally dragging him to the prison as the others kicked him from behind. A posse of armed guards had been stationed around the prison, where the Ephors were waiting along with those members of the Gerousia known to oppose Agis. Once Agis was before them he was ordered to give an account of himself.

The king, relates Plutarch, smiled bitterly. Amphares advised him it would be better to weep, considering what was in store for him. Agis spoke calmly, insisting that he had only wished to govern according to the rules laid down of old by Lykourgos. 'Do you repent of your rashness?' one Ephor demanded.

'Even though I might suffer the heaviest penalty, I can never repent of so glorious and just a design,' Agis replied.

The penalty, of course, was death. Night had now fallen, and Agis was taken to a sinister place called the Dechas, the room in the prison where condemned criminals were hanged. Even then, such was the respect accorded to Agis by great numbers of people that the law enforcement officers and soldiers under them hesitated to lay hands on him, 'believing it an illegal and wicked act to lay hands on a king.' The thuggish Demochares, shouting a string of curses, personally seized hold of Agis and pushed him into the dreaded room.

By now news of Agis' arrest had spread throughout Sparta, and a crowd of supporters had gathered outside the prison with torches demanding that the king be given a fair hearing before the people. Among them were Agesistrata and Archidamia. The Ephors, fearing that the king might be taken out of their hands, decided to execute him at once. At this, one of the law enforcement officers broke down and wept. In terms similar to those of Christ three centuries later, Agis turned to the sobbing man. 'Friend,' he said, 'don't cry for me, an innocent man who dies by the lawless acts of evil men. My condition is much better than theirs.' Then, not showing the slightest fear, 'he offered his neck to the noose.' He was not yet in his mid-twenties.

After the deed was done Amphares went to the prison gate where he found the king's mother Agesistrata anxious for news. The woman was under the impression that Amphares was still her son's friend. Raising her up from where she had fallen at his knees, he led her and Archidamia inside. Amphares ordered the gate locked behind them.

Archidamia, the venerable royal grandmother, was despatched at once. Agesistrata in her turn was led into the Dechas. The sight that met her was her mother hanging dead from the noose and her son lying dead on the ground. Wordlessly, as befitted a Spartan queen, she helped the law enforcement men take down Archidamia's frail body, covered it with a robe, and laid it by the body of Agis. 'Oh, my son,' she said, caressing and kissing Agis' face, 'it was your mercy and goodness that were too great that brought us to this fate.'

'Since you approve of your son's actions,' Amphares broke in roughly, 'then it's only fitting you share his reward.'

Agesistrata hardly expected anything else from such men. She calmly rose up and took her place under the noose. 'I pray this may redound to the good of Sparta,' she said.

The three bodies were placed on public view, and such was the public revulsion and anger that Leonidas and Amphares became the most hated men in Sparta. Yet no-one dared rise against them. 'So wicked and barbarous an act,' writes Plutarch, 'had never been committed in Sparta since first the Dorians inhabited the Peloponnese.'[5] With the people duly cowed, Agis' remaining vocal supporters fled into exile. For the next dozen years Sparta would fall back into the old order. Yet the memory of Agis IV would live on and not least in the Eurypontid house, which would pick up the torch that Agis had dropped.

### Eudamidas III (241–228) and Archidamos V (228–227)

Agis IV died young, but not too young to have left a son, who succeeded him as Eudamidas III. The new king's thirteen-year reign was unremark-able, which is hardly surprising as the judicial assassination of his father, grandmother and great-grandmother proved a shock to the Spartan system that benumbed the society from top to bottom. As Eudamidas was an infant king under guardianship, the royal decision-making was left to Leonidas. The record shows that when Eudamidas reached maturity he was married, though there appear to have been no children.

The real action in Greece was taking place elsewhere, and the protago-nist was Aratos, who now set his sights on capturing Athens, more for the prestige of the place than out of any sober strategic consideration. In 239 the Macedonian king Antigonos II Gonatas died, to be succeeded by his son Demetrios II, who reigned ten years. When Demetrios died the Athenians made a successful bid for liberty, helped by Aratos who was sick at the time and had to be carried to Athens in a litter. The Macedonian garrison in Athens was bribed to leave. While at Athens Aratos received an invitation from the Argive leader Aristomachos to help him invade Lakonia. Aratos at first declined, but gave way after Aristomachos insisted. Nonetheless, he distrusted Aristomachos' motives and when he came on the Spartan army at Pallantion he advised against an attack. For this he came under strong criticism at home, but was nonetheless re-elected general-in-chief of the Achaian League.

While all this was going on, Eudamidas III died of an unknown cause and the Eurypontid throne passed to Agis IV's brother Archidamos, who became Archidamos V. During his nephew's reign he had lived outside Sparta, fearful of the faction that had killed his brother. By 228 politics had changed. Machinations by Aratos had weakened the Ephors as part of a softening-up process for a hoped-for conquest of Lakedaimon. Besides, in 236 the Agiad throne passed to Leonidas II's son Kleomenes III, who was as different from his father as day is to night. Kleomenes made no secret of his social concerns, and is believed to have helped secure Archidamos' recall. But hardly had Archidamos V enjoyed a year of rule than he was assassinated, probably by the thuggish party that had done away with Agis IV, who feared the possibility of a Eurypontid vendetta against them.

Few, if any, in Sparta would have realized it at the time, but the death of Archidamos V marked the end of the 900-year Eurypontid royal blood-line. He was the twenty-eighth Eurypontid in direct descent from the semi-mythical Prokles. The house had produced kings of varying ability and visibility, from Charillos and Theopompos through Demaratos and Agesilaos II to Agis IV. Those of the Eurypontid kings who made their mark did so on the conservative side, upholding the Ephors and championing a muscular foreign policy. With shaky hindsight, though, we can detect a trend towards greater personal assertiveness and statesmanship in the Eurypontid house starting with Archidamos II, who foresaw the destructiveness of the Peloponnesian War and tried to avert it, and his nephew Agesilaos II, who put his interventionist idealism to use wherever he could in the Greek world. Then, after a couple of centuries of quiescence in both houses, came Agis IV who all-too-briefly but effectively redefined the Eurypontid house just before its extinction.

## Kleomenes III (236–222) and Eukleidas (227–222)

Given the unshakeable togetherness of the two royal houses of Sparta over nearly 900 years, it seems fitting that both would fizzle out at approximately the same time. When the life of the luckless young Archidamos V was snuffed out along with the Eurypontids in 227, it fell to the twenty-ninth linear member of the Agiads, Kleomenes III, who had been reigning for nine years, to take up the burden not only of Spartan royalty but of the revolutionary movement it had lately championed. Some commentators have likened Agis IV and Kleomenes III to the Gracchus brothers of the Roman Republic, the one taking up the torch of popular liberty from the other and eventually suffering his fate.

Kleomenes, the son of Leonidas II, was a teenager during the horrific events surrounding the murder of Agis IV. To tie up the resulting dynastic loose ends Leonidas II ordered Kleomenes to marry Agis' young widow Agiatis. Leonidas' motive was not only to get the Agiad house 'on side' but also to get his hands on Agiatis' considerable estate. Agiatis herself was, in Plutarch's description, 'the most youthful and beautiful woman in all Greece,' and highly-regarded in her public and private life. The teenaged Kleomenes thus became not only Agiatis' second husband but also the stepfather of the infant Eudamidas III of the Eurypontid house, in what was perhaps the most curious domestic arrangement Spartan royalty had ever experienced.

Kleomenes' naturally sensitive and generous character enabled the unusual marriage to work. He had great regard for the late Agis (though he must have kept it secret) and believed that by taking care of his widow he could honour his memory. Agiatis herself returned the appreciation, and she would spend time explaining to Kleomenes what Agis had dreamed of accomplishing. Kleomenes took the lessons very much to heart. And he burned with inward rage at what he heard. For though Plutarch describes him as a 'generous and great soul,' he took the world more darkly and seriously than

Agis had. Add to this 'an impetuosity and violence in his eagerness to pursue anything which he thought good and just,' and the stage was set for another attempt at overturning the status quo.

The Sparta of Kleomenes' late teenage years lay prostrate, stunned from the horror of Agis IV's murder. It was dangerous to even mention the old austere ideals of Lykourgos in public. Long gone now were the *agoge* of boys and girls, the institutionalized equality of citizens, and of course the ban on gold and silver. To even speak of such traditions as the old war-songs of Tyrtaios and the manly virtues of courage and endurance was tantamount to treason.

> The citizens lay dissolved in supine idleness and pleasures, the king [Leonidas II] let everything take its own way, thankful if nobody gave him any disturbance, nor called him away from the enjoyment of his wealth and luxury. The public interest was neglected, and each man intent upon his private gain.[6]

Kleomenes studied philosophy under Sphairos of Borysthenes, a Stoic who upheld the old ideals of self-discipline and what today might be called character-building. Sphairos had a theory that modified some of the rigours of the old *agoge* and mixed them with an egalitarian outlook. Some recent writers have called Sphairos a proto-communist, though without the theoretical prejudices and institutionalized class hatreds of Marxism.[7] Stoicism, warns Plutarch, is a good philosophy for a calm and reflective person, but in the head of a firebrand, as Kleomenes was, it can easily lead to danger. Sphairos, at any rate, was impressed by the young prince's spirited temperament. It's a moot point whether his instruction or the words of Agiatis were more influential in forming Kleomenes' outlook. But by the time he succeeded to the Agiad throne in 236 he was well and truly converted to Agis' ideals, and seethed with impatience to put the Spartan state to rights.

Wherever Kleomenes looked he saw general corruption and indifference, the poor becoming poorer, and few if any young people with either the inclination or ability to be trained for war or any civil office. What rankled the most was that after a couple of centuries of declining royal powers and prestige, the Spartan kingship languished as a powerless, purely ceremonial office completely under the thumb of the Ephors. From a close friend (Plutarch terms him a 'lover,' though the word should not be taken in its present exclusively sexual or gay sense) named Xenares he tried to glean more information, showing such emotion as he listened that Xenares drew away in embarrassment.

His friend's sudden withdrawal shocked the impressionable Kleomenes into a psychological withdrawal of his own. In Plutarch's account, an incipient paranoia seems to have overcome him. He believed that everyone was avoiding him because he was a fanatic about Agis' ideas and they were consequently afraid of associating with him. And he probably wasn't far wrong. But he had his faithful wife, and so continued his own plans in secret.

But other, more urgent business beckoned. Aratos of the Achaian League was now bent on subjugating the whole of the Peloponnese, to form a southern counterweight to Macedon's control of the north. To Aratos the new king of the Agiad house was an inexperienced stripling, and thus to be taken advantage of. In 228 Achaian forces attacked the Arkadians as a first step aiming at Sparta. The Ephors sent Kleomenes with a force to hold the Belbina pass at the northern end of the Lakonian valley. Aratos responded by marching to take Tegea and Orchomenos by a surprise night attack. But his allies acting as fifth columns in both towns lost their nerve, failed to open the gates, and Aratos was stymied.

It was now the turn of Kleomenes to feel contempt for his older and more experienced adversary. In a sarcastic letter to Aratos he asked him where he thought he was going at night. Aratos, unfazed, replied honestly that he intended to reach Belbina to confront the Spartans. Kleomenes wrote back that if that was the case, why was Aratos' army carrying torches and ladders? Aratus took the barbed exchange in good humour, but inside him an alarm bell sounded. 'What kind of young fellow is this?' he asked Demokrates, a Spartan exile in his army. (Any Greek army could be expected to contain hopeful men from the city that was being attacked, anxious to be reinstated even with enemy help.)

'He's a young eagle,' Demokrates replied. 'If you've any designs on Lakedaimon, start before that eagle's talons are grown.'

Kleomenes might be eager to tackle Aratos, but the Ephors were in two minds. Shortly after the exchange of letters between Aratos and Kleomenes the Ephors ordered the king home. On the way he took the town of Kaphyai, which impressed the Ephors enough for them to countermand the withdrawal order and send him back north into Argive territory. Aristomachos, the Argive leader and ally of the Achaian League, came out to meet him with 20,000 infantry and 1,000 cavalry. Kleomenes' force numbered not more than about 5,000, but he fearlessly confronted Aristomachos at Pallantion. Aratos was there, and when he saw the determined Spartan stand he ordered a general retreat. He may also have been unwilling to give the credit to Aristomachos. His soldiers couldn't believe it. It was a moot point who jeered louder at Aratos, the Spartans or his own Achaians and Argives being led off the field.

The bloodless triumph raised Kleomenes' standing in Sparta. He was fond of repeating the popular dictum that a Spartan should ask not how many the enemy were but where they were. His next campaign was to aid Sparta's allies in the northwest Peloponnese, the Eleans, against an attack on them by Aratos. This time Kleomenes fell on the Achaians as they were withdrawing, sweeping them from the field with great slaughter. Aratos slipped out of that debacle by leading a force across the Peloponnese to Mantineia and taking the city by assault. Kleomenes would doubtless have marched to meet this new threat had not the Ephors had another change of heart and halted hostilities.

The see-sawing of the Ephors started Kleomenes thinking that it would be nice to have the full strength of Sparta's dual kingship back in place to offset the Ephors' influence. His thoughts naturally fell on Archidamos of the Agiads, the brother of the late Agis who he admired so much. Archidamos, in exile in Messenia, was invited back. His return threw the faction that had murdered Agis into a panic. In Plutarch's account some of them pretended to receive him cordially as he arrived privately in Sparta and escorted him to his house, in an apparent attempt to lull his suspicions. Less than a year later Archidamos was murdered (see Archidamos V above). There was an attempt to put the blame on Kleomenes. Plutarch hints that a consent to Archidamos' being put away was somehow forced from him, but in view of Kleomenes' hopes for a united kingship and high regard for Agis, active complicity must be ruled out.

Kleomenes nonetheless had powerful factors working in his favour. One was his mother Kratesikleia, Leonidas II's widow, who was quite happy to remain single yet for her son's sake married a wealthy and influential Spartan named Megistonous whose backing might well be required in the struggles to come. Kleomenes' early victories in the field ensured his popularity with the citizenry. Besides, with the Eurypontid house vacant and uncertainty over who should fill the gap, he was in effect the sole king of Sparta with all that it implied.

Now was the time to strike a blow against Aratos and his allies in the Peloponnese. It appears that Kratesikleia's new husband bribed the Ephors into sending Kleomenes against Megalopolis in 227. He took a town called Leuktra (not to be confused with Leuktra in Boiotia, the site of the battle of 371), and found Aratos yet again lined up opposite him. Aratos' first attack pushed the Spartan line back, but a deep watercourse prevented him from pressing a pursuit. Lydiadas, his Megalopolitan commander, disregarded orders and led his cavalry across in chase. But his columns soon became entangled in a wilderness of vineyards, bushes and ditches and came to a disorganized halt. This was the signal for Kleomenes to bring up his Cretan and Tarentine contingents and drive the Megalopolitans back, killing Lydiadas and a lot of his soldiers.

When the body of Lydiadas was brought to him, Kleomenes displayed the first of those eccentric moments that were to characterize the rest of his reign. He ordered the corpse to be dressed in a purple robe and crowned, and sent in a procession to the gates of Megalopolis. The way Plutarch describes the event, we're not sure if it was a magnanimous or mocking gesture. The latter would be quite likely, given Kleomenes' previous sarcastic exchange of messages with Aratos. Yet Lydiadas had been an ex-tyrant who had changed his ways and become a democrat. Therefore Kleomenes, one thinks, might have had reason to honour him.

Back at home Kleomenes suggested to his stepfather Megistonous that it would be good for Sparta if the Ephorate were abolished and its collective wealth put into a common public fund. The renewed equality of citizens, he argued, would help bring back national glory and Sparta would again be the strongest power in Greece. Megistonous liked the idea and began to sound out a few close associates of his. Security, of course, was not very good. Somehow the Ephors got wind of the idea; one of them claimed to have dreamed that the Ephors' chairs had been removed from their usual position and in their place stood a single chair, and to have heard a voice saying, 'This is best for Sparta.'

What happened next is not clear. Almost certainly Kleomenes became suspicious that the Ephors had cottoned on to his plans. At some point, while on campaign in Arkadia, he was told that the Ephors were about to move against him. Leaving the suspected pro-Ephor part of his army on garrison duty, he led the more reliable mercenary portion down to Sparta to quash the conspiracy. He arrived at the outskirts of Sparta at sundown, calculating his arrival at the hour when he knew the Ephors would be sitting down to dinner. Kleomenes sent an officer, Euryklas, to the Ephors with a despatch from the front. Behind Euryklas came four of the king's close associates and some soldiers, all armed with swords. While Eurkylas was reading out his message the others ran up and cut down the Ephors, plus about a dozen other men who tried to come to their aid. It was all over in five minutes – the shortest civil war in history.

One Ephor, Agylaios, was wounded but played dead until the assailants left, when he crawled to the nearby Shrine of Fear and lay there all night. When he emerged in the morning he was allowed to leave Sparta along with many others who preferred to leave after Kleomenes' spectacular coup. The end of the 600-year-old institution of the Ephorate was as sudden as it was overdue. Kleomenes replaced the Ephors with a board of *patronomoi*, or 'fatherland-guards', who continued the Ephors' administrative duties without their policymaking powers. To give a semblance of unity to the state

Kleomenes placed his younger brother Eukleidas on the vacant Eurypontid throne as an ineffectual figurehead.

Now Kleomenes III was the tyrant of Sparta in all but name. He no doubt thought it necessary to act autocratically in order to enforce his plans for radical economic and social reform. The fate of Agis IV was not going to be his. But was he indeed committed to reorganizing society for its own sake? 'Kleomenes was first and foremost a soldier; what attracted him most in Agis' reforms was the promise they gave of a bigger and better Spartan army.'[8] Which was uppermost in his mind – society or national power – will never be known. Yet what was obvious in 227 is that never before, with the possible exception of the very earliest kings, had a Spartan king so arrogated absolute power to himself in so sudden a resurgence.

If we are to believe Plutarch, the anonymous Ephor's dream came literally true. One of Kleomenes' first acts after doing away with the Ephors was to do away with the chairs they sat on, replacing them with a throne which he designed himself and on which he would sit to give audience like a king ought to do. Justifying his action to the people, he said he was acting in accordance with the instructions of Lykourgos who had worked out an effective government without the need for Ephors. As Lykourgos had entered Sparta and carried out his reforms only by fear and the threat of force, he was compelled to do likewise.

He declared the land of Lakedaimon to be the common property of the whole citizen body. He cancelled all debts and selectively admitted non-Spartans into the citizen body so as to build up an army of free Spartans with the numbers and the will to defend their home from marauders such as the Aitolians. He and Megistonous promptly gave up their wealth to the common fund, followed by the entire citizen body. As Plutarch relates it, it would seem that all of Sparta eagerly seconded the decisions. Yet we can be sure that at least some of the old creditor class was horrified by what was going on but dared not raise a voice. No doubt the likes of Amphares and Demochares were still about, even though many of that ilk had been banished.

We have no details of Kleomenes' division and re-allocation of lands, so we may assume it was roughly along the lines of Agis IV's scheme to create 4,500 equal plots for the citizens and 15,000 for the outliers. By a quick selection process he formed a 4,000-man standing army. In the first real innovation in Spartan military tactics in centuries, the soldiers would use not the traditional spear but the Macedonian *sarissa*, a much longer weapon that needed both hands to hold and use. The left shield-arm would be freed thanks to an inside band, instead of the traditional handle, to slip the forearm through.

After forging this new model army, as it were, Kleomenes turned his attention towards reviving the Lykourgan *agoge* so long left in neglect. His teacher Sphairos was still in Sparta and found himself employed as combination minister of education and sports. Once more the school grounds echoed to the commands of exercise instructors; once more the common halls resounded with the noises of pubescent boys and girls arranged into the *agelai* of old. The revival of the *agoge* under Kleomenes III is a controversial issue, with some authorities claiming that it was even more rigorous than the old one. The flogging of teenage boys at the altar of Artemis Orthia east of the city can probably be attributed to this period. This ordeal, which has been exaggerated by modern authors, appears to have been a test of endurance, a neutral toughening-up exercise rather than a specific punishment. As such it would not leave a residue of resentment. A few boys reportedly did not survive the flogging. This was almost certainly because of some bodily weakness such as a hidden heart condition, and served as a crude process to winnow out those who would probably have died young anyway.

There were, of course, the complaints and grumbles. But Plutarch assures us that the Spartan majority were glad to have a sense of purpose restored to them. With his brother Eukleidas occupying the Eurypontid throne – and thus maintaining what was by now the legal fiction of a dual kingship – Kleomenes now felt confident enough for another crack at his threatening enemies in the Peloponnese. After all, there was no power like the power of example to show those enemies what they shouldn't tangle with.

Kleomenes may well have felt invincible as he invaded the territory of Megalopolis in 226. His adoring troops wasted the countryside and collected much booty. To graphically display his contempt for the enemy he corralled a company of actors travelling from Messenia, set up a theatre in enemy territory, and sat for a whole day watching plays. The Spartan army, unlike other Greek armies, disdained the traditional entertainment for the troops such as jugglers and dancing girls; the soldiers stuck to their physical training or attended classes given by older men.

Kleomenes kept to the austere example himself. In the tradition of the noblest kings of Sparta he resisted the inevitable temptations to display the near-absolute power that he undoubtedly wielded. His house was no bigger than anyone else's. It contained no elaborate furnishings or army of servants. The admiring Plutarch paints an attractive picture of his everyday demeanour:

> When they ... saw no purple, no robes of state upon him, no couches
> and litters about him for his ease, and that he did not receive requests
> and return answers after a long delay and difficulty ... but that he rose

and came forward in any dress he might happen to be wearing, to meet those that came to wait on him, stayed, talked freely and affably with all that had business, they were extremely taken, and won to his service, and professed that he alone was the true son of Herakles.[9]

He ate frugally, shunning dining rooms and other formalities, basing his diet on the traditional Lakonian bread and the infamous black broth. He did, admittedly, indulge in slightly better fare if some envoy was present. Even then, condiments such as sauces and desserts were absent. There might be a little more wine for special occasions, but it was considered polite in Spartan society to refuse it. There was no need of music or other entertainment in Kleomenes' household, for he was an entertainer himself, telling funny stories and debating serious points with equal facility. He thus had no need to ingratiate himself with influential men through gifts or bribes, believing such things to be moral traps. At all times, we are told, he was agreeable and modest in his dealings.

Kleomenes' fame had spread widely, and the first to seek his help in the Peloponnese were the Mantineians, who had expelled their Achaian garrison. Not even waiting a day, Kleomenes marched up to Tegea as the neighbouring Mantineians gratefully restored their old polity. From Tegea he moved in an arc through the mountains of Arkadia to enter Achaian territory. His intention now was to deal with Aratos once and for all, and if possible remove him as a rival for the leadership of the Peloponnese. Aratos' general Hyperbatas moved out with a force to meet Kleomenes at the town of Dymai. The Spartans found themselves in a potentially dangerous position, sandwiched between Hyperbatas and hostile Dymai. Kleomenes, typically, acted before anyone else, luring the Achaians into an attack that cost them heavily. After that victory Kleomenes moved into Elis, liberating a town there from Achaian control.

Aratos was in a corner and knew it. Pressed to assume the supreme generalship in place of Hyperbatas, he declined it. Kleomenes confidently sent ambassadors to Achaia with a generous call for submission in return for benefits for Achaia's cities. It was a sensible move. The current Macedonian ruler, Antigonos III Doson, coveted the fortress of Acrocorinth and was prepared to negotiate with the Achaians for it. Aratos himself may have opened secret contacts with Antigonos Doson. It would explain the Achaians' delay in replying to Kleomenes' overtures. Aratos invited Kleomenes to meet him at Lerna near Argos, with a 300-man bodyguard only. On his way to Lerna Kleomenes drank too much cold water after having exerted himself on the march, and as a result coughed up blood and lost his voice, forcing him to return home.

When he recovered he arranged the meeting with Aratos, whose condition was that the king should arrive at Argos alone, leaving his army outside the walls. Kleomenes was affronted by this and accused Aratos of bad faith. The communications between the two leaders deteriorated into a series of insulting messages between Aratos and Kleomenes, that master of the epistolary put-down, which even maligned each others' wives!

Aratos now was confused and afraid, seeing 'the Peloponnese shaking and its cities everywhere stirred to revolt by restless agitators.' His vision of uniting southern Greece against the Macedonian dynasty was crumbling. His reverses at the hand of Kleomenes, a man young enough to be his son, added to his bitterness. He also greatly feared Kleomenes' economic and social revolution. Kleomenes resumed his campaigns in Achaia, detaching its towns one by one. Then Argos itself fell to him. It was this last event probably that caused Aratos to abandon what sense of honour he had and actively defect to the Macedonian cause. The first move in this act of treachery was to invite Antigonos Doson's forces to occupy Achaia. His second move was to happily adopt Macedonian habits.

Inevitably, news of Kleomenes' radical reforms had spread far and wide, and a good number of Achaians began agitating for debt cancellations and land redistribution on the Spartan model. Many were also incensed at Aratos' sudden love affair with the despised Macedonians. Kleomenes, well-informed of these currents, took advantage of them by another invasion of Achaia. By 225 Aratos' influence had shrunk to Achaia, Sikyon and Megalopolis. In that year the Nemean Games were held. These were one of Greece's regular athletic contests on the Olympic model, a meeting point for all Peloponnesians. While Argos was busy organizing the Games Kleomenes made a surprise appearance before the thronged city, occupying a strategic point and forcing the Argives to accept a Spartan garrison and deliver twenty hostages.

Thus a Spartan king, after six centuries of fruitless attempts and countless battles, finally brought arch-foe Argos under his city's heel. Plutarch credits Kleomenes with 'raising Sparta to her ancient place as the commanding state of Greece.' The competence of the Spartan and Lakedaimonian soldiery was boosted by the new atmosphere of optimism in Sparta after the reforms and the huge prestige of the king. The Spartans sensed that they had recovered their old strengths first cultivated by Lykourgos, based on clean living, self-discipline and social equality. These, it was claimed, were the true sources of courage and valour in the field, rather than the fear inspired by tyrants.

Kleomenes' next target was Corinth, where most of the lower classes supported him. As Aratos rode into Corinth to unseat his political foes, those foes lay in wait for him. He walked into the city leading his horse and was at once assailed by a host of vocal critics. He quietly asked them to sit down for a civilized discussion. As he talked he sidled away slowly, as if looking for someone to take his horse's bridle. This enabled him to slip out of the mob's clutches, jump back on his horse and ride up to the Acrocorinth. The Corinthians sent a mission post-haste to Kleomenes at Argos, almost killing their horses with the effort. Kleomenes and his stepfather Megistonous tried negotiating with Aratos on the Acrocorinth, offering to share the garrisoning of the fortress and a good sum of money into the bargain.

Aratos' disingenuous answer was that he was no longer in control of events. The real reason for his refusal was that his master Antigonos Doson was close at hand north of the Isthmus with 20,000 Macedonian troops and 1,500 horses, determined to seize the Acrocorinth and save Aratos' skin. Meanwhile, Kleomenes occupied Corinth but refused to allow his men to seize Aratos' property. Antigonos Doson was doubtless expecting the Spartans to resist him at the Isthmus, but Kleomenes was too clever for that; he posted his defences in the Onea hills to the south, sending out raiding parties to harass the Macedonians, who suffered considerable casualties. The Macedonian king's attempt to land forces at Lechaion, the port of Corinth, came to grief. Antigonos Doson, discouraged, planned to transport his army by sea along the north shore of the Gulf of Corinth to the Heraion promontory and from there attempt another landing on the Peloponnesian coast nearer to Achaia. He found unexpected allies in some disaffected Argives, who were disappointed that Kleomenes had not immediately cancelled all the debts in Argos. Aratos, meanwhile, had slipped out of besieged Sikyon at considerable risk to himself and agreed to hand over the Acrocorinth to the Macedonians.

Kleomenes, hearing of this, sent Megistonous with 2,000 men to straighten out matters in Argos, which was in more trouble that he suspected. No sooner had Megistonous entered the city than he was killed in a counter-attack. Kleomenes at once feared for the safety of Lakedaimon if Argos should once again slip into the enemy camp. Sparta itself was completely undefended, with all its soldiers absent in the field. Abandoning Corinth, which Antigonos Doson immediately occupied, Kleomenes threw the army against Argos, where the Spartan garrison was holding out, but only just. Spartan forces, scaling the walls, relieved the beleaguered garrison while the Cretan archers cleared the streets of resistance.

But the Macedonian army was already visible tramping and galloping down into the Argive plain, in hot pursuit of the Spartans. Kleomenes pulled back his forces and, concealed by the walls of Argos, escaped towards Mantineia. Hopes that Argos was finally brought to heel had been dashed in a surprisingly short time. Riding on Antigonos Doson's coat-tails, Aratos re-established his control over the northern Peloponnese. Among his first acts was to carry out a savage and utterly inexcusable reprisal on Mantineia by massacring its leading citizens and selling the rest into slavery – and keeping one-third of the booty. He abolished the very name Mantineia and renamed the place Antigoneia after his Macedonian boss. As a result Aratos courted yet greater unpopularity among his own people.

A dejected Kleomenes was marching by Tegea on his way home one evening when a messenger from Sparta met him with the news that his beloved wife Agiatis had died. The blow was heavy, but he didn't let it show. In a steady voice and with a clear face he arranged the garrisoning of Tegea. The following day he arrived home to join his mother and children for the funeral and mourning period, at the end of which 'he at once devoted himself to the public affairs of the state.'

These affairs were in a discouraging state. Details of the state of the Spartan economy for this period are lacking, but Plutarch hints at some 'assistance' which Sparta sought from Ptolemy III of Egypt who was known to oppose the Macedonians. The term 'assistance' is usually taken to mean political backing, though the Spartan state could well have been in need of money after Kleomenes' continuous campaigning. The egalitarian redistribution of land and debt cancellation were all very well as radical short-term measures to relieve the people's burdens and make them happier than they otherwise would have been. But, as so many other socialist-minded re-casters of society have discovered from that time to this, the macroeconomic structure of the state can be fatally undermined that way. The reforms of Agis IV and Kleomenes, attractive as they might seem on the outside, were not designed to build up a business class on which a growing economy could be based. When everyone has the same assets and no-one can acquire any more than their share, competition – that oxygen of a market economy – cannot take root. We don't know what the Spartan tax system was or whether the common state fund was enough to finance a war of any length.

Moreover, the social revolutions that Kleomenes hoped to ignite throughout the Peloponnese failed to materialize for two main reasons. First, he found he had to respect the Peloponnesian cities' own systems of government if he wanted to keep them on his side. Second, as a consequence the lower classes in those cities, expecting Kleomenes to deliver utopia, turned against him. With the Spartan debacle at Argos the tide now definitely flowed against Kleomenes. That he probably sought a financial loan from Ptolemy III is arguable from the fact that Ptolemy demanded Kleomenes' mother and at least one of his children as collateral – in effect, hostages. (If such international lending terms seem harsh, they're not very much more onerous than those in force today among governments and financial institutions.) Kleomenes was cast down at this, and his demeanour showed it. His newly-widowed mother, suspecting something was afoot, pressed him to tell her, which he finally did.

'Is that all?' Kratesikleia laughed, likely in an attempt to give her son courage. 'Hurry up and get me on a ship and send this old carcass to where it may be of some use to Sparta before I get too old for anything here.'

The army accompanied Kratesikleia to the ship at Tainaros. There stood a temple of Poseidon, and inside, where no-one could see, Kratesikleia turned to say goodbye to Kleomenes, who could hardly hold back his tears. 'Come on, King of Sparta,' she said, embracing him, 'when we emerge let no-one see our sadness or any emotion unworthy of Sparta. All else is whatever the god decrees.' Drying her own eyes, Kratesikleia walked on board the ship with her little grandson, and at once the captain put out to sea for Egypt.

Once there she found that Ptolemy was playing a wily game, considering an overture of peace from Antigonos Doson, who was also pressing the Achaians to extend peace feelers to Sparta. Kleomenes was reluctant to accept without consulting Ptolemy, not wishing to put his mother and son at risk. Kratisikleia stiffened his resolve in a letter, telling him he should do whatever was in Sparta's best interests and stand up to the Egyptian king, no matter what happened to his mother and child.

By now Antigonos Doson's Macedonian cohorts were occupying Peloponnesian cities one by one. When only Lakonia was left, Kleomenes raised an emergency war fund by selling Spartan citizenship to any Helots who could pay the fee. Two thousand of them responded. In early 222, armed with the *sarissa* in the Macedonian style and carrying five days' rations, they and a number of mercenaries marched with Kleomenes at their head to Megalopolis where the Macedonian and Achaian forces were encamped. His intention was to snatch the city from under the enemy's nose and use it as a bulwark for a *revanche*. First he made a feint at Sellasia, as if to enter Argive territory, and then veered westwards direct for Megalopolis.

Before the Megalopolitans could fully realize what was happening, two Spartan regiments under Panteus stormed an unguarded part of the wall of Megalopolis and hacked away at the defenders. Kleomenes, coming up with the rest of the army, followed Panteus inside. The Spartans overcame all resistance and the citizens fled wherever they could – mostly in the direction of Messenia. The Spartans took upwards of 1,000 prisoners, including the Megalopolitan generals Lysandridas and Thearidas. In Plutarch's account, when Lysandridas was being taken to Kleomenes he called to him while he was still some distance away: 'Now, King of Sparta, is your chance to win even greater glory than you had before.'

The defiant tone of the call was matched by Kleomenes. 'Surely, you don't think I'm going to give your city back to you,' he said.

'That's exactly what I mean,' Lysandridas replied. 'Don't destroy this brave city, but fill it with your allies and friends so you can be the saviour of the Megalopolitans.'

The words made sense to Kleomenes, who could not afford to antagonize anyone at this juncture. 'I don't know if I can trust you,' he told Lysandridas, 'but glory is better than profit.'

Whether or not Lysandridas was sincere in his offer, the people of Megalopolis weren't calling the shots. The man who was calling them was Philopoimen, the new leader of the Achaian League, who rejected Kleomenes' proposal out of hand, and for good measure banished Lysandridas and Thearidas who had first broached it.

Kleomenes gave vent to his fury by demolishing a good part of Megalopolis, but not before looting the city of all its works of art and sending them to Sparta. While that was going on, Aratos and Antigonos Doson were at Aigion on the Achaean coast discussing war plans. Aratos broke the news of the sack of Megalopolis by mounting the speaker's rostrum and breaking down in tears. The meeting broke up at once. Antigonos Doson left his main force in winter quarters and marched with a small force to Argos.

It's far from certain what the Macedonian ruler intended to accomplish by this move. His force would be no match for the Spartans, who were on their way north, burning and pillaging the countryside around Argos at their leisure. As Antigonos Doson stayed holed up in his quarters, Argive citizens mobbed his gate, calling on him to fight like a man or let them do it. Antigonos Doson at first refused to be moved and then moved on Tegea as a first step to a planned invasion of Lakonia. Kleomenes in retaliation renewed his attack on Argive territory, destroying the Argives' cornfields by putting his soldiers to trample on them. Antigonos Doson hurried back to Argos, but remained ineffectual while Kleomenes drove out enemy garrisons from some nearby towns, showing that what Plutarch called his 'genius for command' had not diminished.

But that was Kleomenes' last triumph. It might seem fitting that economic considerations, which were the motive power behind Kleomenes' rapid rise, would in the end prove to be his downfall. Effective warfare at bottom depends on the availability of money to finance its huge demands. Kleomenes himself may have been proud to live in noble modesty, but a state cannot. The Spartan state, run along strictly proto-socialist lines, could develop no financial sinews to carry on a protracted war, much less to become mistress of the Peloponnese. The soldiers might well be content to subsist on the most basic pay and the civilians at home weren't much better off, but how long could that be expected to last? There were, as far as we are aware, no banks or other credit institutions to provide liquidity and oil the wheels of trade. Crucially, the fickle Ptolemy III had stopped his subsidies to Sparta as soon as he heard that Kleomenes was losing the battle for the Peloponnese. Antigonos Doson, on the other hand, could draw on all the ample resources of the Macedonian domain.

But neither was Antigonos Doson free of problems. In 222 a host of semi-barbaric Illyrians, living in what is now Albania and Kosovo, descended on Macedon, plundering and pillaging. Urgent messages arrived for Antigonos Doson to turn around and take his forces home to confront that threat. But just at that juncture Kleomenes was facing him at Sellasia with 20,000 men. The Spartan king had called out his brother Eukleidas, the *locum tenens* of the Eurypontid throne, to lead the army with him. He needed a major victory, and fast, for his soldiers' pay was running out and his mercenaries might bolt any day. Antigonos Doson and his 28,000 men took up the challenge, judging Kleomenes to be a much more urgent danger at that moment than the Illyrians.

Kleomenes had cleverly taken up a position on the main road out of Sparta in a pass between two low hills, Euas and Olympos, both fortified by trenches and palisades. Holding Euas on the left was Eukleidas with about 8,000 *perioikoi* and allied troops; Kleomenes and his Spartiates held Olympos, with 1,000 cavalry and some mercenaries on the road between the heights. Kleomenes' plan was probably to use Olympos as a pivot from which his line could sweep onto the enemy in a scything motion.

Antigonos Doson placed his Macedonians and Illyrian mercenaries opposite Eukleidas. These were backed by Akarnanians and Cretans, with 2,000 Achaians in reserve. He put his infantry opposite that of the Spartans on the road in the centre, backed up by mercenaries and Megalopolitan infantry, while reserving the position on the left opposite Kleomenes for himself with the rest of the Macedonians. Antigonos Doson's hammer-like left wing consisted of two close-order phalanxes thirty-two men deep, with a screen of light mercenary skirmishers in front.

Antigonos Doson spent a few days surveying the land and assessing the strength of the Spartan position, at the same time carrying out a series of feints that didn't deceive Kleomenes, who parried them easily. In the end the Macedonian had to open the action, sending his Illyrian and Akarnanian units behind Euas by a hidden pathway (shades of Thermopylai) to outflank Eukleidas' position. Kleomenes, observing from Olympos, could see nothing but suspected what might be afoot. He asked what Plutarch calls his ambush specialist, Demoteles, to check the Spartan rear for any outflanking action. But Demoteles said it wasn't necessary and advised Kleomenes to concentrate on the phalanxes in front. (Afterwards a rumour arose that Demoteles could have been bribed by the Macedonians.) Then the Macedonian right charged Euas hill, but opened a gap in the centre into which the Spartan cavalry rushed, turning to threaten the Macedonian rear. The Macedonian horse somehow failed to counter the advance, with the result that Philopoimen, the Megalopolitan commander, took it upon himself to repulse the Spartan cavalry advance.

Meanwhile, Kleomenes had given the order to charge down on the enemy from Olympos. His charge slammed into Antigonos Doson's line, driving it back about a kilometre. But things were not going well on the Spartan left. Eukleidas had decided not to follow his impetuous brother's example of charging downhill, where his forces would have the advantage, but to wait on Euas in a defensive position. This allowed the Macedonians to regroup after their temporary discomfiture in the centre. In staggered formation they charged the hill and drove Eukleidas from the summit. Eukleidas also found himself outflanked by the Illyrians and Akarnanians who turned his position, with the result that his formations were cut to pieces. Plutarch reports Kleomenes as calling out to his brother, 'Dear brother, brave example for Sparta's youth, you're lost!' Eukleidas is believed to have fallen along with many hundreds of Spartan soldiers and mercenaries; with him the tail-end of the Eurypontid line was finally snuffed out. To save the situation Kleomenes ordered another assault on Antigonos Doson's front. The lines see-sawed back and forth on Olympos hill, both sides fighting stubbornly, until a timely charge by the Macedonian double phalanx, *sarissai* at the ready, swept the Spartans from the hill. The whole Spartan line then gave way and fled rearwards. Kleomenes himself entered Sparta just before the Macedonian forces got there. Plutarch gives the number of Spartan dead as 5,800 – just 200 less than the whole Spartiates force – which is generally thought to be highly exaggerated. But there is no doubt that the Spartan losses at Sellasia were disastrous.[11]

Many high achievers, as long as they are on a roll, seem to have an unerring talent for making successful moves. Affairs somehow seem to fall into their lap. Yet when they meet with a serious reverse, instead of fighting on, they stop and fatalistically wait for whatever may be in store for them. Kleomenes was one of these. With Antigonos Doson at the gates of Sparta and the city in its direst danger for more than a century, he calmly advised the panicking citizenry to accept Macedonian occupation. The battle-weary king made his way home among women hurrying from their own homes to meet their returning men folk, bringing them water to drink and carrying their weapons for them. His own wife being dead, Kleomenes was met by his Megalopolitan slave housekeeper who at once brought water. The king refused to take a sip but still standing, he put his forearm against a pillar and leaned his head on it. Spending some time like that in thought, he went back out and gathered up some friends. For Kleomenes had no intention of remaining in a Sparta overrun and occupied by its enemies. Waiting for him at the port of Gytheion were ships ready to carry him to his mother and children in Egypt.

Antigonos Doson had only three days in which to savour his conquest of Sparta. The urgency of the messages from Macedon, where the Illyrians were causing great damage, called him back. He was also ill, suffering from tuberculosis and respiratory problems. On returning to Macedon he led his forces against the Illyrians. After winning one battle, the ancient writers claimed, Antigonos Doson shouted, 'Oh glorious day!' so vehemently that he broke a blood vessel and later died.

On the boat to Egypt Kleomenes had plenty of time to brood over his reverses. As they touched at an islet called Aigialeia one of his noble friends, Therykion, remarked to him that the era when a defeated Spartan king would die in battle seemed to be over. Nonetheless, he added, there was still time to decide on what would be the wisest course, that is, to surrender to Antigonos Doson, an action 'not dishonourable to the race of Herakles.' He preferred to face the music at the hands of the Macedonian victors rather than be an object of contempt for Ptolemy's Egyptians. 'Why should we choose [Ptolemy] for our master,' Therykion went on, 'by whom we have not yet been beaten?' Moreover, what would Kleomenes' mother think if he slunk away, 'changed from a prince into an exile and a slave?' The coast of Lakonia was still visible on the horizon. 'Better go back and die with honour,' Therykion said, 'than sit lazily in Egypt,' helpless and out of things.

'You're a coward,' Kleomenes replied. 'There's still hope as long as we're alive to fight another day.' Going back to seek probable death at the enemy's hands purely out of aggrieved honour didn't make sense to him. 'Those that have such an inclination,' he concluded, 'might as well die now.' Therykion took him at his word. When the boat touched at Aigialeia he jumped ashore and ran himself through with his sword.

Kleomenes received a decent welcome in Libya. When he was taken to Ptolemy in Alexandria the Egyptian king treated him at first with cool politeness.

> But when he found [Kleomenes] a man of deep sense and great reason, and that his plain Lakonian way of conversation carried with it a noble and becoming grace, that he did nothing unbecoming his birth, nor bent under fortune ... he was ashamed, and repented that he had neglected so great a man.[12]

Ptolemy made Kleomenes' life comfortable with a handsome annual stipend which was more than enough for his frugal needs. The Spartan ex-king spent his time organizing relief for Greek war refugees who like him had sought new homes in Egypt. All the while Ptolemy fed his hopes that he might one day return to his kingship in Sparta with ships and money.

Matters were proceeding in this agreeable manner when in 221 Ptolemy III died and was succeeded by his son Ptolemy IV, an ineffectual and indolent *roi faineant*, dismissed by Plutarch as 'besotted with women and wine.' When the new Ptolemy could take time off from his partying he would take Kleomenes into his meetings. At one of them Ptolemy revealed a plot to do away with his brother Magas, a more capable character favoured by the army and hence a threat to the throne. Kleomenes properly declined the offer to participate in the plot. When pressed, he advised Ptolemy not to worry too much about Magas, as with Kleomenes in Egypt were 3,000 Peloponnesian mercenaries who would move into action whenever he gave the signal.

Perhaps it was the wrong thing to say. For the weak-willed Ptolemy also began to fear Kleomenes and his mercenaries as a potential threat. The Spartan, it was whispered at Ptolemy's court, was 'a lion among a flock of sheep.' Kleomenes, no fool, was aware of this and kept his wits about him. He kept in touch with news from Greece. Antigonos III Doson of Macedon had been succeeded by a cousin, the young Philip V. Sparta was reportedly engulfed in continual disorder. Kleomenes petitioned Ptolemy to allow him to go home to help his city, but the wastrel king was too busy with his orgies and binge drinking to take any notice. Sosibios, Ptolemy's chief minister, was in a dilemma. He saw Kleomenes fretting more and more at his self-exile, indifferent to gifts and other inducements for him to stay. But he also was worried that Kleomenes might take back to Greece reports of mal-administration in Egypt.

One day Kleomenes was strolling along the quayside of Alexandria when he noticed someone he knew coming off a ship. It was a Messenian named Nikagoras who had once sold Kleomenes a considerable piece of property but claimed never to have been paid for it. Either the king had been short of funds at the time or he had been away campaigning and the matter had slipped his mind. The two met civilly, and Nikagoras said he was bringing some good-quality war-horses to Ptolemy. 'You ought to have brought young boys and music-girls, for that's all he wants now,' Kleomenes chuckled. But Nikagoras hadn't forgotten his grievance about the property and a few days later brought up the matter.

Kleomenes frankly told him he had no money left to give him. This was an odd claim, given the generous stipend we are told he enjoyed. Had he given money away to his mercenaries? Had Ptolemy IV stopped the stipend? To lie to Nikagoras doesn't seem to fit with what we know about Kleomenes' honest character. Whatever the truth, Nikagoras tipped off Sosibios about what Kleomenes had said about young boys and music-girls. The chief minister asked Nikagoras to put the whole thing in writing, which he did. The document was delivered into Ptolemy's hands, and Kleomenes was put under house arrest. He knew very well what that might mean. Opposing Ptolemy IV was a rather dangerous pastime. According to a Roman chronicler he was in the habit of playing dice and nodding as the names of those condemned to death were read out to him by an aide.[13]

One of Ptolemy's favourites, who also had been friendly with Kleomenes, told the Spartan that he needn't worry too much if from now on he buttoned his lip. But as the man was departing Kleomenes overheard him warning the door guards that they had 'a great and furious wild beast' inside. Kleomenes' friends, in the house with him, decided that extreme measures only would now save them – they had no intention of being butchered like sheep at the whim of a despised and effeminate excuse for a king. For they had no doubts now that such a fate was in store for them.

The plan was worked out craftily. Kleomenes' friends prepared the ground by spreading a false report that Ptolemy had ordered Kleomenes freed. It was the Egyptian royal custom for the king to send gifts to those whom he was about to set free, and so Kleomenes' friends arranged for some suitable gifts to be sent to the house to fool the guards. Inside, they prepared a party, with roast meat and wine and merrymaking, to which the guards were cordially invited. This way the guards got drunk and fell asleep. When the moon was up and the guards out cold, Kleomenes put on a coat, unstitching the right sleeve to free his sword arm. He and twelve others, all armed with swords, burst out of the house undetected.

One of the escapers named Hippitas was lame, with the result that he couldn't run as fast as the others. When he saw himself falling back he asked to be killed rather than be a hindrance to the operation. A man happened to be riding by at that hour; he was pulled off his horse and Hippitas put on it. The party then ran through the streets of Alexandria proclaiming liberty for the people. The favourite of Ptolemy who had warned of the 'great and furious wild beast' was cut down as he was coming out of the palace to see what was going on. The police chief of Alexandria was dragged from his chariot and slain. Kleomenes' next objective was the prison, where they hoped to free the inmates and add to their numbers, but the guards had already barred the gates.

Kleomenes' plan had come up against a dead end. Far from what he might have expected no masses of Alexandrines rose up to join the revolt against Ptolemy's corrupt regime. The streets were as dark and lonely as ever. Anyone walking about fled at the approach of Kleomenes' band. Looking about him, Kleomenes realized that all was lost. Could a people be so afraid of liberty? He turned to his friends. 'Die as bravely as becomes my followers and your own past actions,' he told them. Hippitas, the lame one, asked to die first; he was run through by one of the younger men. One by one, including Kleomenes, the rest fell on their swords. The last man left was Panteus, the gallant officer who had been first in the attack on Megalopolis, and Kleomenes' closest friend – and newly-married to boot.

Panteus pricked each man with his dagger to make sure they were dead. Coming to Kleomenes, he prodded his ankle with the dagger point and saw the king turn on his back. Panteus kissed him and sat by him until he was certain Kleomenes was dead. He covered up the body and then killed himself over it. Kleomenes III had been the king of Sparta for sixteen years.

Kleomenes' mother Kratisikleia broke down at the news. His eldest child, not yet ten years old, broke from her tearful embrace, and in an astonishing display of Spartan spirit, threw himself from the roof of the house. It wasn't a very tall building, and the boy was not seriously injured. But as he was gathered up he cried bitterly because he hadn't died with his father. Ptolemy, as was to be expected, had not the slightest sympathy for Kleomenes, and ordered his body to be flayed and hung up. And so that the Spartan royal house would cease to be threat for good, Kratisikleia, the grandchildren and the women of her household were ordered to be executed.

Among those on the death list was the attractive Spartan wife of Panteus, who had escaped confinement by her parents in circumstances worthy of the best romantic novels to follow Panteus to Egypt. The young widow held Kratesikleia's hand and held up her robe as they were led to the death chamber. In scenes reminiscent of the execution of Agis IV and his family, Kratesikleia, who was not afraid to die, asked only that she be despatched before the children. Her wish was not granted. The children were put to death as she watched, probably by beheading. 'Oh, children, where have you gone?' Plutarch reports her as whispering in the moments before the blade fell on her neck. Panteus's widow – it is a pity that her name has not been recorded – cut the most impressive figure, showing no fear or emotion, a Spartan woman to the last. After carefully laying out the bodies as best she could, she calmly rearranged her dress and asked that everyone clear the chamber except the executioner. She did not wish her death to be a public spectacle. Her last request was that no-one should do anything to care for her body. By the manner of her death this unnamed but totally noble lady 'showed that women were no unequal rivals of the men.'

Kleomenes' flayed body hung in public for several days. There came a report to Ptolemy that a large snake had curled itself about Kleomenes' head, guarding the face from pecking birds of prey. Plutarch half-accepts the literal truth of the story, though he suggests a more natural explanation such as a coagulation of bodily fluids oozing from the orifices of the head. Ptolemy's superstitious nature was disturbed, so Plutarch tells us, especially as the snake story got around and the Alexandrines, who had stayed cowed in their homes when Kleomenes was calling on them to rise up, made processions to where his body had been displayed and called Kleomenes a hero and son of the gods.

# Epilogue

In 221 Sparta was sunk in civil disorder. The death of Kleomenes discouraged many who had hoped that his strong character and genius for organization would help him unite the Peloponnese and face up not only to Macedon but also to a vigorous new power from the west that was taking an increasingly active interest in Greek affairs – Rome.

Rome's intervention in Greece, which was destined to become a full-fledged occupation in less than a hundred years, began when Roman ships tried to hunt down a Greek pirate chieftain active in the Adriatic Sea. This pirate chieftain took refuge with Philip V of Macedon, who most unwisely hired him as an adviser. Philip, in fact, imagined he could resist Rome in the Adriatic. It was a futile dream, but Philip compounded his error by securing an alliance with the Carthaginian Hannibal who was embroiled with the Romans in the Second Punic War. That war over, Rome decided to deal more decisively with the incautious Macedonian monarch.

Sparta monitored events carefully. In 219 the Ephors, who had in the meantime reconstituted themselves as Sparta's main arm of government, placed a boy purported to be of the Agiad house on the throne as Agesipolis III. This left open the Eurypontid post, which was eventually filled by one Lykourgos, who openly bought the kingship – and its pedigree of descent from Herakles – by paying each Ephor one talent. This Lykourgos displayed some ability by attacking Achaian forces in the Peloponnese and regaining the Lakonian east coast from the Argives. Yet the buyout of the Eurypontid kingship by the commoner Lykourgos rankled in some high circles. One Spartan named Cheilon decided to act. Taking several leaves out of the late Kleomenes' book he took up the defunct causes of land redistribution and debt cancellation. Gathering up about 200 followers, Cheilon burst into the Ephors' chamber while they were at dinner and imitated Kleomenes by butchering them Cheilon next moved to arrest Lykourgos, but the king-by-purchase managed with the help of his servants and neighbours to escape to Pellana.[1]

Cheilon, according to Polybius, then entered the main square offering to reconcile the opposing factions by proffering his hand to both. He found few, if any, takers. Perhaps the memories of the economic slump under Kleomenes were still fresh. Getting the message, Cheilon in turn fled to Achaia. Lykourgos, given a reprieve, led some expeditions against Tegea and Messenia that didn't amount to much.

The following year Philip V of Macedon invaded Lakedaimon with an army, bypassing Sparta to the east and occupying Amyklai. Laying waste the land as far as the sea, including some of the best farmland in Lakonia, Philip turned to meet Lykourgos near the Menelaion, the old ruined hilltop palace believed to be the tomb of Menelaos and Helen, just southeast of Sparta and overlooking the Eurotas River. Lykourgos had 2,000 men defending the space between the city and the river. By damming the river downstream the Spartans turned that space into a quagmire. Nonetheless, Philip attacked the low heights the Spartans were occupying, driving them back and killing many. Lykourgos, fearing the Ephors' fury, fled to Aitolia along with his household.

A year later the Ephors forgave him and invited him back. He returned, but not before engaging in some rather meaningless campaigns against Megalopolis and Messenia. That was in 217. In that year or perhaps later, Lykourgos got his young co-king Agesipolis III exiled on some pretext – perhaps after one the Ephors' nine-yearly stargazing exercises. Lykourgos died in 211, leaving his son Pelops as successor. As Pelops was a minor, an ambitious Spartan named Machanidas assumed the regency. Machanidas didn't enjoy his office for very long, for Philopoimen, the extremely able Achaian leader who succeeded Aratos, confronted him in battle at Mantineia – that plain which was a periodic magnet for murderous battles throughout antiquity – in 207 and killed him along with some 4,000 Spartans and allies. Philopoimen marched to the outskirts of Sparta, burning and pillaging.

Amidst the resulting anarchy an adventurer named Nabis seized power in Sparta. Nabis could have been one of the Eurypontid family or one of the disfranchised Spartans demoted to Inferior status, hence his murderous hatred of the upper class which he proceeded to systematically wipe out by murder and banishment.[2] The seized property, as well as the wives and daughters of the victims, were distributed to his legions of mercenaries. The young and helpless king Pelops was sent packing. One modern commentator terms Nabis 'a grisly caricature of the great Kleomenes III.'[3] In one stroke, and with active help of his ruthless wife Apega, he delivered a mortal blow to the 800-year-old Dorian structure of the Spartan city-state, turning it into little more than a bandits' lair.

Nabis the warlord possessed some military ability. Acquiring a navy, he sent it to join Cretan pirates in terrorizing the Aegean Sea. Around 201 Nabis led a marauding expedition into Messenia, only to be driven off by the

Achaians under Philopoimen. But Rome now was looming larger. Philopoimen inflicted another defeat on the Spartans at Skotitas near Tegea in 200, leaving himself more of a free hand against Macedon, now the target of a major campaign by Rome. Philopoimen hoped to bring the might of Rome to bear against Nabis as well. In 197 Nabis seized Argos, instituting a savage pogrom against its upper classes to the delight of the proletariat and peasantry, who benefited from the land and cancelled debts. Apega did her part, literally ripping the Argive women's gold and finery from them.[4]

This atrocity was too much for the Roman Senate. Having neutralized Philip V by military means in 196, it now turned to deal with Nabis. By 195 the Roman general Titus Quinctius Flamininus had taken Corinth. The previous year at the Isthmian Games near Corinth Flamininus had personally proclaimed the Roman gift of freedom to the Greeks at the Isthmian Games, to the wildest cheering. Having established himself as by far the most popular man in Greece, the Roman general convened a conference of as many Greeks as he could get on side and obtained their agreement for a decisive move on Nabis' Sparta. With Flamininus and his mixed Roman-Greek-Macedonian army was the deposed Agiad king-in-waiting Agesipolis III. Nabis fortified his defences with 15,000 mercenaries. By imposing a reign of terror inside the city he could have held out for a long time. But Roman cohorts out-flanked Lakedaimon by sailing around to the port of Gytheion and investing Sparta from the south. Nabis attempted to open negotiations with Flamininus, but the fanatics in the Apella, made up mostly of mercenaries, were vociferous in their opposition. When 3,000 more troops arrived to boost Nabis' force he felt he could afford to reject the Romans' moderate terms.

Flamininus then ordered a general assault on Sparta, fighting his way into the city itself. But Pythagoras of Argos, a mercenary commander in Nabis' service, torched some houses abutting the Spartan wall, toppling a part of the wall and cutting off the Romans inside. For Flamininus it was just a temporary setback. Over the next several days he kept up the pressure on Nabis who was eventually forced to sue for terms. The Roman general resisted the temptation to give in to revenge. His terms, nonetheless, were strict: Nabis should give back the property and women confiscated from the upper classes, abandon possessions such as Argos and parts of Crete, and keep a navy of no more than two unarmed vessels. Nabis had little choice but to submit.

Agesipolis III now had high hopes of being restored as Agiad king. But his hopes soon crumbled as the process of restoring confiscated properties proved to be insuperably difficult. Nabis was still technically the ruler of Sparta, enjoying considerable support from the lower classes. He acted on his simmering hatred of Rome in 192 when he tried to recapture Gytheion.

This triggered the intervention of Philopoimen's Achaians, who smashed Nabis' army at Barbosthenes (modern Vresthena?) near Sellasia. Nabis fled with the surviving quarter of his army to Sparta. Flamininus, however, didn't want to eliminate Nabis entirely; the Spartan tyrant was potentially useful as an ally against the Achaians. Flamininus forced Nabis and Philopoimen into a truce.

Nabis was crafty but unwise enough to call in the aid of the Aitolians, that warlike people of the northwest who had a long habit of causing trouble for the more settled Greeks. The Aitolians sent Alexamenos with 1,000 troops and thirty cavalry to Sparta, but with secret orders to capture the city rather than help it. They arrived as Nabis was on horseback drilling his forces on a parade-ground. Nabis' joy turned to terror as the Aitolian cavalry surrounded him, pulled him from his horse and lanced him repeatedly with their spears. Alexamenos then ordered a general pillage which was only stopped by the fierce resistance of groups of Spartan citizens and soldiers who in turn massacred Alexamenos and a good portion of his force.

Hearing of this, Philopoimen hastened to enrol Sparta in the Achaian League. But he hadn't counted on the ordinary Spartans who, angry because of the loss of their port, were in no mood for joining their enemies. It took the diplomacy of Flamininus to defuse the tension, but in 189 the fear of Achaian domination was such that Sparta officially requested to be placed under the protection of Rome. Fulvius, the Roman consul on the island of Kephallenia, referred the request to the Senate. But that body, discouraged at the complexity and confusion of the Greeks' quarrels, was in a non-interventionist mood; its reply was essentially that Sparta and the Achaian League should patch up their differences by themselves. In practical terms, that meant that Philopoimen could do pretty much what he liked, which he did, capturing Sparta and hounding the partisans of Nabis. The city walls were demolished and the old institutions of Lykourgos formally abolished. A half-hearted protest from the Roman Senate made not the slightest impression on the Achaian leader.

In 188 Philopoimen perished in battle against the Messenians. His successor, Kallikrates, allowed the Spartans to rebuild their walls and reinstitute the Lykourgan system. This gave Sparta a precious thirty years of peace. During this time, however, Macedon and the Achaians continued to snipe at each other until Rome finally lost patience. In 146 an Achaian force, fighting bravely, was nonetheless soundly thrashed by the Romans under Mummius at the Isthmus. Corinth was razed to the ground. The Roman Senate formally annexed the greater part of Greece.

Sparta under Roman domination was allowed (like Athens) to keep a semi-free status. The Ephors and other state bodies continued to function as before, though the members of the Gerousia were restricted to fixed terms and no longer allowed to stay till they died. The senior Ephor, or Patronomos, had the function of head of state. This way Sparta survived through the Roman Empire. When Nero visited the leading Greek cities he avoided Sparta as still sticking to the Lykourgan norms which he highly disapproved of. In this state Sparta entered the 1,000-year Byzantine Christian era, followed by more than 400 years of Ottoman Turkish rule, until in 1829 it became a part of the free modern Greek state – its name and pride unaltered. The Romans may have let Sparta keep most of its time-honoured institutions. But the kingship, conspicuously, was not among them. What had happened? The answer is not as clear as we would like. Pausanias is hardly helpful when he notes simply that after Kleomenes III 'Sparta ceased to be ruled by kings.'[5] Luckily, other sources have a few more scraps of information.

Great hopes were pinned on Pelops when he was born to king-by-purchase Lykourgos around 210. The very name harked back to the beginnings of civilization in the Peloponnese. In Greek tradition Pelops was a mythical figure just a couple of generations removed from Zeus himself, the one who gave his name to the Peloponnese, which means literally 'Pelops' Island.' But Pelops was not yet a teenager when in 199 Nabis had him eliminated, probably by murder.[6] Nabis, who probably falsely claimed descent from Demaratos, then proclaimed himself king of Sparta, though history has never recognized him as such.

As for Agesipolis III, Polybius claims he was a son of Kleomenes III who escaped the massacre of his family. Said to be born around 219, if that is the case he would have spent his infancy in Egypt. His paternity seems to have been generally accepted by the Spartans, including Nabis, who could have had him on a hit list, as we next hear of him living among Spartan exiles in the Peloponnese and assuming some sort of leadership position. In his mid-twenties, as we have seen, he accompanied Quinctius Flamininus on his march to Sparta. Nabis' successful defence dashed his hopes, and he retired to exile near Megalopolis, a leading member of the so-called Free Lakonians (*Eleutherolakones*), who opposed the regime at home.

In 183, according to Polybius, who was diplomatically active at the time, the Free Lakonians sent Agesipolis to Rome to plead before the Senate that the exiled Spartans be allowed to return home. He never made it. Somewhere in the Adriatic his ship was intercepted by pirates and he was killed.[7]

From the evidence available, it seems that there was no specific moment in which the Spartan government or people decreed that the kingship should be no more. The ancient institution was just allowed to fade away. Social conditions had changed so much, through incessant unrest and warfare, that the kingship and what it symbolized had become irrelevant. After

Kleomenes III the Agiad and Eurypontid thrones were occupied by in turn a fraud (Lykourgos), and youths with a title but no power (Pelops and Agesipolis III). Moreover, from the middle of the second century onwards Sparta was, in name if not fully in fact, subject to Rome and hence had no practical need of a head of state as a figurehead.

When the Roman republic was divided after the assassination of Julius Caesar in 44, Sparta, along among the Greeks, was wise enough to throw in its lot with Octavian and Anthony against the usurpers Brutus and Caius Cassius. This saved the city from the inevitable reprisals by Rome. A Spartan admiral named Eurykles distinguished himself at the battle of Aktion in 31, coming within an ace of personally capturing Mark Anthony's ship. A grateful Octavian – now Augustus Caesar – offered to make Eurykles the ruler of Sparta. But Eurykles, an adventurous spirit, preferred to seek his fortune in Judaea as Sparta for a century had maintained friendly relations with the Jewish kingdom. The Jewish historian Flavius Josephus preserves a cordial correspondence between King Areus I and the Hebrew high priesthood as early as 310. Certainly the two nations were similar in their sobriety, self-discipline and sense of unique destiny. There is evidence that Eurykles advised King Herod of Biblical notoriety, became wealthy and retired to his estates in Lakedaimon. There he frittered away his assets and began to oppress the Spartans, with the result that Augustus had him exiled. Such was the end of the last known leading figure of ancient Sparta.

Soon after the modern Greek state was established in 1829, the capital was set up at Athens, but Sparta was not forgotten. In 1868 King George I of Greece designated his newly-born son and heir Constantine (the future Constantine I) as Duke of Sparta. The move came up against some parliamentary opposition, as all noble titles were illegal. The usage, though allowed in the end, fell into disuse early in the twentieth century. Yet, nearly forty years after the abolition of the modern Greek monarchy, the kingly tradition lives on in Sparta. To this day is it the most pro-royalist region in Greece.

# Standing down

It was in March 1996 that the Mayor of Athens, Dimitris Avramopoulos, decided that a generous gesture to the city's ancient foe might be in order to revive the Greeks' historical consciousness. It was found that the Peloponnesian War had technically not ended, since at the conclusion of the war in 404 BC Sparta and Athens had signed no formal treaty of peace – at least no recorded one. Why not formalize things 2,400 years later?

The conservative city council of Sparta, headed by Mayor Demosthenes Matalas, eagerly took up the cause. The result was the ceremonial signing in Sparta of a 200-word pledge of 'unbreakable ties' between the two cities. Mr Avramopoulos was made an honorary citizen of Sparta. On 13 March 1996 *The Times* of London reported the event, under my byline, with the headline: 'Sparta and Athens bury the hatchet.'

# Sparta's Kings: Timeline

## Mythical era (c.2000–1250 BC)
Lelex
Myles
Eurotas
Lakedaimon
Amyklas
Kynortas
Oibalos

## Semi-mythical era (c.1250–1120 BC)
Tyndareos
Menelaos
Orestes
Tisamenos

## Historical era (c.1120–199 BC)

| Agiad | | Eurypontid | |
| --- | --- | --- | --- |
| Eurysthenes | | Prokles | c. 1103–1060 |
| Agis I | | Eurypon | c. 1050–1000? |
| Echestratos | | Prytanis | c. 1000–950? |
| Labotas | | | |
| Doryssos | | Polydektes | |
| Agesilaos I | | Eunomos | |
| Archelaos | | Charillos | c. 950–c. 760 |
| Teleklos | | Nikandros | c. 790–c. 750 |
| Alkamenes | c. 750–c. 730 | | |
| Polydoros | | Theopompos | c. 730–c. 700) |
| Eurykrates | | Anaxandridas I | |
| | | Archidamos I | |
| | | Anaxilas | |

| *Agiad* | | *Eurypontid* | |
|---|---|---|---|
| Anaxandros | | Leotychidas I | |
| Eurykratidas | | Hippokratidas | |
| Leon | | Agasikles | *c.* 700–*c.* 550 |
| Anaxandridas II | *c.* 550–520 | Ariston | *c.* 550–515 |
| Kleomenes I | 520–490 | Demaratos | 515–491 |
| Leonidas I | 490–480 | Leotychidas II | 491–469 |
| Pleistarchos | 480–459 | | |
| Pleistoanax | 459–409 | Archidamos II | 469–427 |
| Pausanias | 409–395 | Agis II | 427–399 |
| Agesipolis I | 395–380 | Agesilaos II | 399–360 |
| Kleombrotos I | 380–371 | | |
| Agesipolis II | 370–370 | | |
| Kleomenes II | 370–309 | Archidamos III | 360–338 |
| | | Agis III | 338–331 |
| | | Eudamidas I | 331–305 |
| Areus I | 309–265 | Archidamos IV | 305–275 |
| Akrotatos | 265–262 | Eudamidas II | 275–244 |
| Areus II | 262–254 | | |
| Leonidas II | 254–236 | Agis IV | 244–241 |
| (Kleombrotos II | 242–241) | Eudamidas III | 241–228 |
| Kleomenes III | 238–222 | Archidamos V | 228–227 |
| | | Eukleidas | 227–222 |
| Agesipolis III | 219–217? | Lykourgos | 219–211 |
| | | Pelops | 211–199 |

# References and Chapter Notes

The basic facts about the lives of the kings of Sparta are contained in the following primary sources:

Herodotus, *The Histories*
Thucydides, *The Peloponnesian War*
Xenophon, *Hellenika*
Pausanias, *Description of Greece (Sparta, Aratos of Sikyon)*
Plutarch, *Parallel Lives* (specifically: *Agis [IV]*, *Agesilaos [II]*, *Kleomenes [III]*,
    *Aratos, Theseus, Themistokles, Aristides, Perikles, Alkibiades, Lysandros*
Plutarch, *Apophthegmata Laconica* (Loeb Classical Library, available online)

All subsequent accounts derive from these. Other works referred to are named in full in the individual notes in each chapter. I have also made use of modern Greek scholarship, a hitherto underrated source. Some of the best is contained in the first five volumes of *History of the Greek Nation (Istoria to Ellinikou Ethnous)*, a composite text published by Ekdotike Athinon. I include references to three volumes: IEE2, IEE3a and IEE3b, with the particular author.

For quotes from the *Iliad* I have relied on the translation of Richmond Lattimore, which I consider to be the best. Plutarch's lives of the Spartan kings are available online in their original English translation by John Dryden, whose monumental prose I have decided to use in my quoted material.

During the writing of this book a remarkable volume was brought to my attention: *Sparta Through the Centuries (I Sparti dia mesou ton Aionon)*, by a Spartan schoolmaster named Panayotis Doukas and published in New York in 1922. Written in quasi-ancient Greek, the 900-page doorstopper was the product of more than twenty years of labour by Doukas who brings to the page the stern atmosphere of early Sparta and how a latter-day Spartan has viewed it through a lens which is mercilessly candid in true Spartan style.

# Chapter 1
1. Durant, W., *The Story of Civilization*, Vol. II: *The Life of Greece*, New York: Simon & Schuster 1939, 87
2. For example in the Bible, where the Israelites demanded 'a king to judge us like all the nations.' (1 Samuel 8)
3. Doukas, 129
4. Paus. 3.1.5
5. Plu. *Theseus* 31–34
6. *Iliad* II, 581–582
7. Strauss, B., *The Trojan War*, New York: Simon & Schuster 2006, 23–24
8. *Iliad* III, 21–29
9. *Op. cit.*, 180
10. Strauss, 17
11. Her. II.112-120

# Chapter 2
1. For more on Herakles, see Grant, M., *Myths of the Greeks and Romans*, Penguin 1962
2. Paus. 3.1.7-9; Her. VI.52
3. Doukas, 62–65
4. Paus. 3.2.2
5. *Op. cit.*, 3.7.2
6. Her. VIII.137
7. Hammond. N.G.L., *A History of Greece to 322 BC*, Oxford University Press 1967, 141
8. Plu. *AL* 395
9. Plu. *Kleomenes* 10
10. Paus. 4.4.3
11. Plu. *AL* 394

# Chapter 3
1. Plu. *AL* 296
2. Sakellariou, M., in IEE2, 52
3. Plu. *Kleomenes* 8
4. Doukas, 135
5. Plu. *AL* 390
6. Paus. 4.6.5
7. Plu. *AL* 328
8. *Op. cit.*, 391
9. *Op. cit.*, 394
10. Paus. 3.7.6

11. Plu. *AL* 299
12. Her. I.66
13. Plu. *AL* 347
14. *Op. cit.*, 243
15. *Op. cit.*, 297–299
16. Hammond, 97

## Chapter 4
1. Plu. *AL* 338
2. Her. III.148
3. Paus. 3.4.6
4. A talent of gold is roughly 26 kilos. Translated into 21st century values, it would come out at somewhere in the region of £10 million.
5. Her. V.49-51
6. Pelekidis, C., in IEE2, 285
7. Plu. *AL* 337
8. *Op. cit.*, 341
9. Her. VI.74-75
10. Plu, *AL* 319
11. Her. VII.101-105
12. *Op. cit.*, 237
13. Plu. *Themistokles* 29

## Chapter 5
1. Plu. *AL* 350
2. *Op. cit.*, 351
3. Diogenes Laertius, *History* 3.4.71
4. Plu. *AL* 352
5. *Ibid.*
6. Plu. *Aristides* 12
7. The victorious city-states commemorated the battle by commissioning a six-metre-high bronze spiral column with the names of the thirty-one states that took part. Seven hundred years later the monument was carried to Constantinople by East Roman emperor Constantine I. It now stands in what is left of the Byzantine Hippodrome in modern Istanbul.
8. Plu. *AL* 346

## Chapter 6
1. Plu. *AL* 388
2. *Op. cit.*, 389
3. Thu. I.83-88

## Chapter 7
1. Thu. IV.42
2. Plu. *AL* 315
3. *Op. cit.*, 289
4. *Op. cit.*, 290
5. Doukas, 212
6. Plu. *Alkibiades* 23
7. *Ibid.*
8. Xen. III.3.1
9. Plu. *AL* 289–291
10. *Op. cit.*, 293
11. Plu. *Lysandros* 2
12. Sakellariou in IEE2, 332
13. Xen. III.3.11
14. Paus. 3.5.5
15. Plu. *AL* 385

## Chapter 8
1. Plu. *Agesilaos* 1
2. *Op. cit.*, 2
3. *Op. cit.*, 9
4. *Op. cit.*, 11–12
5. *Op. cit.*, 18
6. Plu. *AL* 302
7. Plu. *Agesilaos* 24
8. Plu. *AL* 336
9. *Op. cit.*, 302
10. Plu. *Agesilaos* 51
11. *Op. cit.*, 53
12. Xen. VI.5.22-27
13. Paus. 3.10.2
14. Doukas, 227
15. Plu. *Agesilaos* 38
16. *Op. cit.*, 33
17. Plu. *AL* 287
18. Paus. 3.6.1

## Chapter 9
1. Plu. *AL* 343
2. *Op. cit.*, 311
3. *Op. cit.*, 310

4. Diodoros of Sicily, *World History* 17.62.1-63.4
5. Plu. *AL* 321–322
6. *Op. cit.*, 322–323
7. Cary, M., *A History of the Greek World 323 to 146 BC*, London: Methuen 1972, 44
8. Hammond, 651

**Chapter 10**
1. Paus. 3.6.3
2. Cary, 63
3. Paus. 3.6.4
4. Plu. *AL* 295
5. Paus. 3.6.7
6. Plu. *Agis* 24–25
7. Plu. *Aratos* 21
8. *Op. cit.*, 23

**Chapter 11**
1. Plu. *Agis* 9
2. Cary, 153
3. Plu. *Agis* 14
4. *Op. cit.*, 15
5. *Op. cit.*, 27–31
6. Plu. *Kleomenes* 2
7. Cary, 156
8. *Ibid.*
9. Plu. *Kleomenes* 13
10. *Ibid.; Aratos* 92
11. Plu. *Kleomenes* 29
12. *Op. cit.*, 32
13. Aelian, quoted in Macurdy, G.H., *Hellenistic Queens*, Chicago: Ares Publishers 1932, 136

**Epilogue**
1. Polybius, *The Histories* 4.81
2. Cary, 192
3. Doukas, 274
4. Polybius, 18.17
5. Paus. 3.6.9
6. Diodoros of Sicily, 27.1.1
7. Polybius, 24.1

# Index

Achaimenes 52
Acoris 116
Adeimantos 97
Agamemnon 6–11, 36, 104, 139
Agasikles 30–3, 36
Agesandridas 94
Agesilaos I 17–19
Agesilaos II xix, 101, 103–20, 124, 127, 138, 140, 149
Agesilaos (uncle of Agis IV) 142, 145–6
Agesipolis I 107, 110, 117–19, 122, 141
Agesipolis II 123, 144
Agesipolis III 169–74
Agesistrata 142, 146–7
Agiatis 149, 159
Agis I 15–16
Agis II 83–94, 97–9, 101, 103
Agis III 128–31
Agis IV 137–8, 140–54, 159, 167
Agylaios 153
Aigalos 3
Aischines 35
Aithra 5
Akademos 5
Akrotatos (king) 136
Akrotatos (son of Kleomenes II) 133–4
Alexamenos 172

Alexander I of Macedon 63
Alexander III of Macedon (the Great) 129–33, 136–7
Alkamenes 22–3, 27
Alkibiades 89, 91–6, 98, 103, 105
Amompharetos 65–6
Amphares 146–7, 154
Amyklas 3, 17
Amyntas 126
Anaxandridas I 30–3
Anaxandridas II 32, 35–40, 42, 54
Anaxandros 32
Anchimolos 42, 62
Androkleidas 108
Androkles 27
Antalkidas 110
Antigonos I 133
Antigonos II Gonatas 134–6, 148
Antigonos III Doson 156–8, 160–5
Antiochos 27
Antipatros 130–2
Apega 170–1
Aphrodite 9–10
Aratos 138–9, 145, 148, 151–3, 156–9, 161, 170
Archelaos 19–20
Archias 41
Archidamia 138, 142, 147
Archidamos I 31–2, 104
Archidamos II 61, 70, 72–83, 87

Archidamos III 111, 114, 122–9
Archidamos IV 133, 138–9, 152
Archidamos V 140, 142, 148–9
Archidamos (son of Theopompos)
    29
Areus I 133–6, 138, 141, 174
Areus II 136, 138
Argeia 14
Arimnestos 66, 72
Ariobarzanes 114
Aristagoras 45–6
Aristides 65, 71
Aristodamos 107
Aristodemos (Dorian ruler) xviii,
    14–15
Aristodemos (Messenian general)
    28
Aristodemos (Spartan soldier) 61,
    66
Aristokles 91
Aristomachos 12–13
Aristomachos (Argive leader) 148,
    150
Aristomenes 32
Ariston 34–5, 38–9, 48–50
Aristophanes 84
Aristotle 34, 75
Arkesilaos 19
Artaxerxes I 75–6
Artaxerxes II Mnemon 105–6, 110,
    115, 120, 124
Avramopoulos, D. 175

Brasidas 80–2, 84–5, 87–91

Chabrias 116
Charillos (Charilaos) 17, 19, 20, 23,
    148
Cheilon 169–70
Chileos 64
Chilon 35, 40

Chilonis 134, 137
Chremonides 135
Churchill, W. 50
Croesus 38, 41
Cyrus I (the Great) 38, 54
Cyrus (brother of Darius II) 95–6

Damis 132
Darius I 46, 50–1, 54–6
Darius II 93–5
Deinicha 125
Deinon 122
Demaratos 34, 44–6, 48–54, 56,
    58–9, 68, 113, 173
Demetrios of Phaleron 133
Demetrios Poliorketes 138
Demetrios II of Macedon 148
Demochares 146, 154
Demokrates 151
Demosthenes 84–6
Demoteles 162
Dienekes 60
Diodoros of Sicily 131
Diogenes the Cynic 141
Dorieus 35, 40, 42, 54
Doryssos 17–18
Durant, W. 1

Echestratos 16–17
Egan, R. vi
Elatos 26
Enarsphoros 5
Epaminondas 112–15, 121–2, 126
· Ephialtes 59, 61, 132
Epikouros 141
Epitadas 85–6
Epitadeus 140
Eteonikos 96
Eudamidas I 131–2, 138
Eudamidas II 138–9
Eudamidas III 148–9

Eudamidas (general) 118
Eukleidas 154–5, 162–3
Eunomos 17, 19
Euphaes 27–8
Eupolia 104
Eurotas 2–3
Eurybiades 56, 58, 62–3, 67
Euryklas 153
Eurykrates 30
Eurykratidas 32
Eurylochos 84
Eurypon 15–16
Eurysthenes, xviii, 14–15
Eurytos 61

Flamininus, T. Q. 171–3
Fulvius 172

Gorgo 46, 52, 54, 57–8, 70, 72
Gorgophone 4
Gracchus, G. 149
Gracchus, T. 149
Gras 15
Gryllos 115
Gylippos 93, 100
Gylis 108

Hannibal 169
Hegesistratos 67
Hektor 8
Helen of Troy (Helene) xviii, 5–11,
  34, 92, 170
Herakles xviii, 4, 12–13, 15, 18,
  121, 156
Herippidas 106–7
Hermione 11
Herodotus xix, 10, 14, 18, 24, 34,
  41–60, 62–4, 66, 70
Hetoimaridas 70
Hipparchos 40
Hippias 40–2, 51

Hippitas 166–7
Hippokoon 4–5, 18
Hippokrates 87–8
Hippokratidas 31, 48
Hippomedon 142–3, 146
Hipponoidas 91
Homer 6–10, 16, 37
Hyakinthos 3
Hydarnes 59–60
Hyperbatas 156

Iphikrates 109–10, 113
Isagoras 42–3

Kallikrates (Achaian leader) 172
Kallikrates (Spartan soldier) 65
Kallikratidas 95–6
Kallipides 109
Kassandros 132
Kastor 4–5
Kimon 75
Kinadon 100
Kleandridas 73
Klearidas 88
Kleisthenes 43
Kleombrotos I 111–12, 119, 120–3
Kleombrotos (brother of Leonidas
  I) 35, 61, 64, 70
Kleombrotos II 136–7, 144, 146
Kleomenes I 35, 40–9, 53–4, 67,
  83
Kleomenes II xix, 117, 123, 129,
  133, 136, 141
Kleomenes III xix, 24, 148–70,
  173–4
Kleon 82–4, 86, 88–9
Kleonymos (son of Kleomenes II)
  133–6
Kleonymos (son of Sphodrias) 111,
  122
Kleora 108

Konon 96
Korrhagos 130
Krateros 132
Kratesikleia 152, 160, 167
Kyniska 83
Kynortas 2–3

Labotas 17
Lakedaimon 2–3
Lamachos 92
Lelex 2
Leda 5
Leon 32–3, 35–6
Leonidas I vii, xix, 35, 52, 54–61,
    64, 67, 70, 72, 78, 83, 87, 103,
    127
Leonidas II 136–8, 141–6, 148–50,
    152
Leosthenes 132
Leotychidas I 31
Leotychidas II 48–50, 54, 61–4,
    66–8, 72, 74, 83, 116
Leotychidas (son of Agis II) 103–4
Libys 142
Lichas 36
Lydiadas 152–3
Lykopes 41
Lykourgos (Eurypontid 'pretender'
    king) 169–70, 173–4
Lykourgos (reformer) 19–20, 23–4,
    26, 32, 131, 140–1, 143, 146,
    150, 154, 157
Lysandridas 160–1
Lysandros (general) 95–7, 99–101,
    103–5, 116, 142
Lysandros (son of Libys) 142–4

Machanidas 170
Magas 165
Maiandrios 41
Mandroklidas 142

Mardonius 63–6
Masistius 64
Matalas, D. 175
Megistias 60
Megistonous 152–4, 158
Melesippos 79
Menedaios 85
Menekrates 109
Menelaos 5–12, 36, 43, 85, 170
Menestheus 5
Mummius 172
Myles 2

Nabis 170–3
Napoleon I 54
Nectanebo 116
Nero 173
Nestor 85
Nikagoras 165–6
Nikandros 20
Nikias 87–9, 92
Nikokles 139
Nikomedes 74

Oibalos 3–4
Orestes 11, 15, 36–7

Panites 14
Panteus 160, 167
Paris 6–10
Patroklos 135–6
Pausanias (general and regent)
    64–7, 70–2
Pausanias (historian) xix, 2, 4, 11,
    14–5, 17, 19, 28–30, 32, 40,
    48–9, 98, 118–19, 122–5, 128,
    131, 133, 138, 173
Pausanias (king) 87, 95, 97–102,
    107, 117
Peisandros 106
Peisistratos 37, 40

Pelles 108
Pelopidas 121
Pelops 170, 173–4
Perdikkas III of Macedon 126
Perialla 49
Perieres 4
Perikles 73–5, 77, 79–80, 82, 89, 91
Perikles (son of Perikles) 96
Phalaikos 127
Pharnabazus (admiral) 130
Pharnabazus (satrap) 93, 105–6
Philip II of Macedon 123, 126–9, 134
Philip V of Macedon 165, 169, 170–1
Philippides (Pheidippides) 55
Philokles 97
Philopoimen 161, 163, 170–2
Phintias 27
Phoibidas 118
Pleistarchos 15, 61, 64, 70–4
Pleistoanax 73–4, 77, 84, 87, 89, 91, 94–5, 97–8, 100, 141
Plutarch xix–xx, 5, 18–21, 23–5, 29, 31, 33–4, 36, 41, 47, 52, 58–9, 61–2, 65, 72, 75, 79, 90, 92–3, 95, 99, 103–5, 107, 109, 112–14, 116–19, 123–4, 136–7, 139–40, 143–7, 149–50, 152–5, 157, 159–63, 165, 167–8
Polemarchos 30
Polybius xix, 169, 173
Polydektes 17–19
Polydeukes 4–5
Polydoros 23, 27–31
Polykrates 40–1
Priam 10
Prokles xviii, 14–15, 148
Proteus 10
Prytanis 16–17, 19

Ptolemy II of Egypt 135–6
Ptolemy III of Egypt 159–60, 162, 164–5
Ptolemy IV of Egypt 165–8
Pyrrhos I of Epiros 134–5, 142
Pythagoras of Argos 171

Salaithos 82
Simonides 61
Skouras, S. vi
Sokrates 87, 89
Sophokles 93
Sosibios 165
Sous 15
Sparte 1–3
Sphairos of Borysthenes 150, 155
Sphodrias 111, 119, 122
Sthenelaidas 78
Stratokles 129
Styphon 86

Tacho 115–16
Taygete 3
Teleklos 21–2, 27
Temenos 13
Terpandros 31
Thearidas 160–1
Themistokles 52, 55–8, 62–3, 69
Theopompos 23, 26–30
Theramenes 97
Therapne 2
Theras 14
Therykion 164
Thucydides (historian) xix–xx, 62, 71, 77–9, 84, 86–8, 90, 94, 116
Thucydides (politician) 77
Timaia 92–3, 98, 103
Timomachos 26
Tisamenos 11–12, 14–15
Tissaphernes 93–4, 105–6
Tithraustes 106

Tyndareos xviii, 4–5, 15, 18
Tyrtaios 32, 54, 78, 90, 150

Xanthippos 67
Xenares 150
Xenokrates 132
Xenophon 24, 95, 98–9, 105–6,
    109, 115, 117–19, 122

Xerxes 51–64, 66–7, 70, 75, 114,
    127

Zeus 5, 13, 18, 39, 50, 53, 109, 173
Zeuxidamos (grandson of
    Theopompos) 30
Zeuxidamos (son of Leotychidas II)
    61